Advance Praise for *Lifestyles for Learning*

"Any parent or student who is thinking of entering college must read *Lifestyles in Learning* first before settin All too often colleges have become a vac who is in Division 1 for sports, who ha the latest technology. Susan has melded h ground in nutrition and health, her keen humor, and her experience and knowledge of teaching college students who learn differently, to create a masterpiece of information that puts all the pieces together to teach us what it takes to learn, from the latest in our understanding of brain functioning to what we choose to think about. The successful college student will want to put this on their reading list. I know it's going to become a text for my students."

—Kathy D'Alessio
M.Ed., Academic Advisor, Landmark College

"Going to college is a lot easier than being in college. Susie Crowther has written a delightful book that unravels the college experience. It is smart, witty, and thoughtful. As tasty as junk food but healthy as bean sprouts."

—James W. Pennebaker
Professor of Psychology at the University of Texas at Austin; Author,
The Secret Life of Pronouns

"In *Lifestyles for Learning*, Susan Crowther elucidates the science and art of lifestyle choices for young adults entering the cultural minefield of today's college campus. With humor and refreshing honesty, Ms. Crowther shares her personal tribulations and decades of teaching experience as she takes us through key influences on learning and success: nutrition, exercise, sleep, and stress. For anyone facing learning challenges, her message resonates with the best that positive psychology has to offer: that each of us has control over the choices we make, the kind of life we aspire to lead, and the degree of success we earn."

—Jim Baucom
Professor of Education, Landmark College

"Crowther breaks down the process of learning into an accessible and digestible process, and provides an excellent overview of the circumstances necessary for optimal learning to occur. *Lifestyles for Learning* validates what higher education professionals have long suspected, that academic success requires far more than cognitive intelligence. Crowther brings to the forefront what most educators already know intuitively, that students need to be in balance (physical, emotional, spiritual, and psychological) to truly thrive in college. Higher education professionals finally have a resource that honors this intuition with science. The author's ultimate goal is simple: help students become better learners, regardless of starting point or life circumstances. *Lifestyles for Learning* should be required reading for anyone wanting to better support students as they navigate the collegiate journey."

—Nova Schauss
Academic Advisor & Student Success Specialist

"I love love love the book and want to read it cover to cover and then backwards like the demonic messages on the Beatles white album. Perfect tome for the non-traditional student. It will be Invaluable. Make sure it is required reading for all of your courses."

—Joan McArthur
Author's college BFF

"*Lifestyles for Learning* is a must read for all college freshmen and their parents. This savvy book identifies the multiple areas of stress that every new college student will encounter, and the often most overlooked remedy—creativity. Ms. Crowther explains how today's students are pressured to make career decisions based on old beliefs about financial success and future employment trends, when current research in psycho-neuroscience indicates that happiness and career satisfaction is more easily achieved when such decisions are made from the passions of the heart. Based on case studies and personal experience, she provides concrete examples that demonstrate how the pathway to the heart cannot be accessed through the mind alone.

Through illustrations and exercises, she shows how the arts, particularly a regular practice of visual journaling—journaling with words and images—can be the most direct pathway to the vast well of personal wisdom each of us possess. When students learn early on how to tap into this place of inner knowing that only the heart and soul can reveal, they will begin to re-define their life purpose based on what matters most to them."

—Barbara Ganim
Author of *Art and Healing: Using Expressive Art to Heal Your Body, Mind and Spirit;* and co-author of *Visual Journaling: Going Deeper than Words*

The Essential Guide for College Students
and the People Who Love Them

Lifestyles
for Learning

Susan Crowther

Foreword by Philippa Norman, MD MPH

Illustrations by Julie DuCharme Fallone

Skyhorse Publishing

Skyhorse Publishing books may be purchased in bulk at special discounts for sales promotion, corporate gifts, fund-raising, or educational purposes. Special editions can also be created to specifications. For details, contact the Special Sales Department, Skyhorse Publishing, 307 West 36th Street, 11th Floor, New York, NY 10018 or info@skyhorsepublishing.com.

Skyhorse® and Skyhorse Publishing® are registered trademarks of Skyhorse Publishing, Inc.®, a Delaware corporation.

Visit our website at www.skyhorsepublishing.com.

10 9 8 7 6 5 4 3 2 1

Library of Congress Cataloging-in-Publication Data is available on file.

Cover design by Julie Fallone.

Cover photo by Susan Crowther. Interior and cover art by Julie Fallone.

Print ISBN: 978-1-63450-392-1

Ebook ISBN: 978-1-63450-858-2

Printed in the United States of America

Dedication

For Lucas
Be the chessboard, son.

Foreword

From the earliest years of childhood, we prepare students for the academics of college. Yet, students head for campus unaware of potential threats to their well-being. With more demands on their time, sleep becomes an inconvenience, leading to reliance on caffeine and sugar to push through fatigue. Drinking and drugs are interwoven into college social life, making it difficult for a student to know if they (or their friends) are being social or becoming dependent. Many students silently struggle with depression, unaware of how to ask for help. In a relatively short time, a student's life can become unstable. Brain science informs us that young adult brains are vulnerable - actively rewiring, unplugging old connections and rebuilding new ones. The abrupt changes in lifestyle are stressful and divert brain activity to survival rather than learning.

It's no wonder that many look back on their college years and ask, what could I have done differently?

As I think back to my own college experience, I recall years of stress, sleep deprivation, and and burnout. Now, as an integrative physician with a focus on nutrition and brain health, I see young people experiencing the same pressures. What has changed? We desperately need a new way to help students navigate college years.

Susie's book, *Lifestyles for Learning*, offers a completely revolutionary approach, guiding students to the understanding that their whole being—soul, body, and mind—will be affected by the college experience. After all, students are more than their brains. She guides students to defend their opportunity to learn by choosing to nourish their health. Crowther reframes brain science, creating a narrative that helps students see that the emergence of self-responsibility is parallel to the brain's natural process of reorganizing itself. As self-motivated young adults, they can anticipate and better understand the challenges of college life and thrive as they engage fully in all that college has to offer.

Susie is experienced in helping students shift into self-reliance. She worked for 15 years as a college professor, advisor, and tutor, creating a course on college health for learning-disabled students. Susie uses analogies and stories that make the science of wellness accessible and easy to remember. For example, "Sleep Your Way to an A" helps students understand why the brain needs sleep to form memories. An experienced chef, Susie created the concept of FARE WELL foods (Fresh, Ripe, Whole, and Local) to help students understand how to nourish their brains and fuel learning.

As you read *Lifestyles for Learning*, you'll feel like you are sitting with a friend who is a great storyteller: knowledgeable and down to earth with a great sense of humor. Susie's book is a welcome guide you'll want to refer to again and again. If you are a student, it will shorten your learning curve and help you feel healthier, enjoy learning, and make the most of your college years. If you are a parent or counselor, it will provide insight and support for your student's health and well-being.

College really is an incredible opportunity. I am thrilled about Susie's new book because I truly believe it will help students achieve all they desire from their college experience. Enjoy it in good health!

Philippa Norman, MD MPH
Integrative Physician
Chicago, IL

The Essential Guide for College Students
and the People Who Love Them

Lifestyles

for Learning

Welcome

Imagine you are living your life, and it is a good life. You have a lovely clean home. You have a personal chef, live-in maid, gardener, and chauffer. You have pets: a dog and cat, maybe a fish or lizard, too. Meals are prepared, *three square meals a day*, plus pancakes and bacon on Sundays. The cupboards and refrigerator are well-stocked with your favorite foods and healthy snacks. Your home contains comfortable couches, pretty painted walls, decorated rooms, houseplants, and full-spectrum lighting. There is a roomy shower and Jacuzzi bathtub that you use whenever you want.

You have close friends whom you have known for years. You have unlimited time with them and spend your days swimming, riding bikes, going to all your favorite places, and just hanging out. Your community of coaches, teachers, and family members gives you a strong sense of belonging. You are happy, secure, and loved.

One day, rather abruptly, it all stops. You must leave. You are given a short amount of time and space to pack, and you may pack only what is necessary. Someone forces you into a car and takes you to another place, somewhere completely unknown.

When you arrive, you are put into a cell—a tiny room with bare walls and floors. There is a skimpy foam rectangle for a bed, a single table and chair, a bare floor, and concrete walls. Strangers are in the room. They don't know where they are, either. There are strangers everywhere. No one knows anything. You don't know where anything is. You don't know where to go or what to do and there is no one to tell you.

Everyone is crazy in this place. They have strange habits, so different from yours. They do things you've never done. They are loud and scary, staying up all night, screaming and crying. They are threatening, ignoring your boundaries, stealing and lying all the time. It never stops. You are surrounded by people, and yet, you are completely alone. You feel like a ghost in your own skin.

People run your life. You are forced to do things that you do not want to do. You don't know how to do the stuff they expect. No one is helping you. You have to do what they say or you will be in grave trouble. You are judged and punished when you do things the wrong way, even though you don't know what it is you're supposed to be doing.

You are tired all the time. You have intense headaches and stomach aches. The pain is constant and unbearable. You have insomnia and are so exhausted that you explode with anger for no reason. You often don't feel anything. You cry a lot when no one is around. You suffer hair loss and weight gain. You look in the mirror and don't recognize who you see. You stop looking.

You begin drinking and taking drugs. Sometimes this brings sleep. Sometimes, after drinking your sorrows away, you awaken with feelings that you have done something very wrong yet can't quite remember. You sink even lower into depression and begin to have thoughts of suicide. A time or two, you attempt it, but only half-heartedly. Ironically, you cannot seem to muster the courage to end your life. Exhausted, confused, and alone, you give up. The work you are forced to do becomes unbearable. You hate the work, but have no power to leave. You are a slave, stuck in this prison.

You are stuck here for years—about four or five, depending on your major.

* * *

Welcome to college.

Contents

Ditat Vitae

**Defend Your Education
Defend Your Health**

Prologue

When I was twelve years old, my whole family took the Mensa IQ test. I scored the highest—a gorgeous 164, which really pissed off my father and brother. Academically oriented, I loved reading and writing, aced test-taking, and excelled in classroom activities. I ranked 9th in my high school graduating class, with a 91% grade average. So, why did it take me twenty years to complete college? The obvious answers were that I was unprepared, didn't attend classes, and didn't do the assignments. But, the *reasons* for the italics—the real answers—are revealed in this book.

In essence, it was due to lifestyle factors. I didn't regulate my sleep. I experienced high levels of stress. I drank alcohol and did drugs. I smoked cigarettes. I gained weight. I didn't move my body. I didn't go outside. I cut myself off from friends and family. I basically stopped being me.

I did do one thing. I wrote. I sat on my dorm room bed and wrote and kept writing. Then, I got a job. Writing and working got me through that time. Without the emotional release of journaling and the sense of purpose with cooking, my identity would've shattered completely.

* * *

Several years later, my husband and I embarked on a West Coast tour, promoting my first book, *The No Recipe Cookbook: A Beginner's Guide to the Art of Cooking* (Skyhorse Publishing, 2013). Along the way, we discovered a small town in California named Weed. Being college educators and parents of two young men in their twenties, we totally had to make the stop.

There's not much to Weed. It spits out a few ratty restaurants and kitschy shops. The highlight of the town is a head shop featuring, well, All Things Weed: "I Heart Weed" emblazoned T-shirts, posters, key chains, mugs, book bags, ash trays, bongs, and thongs. We bought our sons Weed T-shirts. For our younger son, still in college, we bought a college-logo-style shirt stating, "Weed University: College of Higher Education." The shirts came with free gifts: a beer pong ping pong ball and book of matches with "I Love Weed" inscriptions on them.

I like to joke around with my boys, presenting a bit of the "If you can't beat 'em, join 'em" kind of attitude. However, as I think about these gifts, beyond the haha-jokey-cool aspects, I reflect more somberly about young adults in college and their culture. For years, I have taught students with learning disabilities (LD), in courses exploring educational psychology content: factors affecting learning, intelligence styles, media literacy, psychoactive substances, and stress management. We've explored LD diagnosis, LD law, advocacy, strategies, and accommodations. **What all these topics have in common is health and wellbeing: how students live, what choices they make, and how these choices affect learning. In short, we explore the culture of college lifestyle.**

In these courses, we read that the drug culture for college students is less prevalent than the mainstream media leads us to believe. Some studies reveal that almost one third of surveyed college students report never drinking alcohol or smoking pot (Botvin, Life Skills). Personally, I've never met this third. During my teaching career, I raised two boys into young adults. I know about their lifestyle and observe different data. The students I encounter admit to using both substances, at least several times. At least half admit to smoking cigarettes, and I've caught some "non-smokers" in the act. Both of my sons have smoked pot and drunk alcohol. One son smokes cigarettes. These behaviors are what they *admit* to an authority figure. Recall the Cockroach Theory: for every one you see . . .

Optimistic studies reveal how young adults are making smarter choices than we're led to believe by the omnipresent media influences. I'm not seeing the smarter choices. I don't see them in my own children, after bombarding them with healthy guidance, but at least they are making the *choice* to discard health. With most of the college students I see, there isn't even a general understanding of health and wellness, allowing them to make an intentional choice. One of my advisees thought a diet of Twinkies and Captain Crunch was sufficient. I see students moving from their homes to their dorms without any knowledge of self-care, and quite frankly, it scares the hell out of me.

Good health is no laughing matter. Gaining our sons' approval with Weed T-shirts is not the answer to the cold reality that drugs and alcohol are the tips of the iceberg—the iceberg of lifestyle factors affecting young adults' health.

* * *

It has taken thirty years to understand what happened to that intelligent eighteen year-old girl who failed so miserably. Working with college students was the catalyst, showing how significantly lifestyle factors impeded their academic performance and validating my own experience. Next, an article in *Psychology Today*, "Perils of Higher Education: Is College Bad for the Brain?" (Kotler, 2005) awakened an epiphany. The cover photo shows a graduate in his gown chugging a beer stein so large it completely conceals his face. There was something captivating about that image and the article's title; I couldn't take my eyes off them. That article prompted the creation of a wellness course. I understood how lifestyle factors affected academic health, but it took that trip out west to crystalize what had been brewing all along. The Weed T-shirt became the inspiration for this book you are now reading. I owe a debt of gratitude to my students for opening my eyes and heart. I am also in awe of life's sweet serendipity, which introduced me to the article and T-shirt.

Lifestyles for Learning discusses health simply. My struggle in higher education motivated the writing voice to remain accessible. A dear colleague says to her students, "If you're bored writing it, I'm bored reading it." We feel that way about research papers, yet seldom reveal the sentiment. Research papers are the emperor's new clothes. Who are they trying to reach? Certainly not the people who need the message.

My goal was to write a book that people could *get*. I hold no PhD, am not a full professor nor authority in the field of learning disabilities. What I am is a college graduate, health educator, college instructor, and mother of two college-attending sons. I gained wisdom from my own failures. Through hardships and successes, my sons and all those dear students taught me why this college thing is so hard. We are all part of the scar clan, and we welcome you, with your own scars.

This book is intended for young adults considering, entering, and attending college. It hopes to inspire young adults; educators, therapists, and practitioners trying to understand these students; and the family and friends who love them. Ultimately, this book shares how particular lifestyle factors affect *performance, in general*: school, career, relationships, or wherever you may find yourself in this great big minefield of Higher Living.

Lifestyles
for Learning

THE CULTURE OF COLLEGE

"I imagine that one of the biggest troubles with colleges is there are too many distractions, too much panty-raiding, fraternities, and boola-boola and all of that."

—Malcolm X, *The Autobiography of Malcolm X*

"College has become too abstract. People need to be learning how to do things, rather than be forced to contemplate abstract concepts, graduating devoid of any practical skills. Too many kids aren't learning how to work."

—Temple Grandin, on college

"College has given me the confidence I need to fail."

—Jarod Kintz, *This Book Has No Title*

Welcome to college: the best and worst thing you will ever do in your life. Forget the ads and promises; you have no idea what you're getting into. College hurls students into never-before imagined freedom, independence, and choice. Freedom comes at a cost, tantalizing students with unprecedented opportunities to manipulate and compromise every area of their young adult lives.

A college student is the Phoenix Rising. The child in you collides with the adult you will become. Everything shatters: identity, personality, philosophy, monogamy . . . you name it, it changes. Every aspect of development is knocked off balance: physical, physiological, emotional, social, residential, financial, psychological, and spiritual. There are surely a few more *"-als"*: cultural, financial, geographical, vocational, sexual . . . in short, auto-biographical. Name an area of life, and college challenges it. **College may well be the singularly most volatile time in a person's life.**

It's *supposed* to be. The goal of college is to create what late educator John Dewey called "**disequilibrium**"—a knocking off balance, challenging one's patterns and paradigms, in order to grow. That is a required part of the academic experience. Surely, all education encourages disequilibrium, but college imbalances *everything*. College reshapes our world, and it is a spectacular transformation; however, without guidance, it may be as terrifying as a bad hallucinogenic trip lasting for years.

Attending college is bad for your health. All lifestyle factors come under attack: eating habits, daily movement, sleep cycles, social support, creative outlets, and coping strategies. Chemicals in the body change dramatically, with substance experimentation and medication modification. Sexual activity explodes, accompanied by sexually-transmitted diseases, love, and unplanned pregnancies. College is a breeding ground for untamed bacterial and viral havoc. Students herd into health services, documenting illness rates that rival epidemics. College is the opposite of a healthy lifestyle: mentally disorienting, physically disturbing, emotionally draining, and and soul crushing.

Statistically, young adults face more depression, anxiety, eating disorders, and drug addiction than in any other time in their lives. Schizophrenia, the debilitating disease of delusion, emerges most often in young adult years. Suicide rate is highest in young adults between the ages 16-21. It's no accident that young adults pay the highest car insurance rates. A college student's lifestyle is a potential viable threat to their survival and, certainly, to their successful academic performance.

The career that students have held for thirteen years—attending school—changes drastically. The job description changes and, more importantly, the boss changes. From the nanosecond that parents say goodbye, they are fired. Suddenly the child is in charge, but the promotion comes with two hats: employer *and* employee.

The college student is the CEO of her life. Every decision is her own. This may sound empowering, and it is, but it is also devastating. At the same time she becomes her own boss, she loses her office manager and personal assistant—the great and powerful Mommy. Every single task of her daily life, managed until that kiss goodbye, is now up to her. That kiss changes everything.

* * *

With the new job title comes a new identity. College students are systematically interrogated and expected to have all the answers:

"What's your major?"
"What's your GPA?"
"Are you seeing anyone?"
"Do you have a part-time job?"
"Who's paying for your education?"
"What are your plans after school?"
And, the ever-popular: *"What are you gonna do with your life?"*

College students don't know where their campus mailbox is, much less what they're going to do with the rest of their lives. It's a moot question, anyway. No one knows what he's going to do with the rest of his life! It's common for people to major in one field and work in some totally unrelated field. Hardly anyone wears one vocational hat anymore. We play musical chairs, bopping along from one career to the next (when we're lucky enough to secure employment). Nonetheless, we expect students to identify their paths after receiving their high school diplomas, as if their lives' vocations are etched in ink next to their names.

If only it were that tidy, but it's not. For those who have earned your degrees, think back. Remember college? Mmhm. Okay, now *really* remember it. Hold on a second. Put down your phone . . . reflect for a moment. College. Is it all coming back? Just a bit more . . . Ahh, *now* you're there. Now you got it.

College demands all of you and expects you to defend it. College demands that you know who you are, what you want, and how to get it.

College is serious stuff.

BA Is the New GED

It's also serious business. Since the twenty-first century, college has become required reading among first-world inhabitants. If you want a good job, you must graduate college. If you want to make money, graduate college. If you want to be happy, graduate college.

The BA is the new high school diploma, and in fact, the BA is really just a stepping stone to your *real* degree. If you want to make *serious* money and be *seriously* happy, you must acquire *at least* a Master's degree. This is the new truth and this truth is well-marketed. College is Big Business—one of the most reliable forms of commodity we currently have in the States, beyond peddling *mochaccinos*.

The truth is a myth and fantasy, a Hollywood ending. The ideal of college and its original quest no longer exists: the gathering of bright young wealthy male minds to postpone the eventual settling into Daddy's company; the finishing place for society women to meet and marry; and later, the melting pot of intellectual curiosity, stirring ideas, beliefs, passions, and social actions. Institutions are transforming, replacing abstract liberal arts degrees with concrete technical training. Online models and distance learning now pervade higher education.

Regardless of the shape, today's college is considered prerequisite to "making it" in the world, securing the perfect career and social status. In the US, college has evolved into a coming-of-age symbol, like a car or trip to Europe. It's something kids get when they graduate, because they're supposed to. It's not only kids who believe this; parents readily embrace this mindset. *If you're good parents, you send your kid to college.* The epidemic of college continues to spread, despite the financial and lifestyle burdens it creates.

At a time when we are outsourcing work opportunities, college is becoming one of the last great domestic products. It's the last, best toy children receive before they are thrust into the real world. Increasingly, for both parents and their children, college is becoming a place to put off the inevitable, more pause than prepare. College is a holding tank before dealing with the reality of adult life.

You'd think this overzealous enthusiasm would be due to universal financial accessibility, but nothing is further from the truth. Our nation holds the highest college debt of any westernized country with some of the lowest financial assistance for higher education, while offering the least amount of job security. The only thing a college degree guarantees is student loan debt; still, college graduates earn a sense of entitlement with their degrees. *They're college graduates, for Chrissake—better than a T-shirt Folder at the GAP or 'Za Slinger at Dominos!* Only, they're not. College students graduate, only to find themselves competing in the workforce for the same jobs as younger, less qualified applicants who make better candidates, because they have lower expectations and are willing to work for less money. If they're lucky enough to secure a job, college graduates use their hard-earned paychecks to pay down their never-ending student loans.

The harsh reality is that a college degree no longer implies success. More young adults are applying to, transferring from, and dropping out of college. For those that do graduate, more young adults are unemployed and living at home.

College is hard enough when you are qualified and prepared, but if you are a student who has learning challenges, attending college is akin to paddling your way out of a tsunami. That does not stop learning-challenged students from applying to college. In fact, their numbers are increasing, becoming an integral part of the higher learning population.

Learning disability (LD) laws have initiated a surge of support centers and learning accommodations. In addition to accommodations, colleges also institute policy changes: pass/low pass/fail grades and forgiveness policies for failed classes. Critics challenge how assignments are modified and grades inflated. It's tempting to blame learning-challenged students, but that may be too easy. More likely, expectations have shifted; college is a universally encouraged choice for anyone graduating high school. Some states are implementing free community college incentives. Whatever the reasons, scholarly expectations have been reducing for decades. Graduating from college isn't the rigor it used to be.

Colleges are becoming the thing they once loathed—degree factories. However, this should not be viewed as a stigma. Factories are places that manufacture a product. In this case, the factory manufactures a degree. It's not an evil conspiracy, but rather, good business sense. If more learning-challenged students are coming of age, and more non-traditional students are applying to college, then colleges need rebranding to accommodate new demands. For busy people, veterans, working parents, and distance learners, online and for-profit schools have burgeoned on the scene.

In a business model, when the customer changes, the product often follows suit. Colleges currently follow business models and are transparent about this shift. Following a business model, colleges modify expectations in order to keep the customer happy. If a student fails, college revenue fails. Schools receive funding for graduation rates, versus enrollment. Colleges, like all businesses in a shaky economy, shift from being product-driven to profit-driven. It's not solely the colleges' fault; all businesses rely on creative problem-solving to stay afloat. Our economy drives our motivation.

The problem isn't that colleges now embrace business models nor is it that expectations are changing. **The problem comes when people buy a product that they cannot afford and do not use.** College students' minds are garages filled with expensive unused toys. During a recent presentation, Temple Grandin, popular learning disabilities advocate, summed it up candidly: "College has become too abstract. People need to be learning how to *do* things, rather than be forced to contemplate abstract concepts, graduating devoid of any practical skills. Too many kids aren't learning how to work."

* * *

I can hear my students, now. "Geez, way to be hating on college, Mrs. C." Guess what? I'm all for college! I went to college. My husband went to college. Our sons went to college. My brother and sister went to college. My folks were educated beyond their Master's degrees and held professional careers. I *teach* at a college, for Pete's sake. I live and breathe higher education.

But, college is not for everyone. It never was and never will be. For the money it costs versus the outcome it yields and lack of job security it provides, college is no longer viable in many situations. College is certainly not for the person who is unqualified or unprepared.

It may not be worth it if attending puts one in debt for the comparable cost of purchasing a house. It is also not worth it if the only reason someone goes is because someone else believes they should go.

Crazybusy Culture

What's happened to the typical college student? How are students different than they were years ago? Every generation experiences dramatic change. Due to its malleable nature, a child's brain may be neurologically different from his parents'. Brains wire uniquely; this "wiring" is what psychologists call nurturing. It's all that life-stuff we do to the brain after nature has formed it. How has the nurturing changed for today's college students?

One major change is the family environment. Contemporary home life is completely different than the last generation's. The nuclear family—spouses who marry, have their own biological children, and remain married—is nearly extinct. These days, it's more conventional for spouses to divorce than remain married. Many couples have children out of wedlock, and single mothers are the norm. Alternative child-acquisition techniques such as adoption and fertility intervention are commonplace.

During my Master's degree program back in 2000, I participated in a student panel, *Diversity Within the Family Unit*. At the time, I was a divorced mother of two half-brothers and never married the second son's father. Starkly aware of my "colorful predicament," I figured the college invited me as the resident freak.

How wrong I was. In addition to me, the panel represented: a lesbian couple; a couple whose husband had transgendered into a woman (which might make them a lesbian couple, too); a single mother who had chosen artificial insemination; a couple who had intentionally adopted several severely disabled children; and an elderly couple who were raising their granddaughter, due to their drug-addled daughter's inability to parent.

There was one freak show representing. Let's call her Lisa, since that is not her name. (This is Martha Beck's joke, from her bestselling memoir, *Expecting Adam*, and it's wonderful. Thank you, Martha.) Lisa is a Christian woman who married her high school sweetheart, bore three healthy children, and has remained monogamously married to this day.

You would've thought Lisa entered the panel wearing only edible panties while huffing on a crack pipe. During the Q & A, someone asked Lisa if she was a virgin when they married. Her affirmation caused deep snorts, smirks, and a few indiscreet elbow jabs at neighboring participants. Lisa's marital virginity and serial monogamy caused a flurry of curiosity. The glaring audience began asking her barbed questions, each one more directed and judgmental than the last. With every hesitation (Lisa is a nice woman, after all), the audience grew more brazen and vindictive. The whole scene felt very lynch-y. I kept scanning the audience, the panel, and Lisa, barely restraining from screaming aloud, *"Why the hell are you-all getting so upset? She's the only normal one here!"*

Lisa touched a nerve, and remember, this was back in 2000. Since then, family dynamics continue to grow more interesting. Ask any adult in the United States how they are, and they will respond, "**Crazybusy**." There may be cutesy versions: "I don't have a minute to spare; I don't have time to breathe; I'll sleep when I'm dead; I'm out flat, out of control, out of my mind."

In my generation, people used to be busy. Somewhere between 1980 and 2000, people progressed from busy to *crazy*busy. Nowadays, being so busy that you incite mental illness isn't impressive enough to warrant attention. You have to be *so* busy that you have no time to inhale oxygen into your lungs and exhale carbon dioxide back into the atmosphere.

The truth may be that people want to avoid weird people and icky obligations, and the polite way of doing so is to say, "Gosh, I'd love to, but I'm busy." Eventually, everybody used that particular nugget. Being busy was no longer a viable excuse, so one had to up the ante, declaring, "Gosh, I'd love to, but I'm *crazy*busy." Then, in an effort to cover one's tracks, one had to *become* crazybusy to make one's excuses appear legitimate. The moral of this story is to heed the late Kurt Vonnegut's advice: "We are what we pretend to be."

* * *

Life is transient and global and constantly changing, and that is an exciting concept; but, in order to create this zesty new world, some things had to give. Extended families are *really* extended. People can live anywhere in the world, so families have scattered. Where relatives used to stay close—geographically, therefore emotionally—contact is reduced to the occasional yearly visit. Kids grow up without knowing their extended family and learning from them. Kids used to learn how to *do* things: cook, garden, care for animals, fix cars, and build stuff. They would learn special skills that their families loved: playing music, fishing, skiing, camping, and constructing model trains and planes.

Family meals have drastically changed. Moms would cook and kids would help, and everyone would eat together. Meals were an opportunity to be together, sharing stories and telling about the day. Mealtime was a communal time to bond, laugh, argue, and resolve issues. Cooking and eating are at the core of our existence, yet are ignored in our modern way of life.

Eating has taken on a more robotic and dismissive quality these days. "Fast food, on-the-go, grab 'n' gulp, in-and-out, convenience"—these are the phrases that describe our relationship to eating. Today's meals are in-transit: in the car, on the field, and in rehearsals. Meals are shoved into our bodies on the way to appointments and activities. Eating has taken on a perverse stigma. It is a cumbersome interruption of our workflow, rather like stopping to refill the car with gas. Every minute spent eating is a minute that could and should be spent being productive and making money. My husband jokes about the American male who eats over the sink.

Ah, in jest there is truth. People eat over the sink, at work cubicles, in class, on the phone, while driving and commuting. Maybe you're reading this book on an airplane while munching on a bag of nuts, which you will later tonight refer to as "lunch."

If eating is a lost art, cooking is dead. No longer a legitimate part of our lifestyle, cooking is demoted to a luxury hobby. Some consider cooking indulgent, and some people even consider it inferior and submissive. *A parent who spends time cooking is an archaic homebody who could be out there in the real world earning a living with a career, really providing for the family.* Some people just think it's too expensive to cook. Consequently, young people miss learning this invaluable life skill.

Learning practical skills from family, like cooking, has been replaced by the modern activities of screens, organized sports, and monitored play dates. Parents spend more time observing their children, yet less time interacting with and teaching them. In the past, when kids weren't learning skills from their parents, they were as far away from their parents as possible. Parents used to kick kids out the door after breakfast with a perfunctory, "Go play," expecting them to return home only for lunch and dinner. The rest of the time was spent playing in the neighborhood.

Life for kids used to be a freer time. They moved their bodies and breathed outside air. Kids learned how to be kids through other kids. They learned social behavior through games like *Kick the Can* and *Capture the Flag* or they made up their own games. Kids made the rules and regulated them, redirecting each other. My father told me that if a parent came by to intervene, kids would gather up their stuff and move to another field.

Parents now organize everything for their Precious Flowers. Today's parents may protest, "The world is more dangerous nowadays. Children need constant supervision." For the majority of US citizens, most of the time, life is not life-threatening. Unless you are growing up near the Gaza strip or in a developing nation (one might consider the urban projects as developing nations), life is pretty peachy with occasional shocking incidents. No child should be observed 100 percent of the time. Even prison inmates have moments of privacy.

My generation grew up with one television. One. It was located in this thing called a "family room," where families converged together, at the same time, in human form. Everyone watched the same thing. Show selection was controlled by adults and TV time limited. If you didn't like the show, you didn't watch television. Video games didn't exist. Only the occasional war movie or western television show would offer that much violence. If you wanted to engage in combat, you did it outside, in person, with the rest of the neighborhood kids. When inside, we played quietly: card and board games, playing with dolls (action figures), puzzles, and reading. Modern quiet time is primarily screen time.

Telephone use was vastly limited, compared to modern modality. Phones were auditory; you talked and listened only, with no texting or photos. Phones had cords attached to separate receivers, so you were landlocked in a room. My friends and I would invent code words during phone conversations. "The stars are shining," was code for "My folks are in the room." If I said, "Apple pie?" that meant, "Did you go all the way?" (Kids, we didn't hook up. We went all the way.) People shared the phone line and scheduled times to talk. (Even weirder is how our folks shared telephone lines with neighbors, which actually seems more like today's internet).

Phones didn't exist in college, except for pay phones. Without cell phones or email, students had to use corded dormitory phones located in the hallways. Students were confined to leaning against the wall, like Will in *Good Will Hunting*, David in *War Games,* and more recently, Piper, in *Orange is the New Black*. Some privileged students had telephones in their dorm rooms, but these phones were corded, too. Because there were no personal cell phones, there were no phone distractions in the classroom. If professors were boring, students had to resort to a rudimentary distractive technique known as "doodling."

Before electronic mail, people wrote letters, with writing implements called pens and paper. You would write a letter, mail it, and wait. A few days later, your recipient would receive it. A few days later, they would reply and mail their letter. And a few days after that, you would receive their reply. I imagine that sounds a bit like the Pony Express did to our generation.

These small details were huge, in terms of communication. You had to actively plan when to have a phone conversation. Parents and long-distance partners would schedule weekly check-in dates, for example, Sundays at 7:00 pm. With no computers or cell phones, there was no texting. Parents could not constantly text, "Where are you?" and "What are you doing?" Contact was not the instantaneous luxury of today; making contact was an intentional act. (While dating, my grandparents would talk weekly on the phone. In anticipation for her conversation, Grandma Esther would dress in a preciously light voile dress, which she accessorized with delicate yellow silk stockings.)

Without screens, students went to the library to study. They relied on printed media for academic information: books, journals, magazines, and articles. The library's resource room was utilized for its informational tomes instead of its contemporary function of hosting napping graduate students. Without computers, there was no Google. One had to physically seek out information, ask someone, or look it up in a book. Family and school were primary sources of information and values formation. Without the web and streaming shows, screens were limited to television's fixed schedules (no TiVo). Students rarely had their own televisions in their rooms; instead, they watched television in the residential lounges. Video games did not exist, so there was no temptation to stay up all night playing.

College was still considered a privilege rather than an expectation, and fewer people attended. Higher education was an expensive lengthy luxury for those who wanted to enter specific professional fields or had expendable funds to expand their intellect. The remaining population worked.

In previous generations, if you were learning-challenged, you typically did not attend college. If you did, you worked twice as hard and still struggled mightily. There were no learning disabilities, or rather, they were not legally recognized. I tell my students, "When I was in high school, there was no ADHD. You were just considered an ass."

Learning disabilities (LD) were legally recognized in 1973, but similar to most civil rights, were slow to gain implementation. For a culture to change, it needs a few million people to shake their heads yes or no, in unison. Back then, most people just shrugged their shoulders at the mention of an LD. In the 80s, knowledge of LD was as rare as AIDS, and news of its diagnosis received as warmly.

* * *

Since the 70s, every decade brought an increase in technology, college attendance, and LD awareness, until a tipping point seems to have been reached. Students are expected to attend college and use technology. Everyone has heard of LDs and many students have *some* diagnosis: an LD; behavioral disorder such as ADHD (Attention-Deficit Hyperactivity Disorder), ASD (Autism Spectrum Disorder), OCD (Obsessive Compulsive Disorder) or CD (Conduct Disorder); some diagnosis that affects the learning process like depression, stress, or anxiety disorders. If students do not have a diagnosis, they know someone who does. Test the hypothesis. Does anyone in your family have at least one such diagnosis? No? Do they know someone? Sure they do.

With an odd combination of crazybusy culture, sedentary lifestyle, and an increase in learning and behavioral diagnoses comes an increase in medication. Most people are medicated these days, and not just the adults. Again, ask around. It's less common to find someone who's on *nothing*. During annual physical exams, the nurse asks me to list all current medications I am taking. I reply, "None," and await the accusatory leer. "*None? Nothing?*" At that moment, I can relate to my friend Lisa. Living medication-free is abnormal. I feel like apologizing for not being on something, as if somehow, I'm neglecting my health.

At a time when it is increasingly more difficult to fund, flourish, and find employment with a college degree, young adults are increasingly expected to attend. The myth is vibrant in today's society, and the pressure is on. One must not only be a college graduate. One must employ a renaissance mentality to one's life. Children are forced from birth to adopt a crazybusy lifestyle just like their parents'. All their lives lead up to college, and their whole life depends on their successful journey through it.

The crazybusy lifestyle worships productivity and parental control, but sorely neglects the key factors necessary to function successfully: food, sleep, stress management, movement, creativity, connection, and moderation. Without these in place, even the smartest young college student may flounder.

COLLEGE: ACADEMIC OR MENTAL INSTITUTION?

"If your son or daughter is in college, the chances are almost one in two that he or she will become depressed to the point of being unable to function; one in two that he or she will have regular episodes of binge drinking (with the resulting significant risk of dangerous consequences such as sexual assault and car accidents); and one in ten that he or she will seriously consider suicide. In fact, since 1988, the likelihood of a college student's suffering depression has doubled, suicidal ideation has tripled, and sexual assaults have quadrupled."

—Richard Kadison, MD, *College of the Overwhelmed*

A Crisis in College

When I was six, I wanted to be a brain doctor. I wanted to be a brain doctor before I had any real idea what that meant. I pictured doing research in a lab with people hooked up to wires and monitors, tracking their thoughts and feelings. I'd spend my days figuring out how we did things and why we did them. Fascinated by the idea, the words rang in my mind . . . *brain doctor* . . . *brain doctor*. I would become famous and travel around the world, helping people. That's what brain doctors did, after all. I was going to be a big, famous brain doctor.

When my friends and I played with Barbie dolls, I played brain doctor. Barbie was Ken's therapist. Ken was really messed up and Barbie possessed keen insight into Ken's suffering. I would prop him up on a couch made out of a small bean bag puppy. Ken lay down on the therapy couch, while Barbie sat on my lap probing his psyche.

When I was about ten years old, two movies were released that profoundly affected me: *The Exorcist* (1973) and *Carrie* (1976). Supernatural concepts such as channeling, possession, and telekinesis invaded my brain doctor fantasy. The vision shifted to paranormal activity. Intuition, E.S.P., and pre-cognition—these phenomena fascinated me. I attempted bending spoons and moving objects with my mind. I pictured what would happen in the future and predicted what cards were when face down. I practiced and practiced, and not much seemed to happen. No matter. I predicted my future with absolute accuracy: to be a famous paranormal brain doctor.

Duke

Did you know that Duke University has a parapsychology department? I did. Back in 1980, it was the only parapsychology department in the United States, and Duke was the only college to offer a bachelor's degree in parapsychology. That was it! *Fait accompli.*

How amazing that a university would have not only courses in parapsychology, but an *actual* department, an actual major. Plus, Duke was such a cool school, complete with a Division I basketball team. Parties and parapsychology awaited me.

I fantasized about receiving my doctorate in parapsychology and spending days in the dreamy world of research: writing grants, conducting experiments and, of course, presenting my astounding findings. My path was clear. I found my calling. Along with brain doctor, the phrase *keynote speaker* entered into my vision. I would chant these mantras as I hummed along the remaining high school days.

A friend and I visited Duke University in early December. She was considering Vanderbilt University and decided to tag along for a fun southern college experience. We stayed in a dorm with a student host. The eerie gothic grey buildings, the mild weather, the humungous basketball stadium, the quaint, cool college town . . . it was perfect. I felt at once excited and serene, at peace with myself and confident that I was visiting my future home for the first time. I glided around campus with arms swinging, the warm winter breeze blowing softly against my toughened Vermont skin.

During the weekend visit, television broadcasts exploded with news that John Lennon had been shot in front of his apartment building, *The Dakota*, in New York City. Not even the news of Lennon's assassination could squelch my ecstasy.

I would be a brain doctor, conducting research on plants and mice and then humans, studying E.S.P. and intuition and clairvoyance and pre-cognition. A pioneer in paranormal science, I'd propel noetic sciences into the twenty-first century, illuminating the sixth sense and forming new theories. I'd be a famous keynote speaker, traveling throughout the world, but mostly in Australasia and Europe. I'd discover fantastic research breakthroughs. Of course, I would write compelling and humorous narratives like Bill Bryson, but my real power lay in public speaking. I'd be a funny, magnetic presenter: the cool, hip scientist who breaks complex ideas down into clear, witty doctrines—*Carl Sagan meets Deepak Chopra meets Malcolm Gladwell meets Louis C.K.*—the kind of person people flock to and quote and tell all their friends about and can't wait to see again.

I apply for early admissions to Duke University. Three weeks later, I am rejected.

Plan B

I had no idea that early admissions was more competitive than regular admissions. *Of course* I should apply for early admissions, because I really, *really* wanted to go! (Rather like a girl sleeping with a guy on the first date, to show him how much she really, *really* likes him.)

Immediately stalled and completely stunned, I had no idea what to do. Duke was the only school to which I had applied. I had not considered rejection. There was no Plan B, no safety school, and no state college. Never once did I seek advice from a guidance counselor, because I didn't need it. I never thought of re-applying for regular admissions, because I couldn't bear that horrible feeling of rejection a second time. I needed a college. An admissions counselor from Bryn Mawr College visited our high school. They presented a slide show in the library. Their buildings resembled Duke's.

I apply to Bryn Mawr. Three weeks later, I am accepted.

* * *

So, we drive down to Bryn Mawr. I start unpacking the car and begin looking around. "Where are all the guys?" My father looked sideways at me and said, "You're joking, right? Bryn Mawr is an all-girls' school."

I wasn't joking. I had no idea. I expected college to be *Duke*: Big State University life, southern hospitality, and hot-buttered rum sipped under blankets, watching football games. What I didn't expect was an all-girl's school. Judging from the look of the typical student, athletics and partying were not high on their priority list.

In senior year, I acquired a new name and pet. Wilma Daniels was my fake ID name, in preparation for barhopping at Duke. You see kids, way back then, Vermont's drinking age was 18, and any respectable high school senior sported a fake ID. The name "Wilma" was weird . . . kooky, silly, and exotic. "Daniels" just flowed. *Wilma Daniels, Wilma Daniels* . . . The name evolved to Willowmina Muffinhead when, during keyboarding class, we were typing business letters and could make up any name. I tried Wilma Daniels, and that was fun to type, then riffed around and discovered Willowmina Muffinhead was even *more* fun. The name sort of stuck. As for the pet, my best friend and I went to the mall during Senior Skip Day. She dyed her hair fuchsia. I bought a boa constrictor and named him Pythagoras.

Here come Willowmina and Pythagoras to Bryn Mawr, looking around and wondering where all the hot boys and buttered rum are. Undeterred, I enter my suite and introduce myself and Pythagoras to my suitemates. Later that week, during a residential hall orientation tea, I stride confidently up to the college president, stretch out my hand, and declare, "Hello. I am Willowmina Muffinhead. You are going to remember me."

Essay

Freshman English ran Monday mornings at 9:00 am. Following a curt introduction, our teacher described the grading process. Every Monday morning at 8:45 am sharp, we would submit a 5-page typed, double-spaced essay on the topic of our choice. The culmination of these graded essays would comprise our final grade.

Piece of cake. I loved writing; in fact, my love of writing coincided with my first crush. It happened in tenth grade with Jon Hayward, a dashing Englishman disguised as an English teacher. Mr. Hayward was mid-thirties, average height, slim build, and brutally handsome. His salt-and-pepper beard covered sweet dimples, which melted into deep dark eyes, but in a playful way, not piercing. He always seemed to be in mid-to-post-giggle. I liked him so much. He liked me, too, understanding my humor and encouraging my nonconformist thinking. We lingered a bit after class, enjoying our company.

Mr. Hayward required students to maintain a daily journal. Journals were the most important part of the class. Entries were to be written daily for at least fifteen minutes. The only rule was that there were no rules. We were to write from the head, heart, and soul. Never had I been given this forum for self-expression in school.

Although I always kept a journal, my entries were daily-log-griping stuff—*sister's-being-a-jerk* fodder. Mr. Hayward would have accepted the daily log style, but I wanted to be noticed. My writing would shock him and he would know me. It was safe sex, but better. Because it was required, I disguised my personal enthusiasm behind the assignment. I thought, *Geez, I must be doing a fine job keeping up with my homework*, not fully realizing the unearthing passion.

I wrote several times a day, sometimes for hours—slash-and-burn observations, hurled anger and bliss, documenting moods like torrential rain. I loved feeling cleaner after a hearty rant. The journal offered a place to take risks, and I played with poetry and short stories. Risks were encouraged, and the enthusiasm became infectious. I noticed how the more I wrote, the more I wrote. My muscles gained confidence. The ability to drop into the writer's well increased as time passed. I awakened the writer and began to listen and share in dialogue. In writing, I found a friend, a true *confidante*—someone who shared my soul and heard me without interrupting, unlike a friend who hijacks the moment to share her own stories.

I eventually forgot about Mr. Hayward and wrote for myself. The writing became vulnerable and touching. This was the writing he respected the most. I began to understand this, too. When I wrote for him, writing was forced, seeking approval. When I wrote for myself, writing flowed honestly. When grading, Mr. H wrote long responses that always ended, "Keep writing." He looked forward to reading my journal. How powerful for a young woman to affect someone whom she admired! It was intimately divine.

> To a very meaningful, decent, heavy, groovey, excellent, veggie, wonky, beautiful lady —
> JH
>
> *In this short life*
> *That only lasts an hour*
> *How much — how little — is*
> *Within our power*
> *— Dickinson*

Jon Hayward enscribes in Susan (Fagelson) Crowther's 1980 Brattleboro Union High School yearbook, Junior year.

In this spirit of writing confidence, I received the news of grading criteria in English Composition, in that first class, on that first day of college. There was a tiny glitch. I had no idea what an essay was. I mean, I knew how to write, and I sort of had an idea what an essay was. Kinda. You know. But, I didn't know what it should, you know, look like. Like, how was a college essay different from, say, an assignment in high school? Was this some new type of special format thingamajig? What about this "topic of our choice?" What was *that* all about? You mean, like *anything* or something *"English-y"*? I got A+s in Mr. Hayward's journals. Could I just submit five pages of that?

Recall that this was 1981. Back then, PCs, laptops, tablets, and smartphones—all of it—did not exist. I couldn't Google "essay" to discover what the professor wanted, nor email her for guidance.

Granted, I could have turned to my classmate sitting next to me or stayed after class, requesting clarification from the professor. I could have called my parents. I could have asked probably anybody at the college, including the janitor (in my experience, college janitors have often earned degrees in higher education). But, come on. We're talking about an eighteen-year-old college student, and female, at that. Expecting a young female adult to seek help is like asking someone from 1981 to imagine a smartphone.

On the following Monday, precisely at 8:45 a.m., all the young English students dropped their essays into the professor's assignment bin outside her office. I slunk into the classroom at 9:00 am, sitting in the back of the lecture hall near the door. The professor began discussing a book we were reading. A few questions were proposed to the class, and a few bold girls answered. I remained silent, never making eye contact with the professor nor diverting my head. I stared into the back of the seat in front of me in a defocused gaze, appearing attentive while remaining motionless. There was pink chewed gum stuck to the lower left side of the seat, and I concentrated on it. By the end of class, I could smell it. Strawberry.

The moment class ended, I abruptly rose from my seat and quickly left the room. I *knew* the professor would be right behind me, calling out, "Hey you! *Yeah, YOU! You didn't submit your essay! Someone stop her!*" Any moment, there'd be a jerking motion as the professor grabbed my shoulder and accosted me in front of everyone.

Nothing happened.

For the rest of the week, I went to my other classes and did the homework. The essay plagued my conscience. The following Monday repeated the pattern: girls dutifully dropped off their papers while I snuck in the back of the room, sitting lower in my seat.

The next week, I began doodling in class.

20 + 6 = 1

Joan, Laurel, and I were the Three Musketeers, the rebels. We detested drinking tea in the dorm lounges, instead opting for booze in UPENN fraternities. Rather than sitting around madly debating social and political justice, we hit the Philly bars, drank all night, and then wolfed down cheesesteaks in the early morning. We were savagely misplaced; Bryn Mawr was a pathetic hoax played upon us. State College gals marooned at a frigid Sister school? We commiserated on how we ended up on a campus filled with uptight hair-lipped feminist lesbians androgynously named Adrianne, Chris, and Terry. While our love of hating Bryn Mawr sustained us, Joan and Laurel found a way to play the game. Through commiserating and rebelling, they still managed to attend classes, hand in homework, and pass exams.

Halfway into the semester, attendance became too painful. I wasn't submitting the papers. The professor never confronted me. It was as if I didn't exist . . . so, I didn't. I stopped attending English class. I was already failing, so why bother trying? Plus, English was held at 9:00 am. On a *Monday.* Come on.

Hell, as long as I wasn't going to English, I may as well stop going to Calculus. Ever since *infinity* entered into the equation, math turned hopeless. Forget it. German was stupid, too. Who takes *German?* What was I thinking? That left art history and psychology, two classes I actually liked. Art history introduced beautiful creations and told stories of tortured geniuses in troubled times. So did psychology, for that matter . . . plus, psychology fed my brain doctor passions. However, the pull was strong and soon I stopped attending, altogether.

I had my own car on campus and took long solo drives, serenaded by Carly Simon and Linda Ronstadt: "You're No Good," "You Don't Love Me Anymore," "You're So Vain." Hours were spent driving around the suburbs of Philadelphia, cranking tunes and singing at the top of my lungs. In the middle of the night, I'd prowl the drive-thru windows, ordering greasy cheeseburgers, French fries, and sausage pizzas, then hit the convenience stores for Hostess cakes, honey buns, and half gallons of ice cream. I'd eat the fast food and desserts while driving, then finish with ice cream in the parking lot. Before the carton was completely empty, the ice cream would start melting. I'd shove all the wrappers into the carton and pack the trash into a fast food bag, then run into the dorm and sneak into one of the bathroom stalls on a floor different from my own.

I stopped talking to my roommates and slept most of the day. Sometimes I would sit in the suite holding Pythagoras while they tried to study. My roommates grew weary and asked if maybe I could find another room. I applied for a single room in Brecon Hall, a remote senior dormitory half a mile off campus. The request was granted.

After rejection from Duke and avoiding the English essay, that Brecon move was the worst academic decision. I hid out, rarely attending class, only leaving my room for the late-night drives. Failure snowballed; the less I went to class, the more fear grew, and the less nerve I had to seek out my professors. The weeks went by. While my classmates went to study in the library, I hid in my room, smoking cigarettes and watching Pythagoras choke mice. I was the snake: cold, calculating, unpredictable, and uncaring. I was the mouse: frightened, doomed, and suffocating under the predator's unwavering grip.

Fall semester culminated with a .7 GPA. (I somehow managed to pass Introduction to Psychology.) Bryn Mawr held a strict academic policy; earning a GPA below 2.0 initiated a "red flag" with academic probation and mandatory counseling. A student without the energy to get out of bed is now faced with this looming challenge. A "pick-yourself-up-by-the-bootstraps-and-get-the-job-done" mentality was needed. I didn't have that. What I did have was a private room off-campus, a boa constrictor, an eating disorder, and a severe case of undiagnosed depression.

* * *

I didn't know what to do, so I went to work. I had already worked in kitchens for five years and liked how I felt when cooking. It comforted, in some natural way. Cooking, like writing, had always been friendly. Opening the Yellow Pages (an actual phone book with yellow pages, for you whippersnappers), I found an appealing name of a catering business: *Chez Bear*. I dialed the number. Bear answered.

"Hello. Do you need any help?"

"What you mean, do I need help? Help weeth waaht?"

"I mean, do you need any help . . . like, in your kitchen?"

Bear had an impatient, short-tempered manner (what accomplished French chef *doesn't?*), so it was serendipitous to find him in a relaxed and talkative mood. We spoke briefly, and he told me to me come over.

"Right now?"

"Yes of course, what you thaaynk?"

When I walked through the door, he tossed me an apron. I put it on and kept it on all semester.

Although it further detracted from academics, the job also rescued me. Campus had become stagnant and vile—*icky*. I always felt like this putrid creature violating Bryn Mawr's pristine paths, a disease infecting the campus. At work I excelled, impressing Bear with fluent common sense and intuitive ways of handling customers and operations. It brought solace in a way that an eighteen-year-old cannot articulate. I simply felt better when I went to work than when I went to class. *Chez Bear* was good and Bryn Mawr was bad.

On April 30, 1982, three weeks before freshman year ended, I packed up my car and left. I didn't tell my parents; I just showed up at home. I have never returned to Bryn Mawr. To this day, even hearing the name makes me queasy. There is such intense shame, so much disappointment, failure, and dread, so much avoiding and lying . . . so much pain. I murdered that fragile young girl. She was doomed the moment she received that rejection letter from Duke.

My shame was not the guilt of literal murder. It did not stem from physical or sexual abuse. The failure was not life-threatening, and my psyche had no need to repress it. As time went on, life brought real issues to deal with. My shame wasn't enough to be acknowledged. Feeling it felt indulgent; however, to this day, it is felt.

I was supposed to ace college! I'm one of the smart ones! Ninth in my high school class! An IQ of 164, a member of the Mensa Society! I was destined be a brain doctor!

What the hell happened?

* * *

First, Do Some Good

It took twenty years and six colleges to earn my Bachelor's degree. I lead with that at the beginning of every semester. "Good morning, students. My name is Susan Crowther, and I am your teacher. It took me twenty years and six schools to graduate from college." Eyes grow wide; a few of them roll. Smiles and frowns emerge. Some kids glance at each other. Sometimes I feel like my friend, Lisa. Mostly, we let out a collective sigh. However they laugh, at me or with me, doesn't matter. Either way, they are laughing. The truth calms my students and helps them feel a bit more at home in their own skin.

They all have failures. Failure is, in fact, a prerequisite to being there. "There" is a college for learning-challenged students, where I taught for many years. These students failed in academics so consistently that their options were to either quit school altogether or come to this tiny village and attend this tiny school to learn how to learn. And maybe, they might also learn to *like* learning . . . a tiny bit. (I no longer teach there, but continue to empathize vocally with struggling students and their parents.)

Learning-challenged students initially were diagnosed with dyslexia and other language-based learning disabilities. Around the mid 1990s, the demographic changed. College campuses began to see an increase in students diagnosed with attention disorders, such as ADD and ADHD (now known as ADHD). Dyslexia is a disorder treated with remediation rather than medication: skills and strategies, intervention and support. However, ADHD is a disorder typically treated with medication. It was and still is common protocol for educational psycho-evaluations to recommend medication in conjunction with academic management.

At the time, current pedagogical climate supported the belief that medication was the first line of defense in achieving academic success. The hypothesis was straightforward: if students failed to take medication, they failed. The philosophy was widely supported as the course of action for ADHD treatment, endorsed by leading brain researchers Drs. Russell Barkley, Thomas Brown, and Daniel Amen.

* * *

Years before teaching, while working at a health food store (Marlene's Market and Deli, from *The No Recipe Cookbook*), I met a blond-haired hippie midwife named Honey. Honey was *the* midwife, delivering all the naturally-born babies in the Seattle valley.

One day, Honey came in to shop. A pregnant customer who was two weeks overdue happened to be there. Part of the excellent customer service at Marlene's Market and Deli is "babying" the customer. We prided ourselves in fully supporting the customer's needs. That included researching particular illnesses with them and, together, identifying just the right foods, herbs, or supplements to help aid in their recovery.

I approached Honey and shared the woman's plight. "What should she do?" I asked. "Take some Blue Cohosh tincture? Raspberry tea? Perhaps a homeopathic remedy?"

Honey said, "Walk."

"Huh?"

"Have her go for a walk," she replied. "If the baby doesn't come, have her go for another walk, up a hill."

"A hill."

"If labor continues to stall, have her walk up another hill. Have her keep walking up hills until a baby comes."

I couldn't believe she would leave it at something so simple, so I pressed her.

Is there any other way to stimulate labor?

Sex.

How to instigate the water sac breaking?

Ride slowly in a truck down a bumpy road.

Having delivered hundreds of babies, Honey understood a simple, powerful philosophy: First, do some good. **Given the opportunity and healthy resources, a body naturally seeks to balance itself.**

* * *

Years later in this tiny village, I found myself on the other side of the fence. My lifelong philosophy meshed with Honey's. It postulated an oppositional stance from the current pedagogical climate, mainly, that **medication is the last line of defense in any healing situation**. Every other lifestyle factor must be considered before subjecting a person to a foreign chemical, especially on a continual basis.

Medication does work, some of the time, for some students; however, medication is never intended to be the first line of defense in any physiological matter. Hippocrates stated, "First, do no harm," and meds are . . . well, meds. They are foreign substances that infiltrate the mind, body, *and* spirit—subtle energy fields surrounding every human. Meds force changes by their very nature. These changes often have a spectrum of effects that are taxing, toxic, or even fatal. Many create additional issues that necessitate more medication. Chronic use may transform a person into a pharmaceutical cripple, unable to self-regulate and dependent upon external chemical manipulation.

Medication can be valuable and has its place in the academic world, but only as a last resort. One must consider every plausible lifestyle aspect of a student's condition before administering diagnosis and medication. The protocol to seeking health in any situation must be to first, do some good. Always apply something beneficial, before you manipulate the body with synthetic chemicals that alter body systems and create toxic by-products. Add goodness and strive to regain balance: a good night's rest, a nourishing meal, a tall drink of water, a much-needed pep talk from a dear friend. Science is increasingly validating the physiological power of simple steps toward wellbeing. In an age of litigious behavior, think of healthy lifestyle practices as GRAS: Generally Regarded as Safe (and Smart).

Attending college is like having a baby, so heed Honey's advice. If you are having trouble studying, take a break. If you are restless, go for a walk. If you're really restless, be active: shoot some hoops or plug into some music and dance in your room. If you are hungry, grab a bite to eat. If you're tired, take a nap. If you're lonely, talk to someone. If you misunderstand an assignment, talk to a classmate. If they can't help, talk to a teacher, Resident Dean, or counselor. You don't need intricate strategies to succeed. You need to show up for class and do some work, every day. Walk up that hill, until the baby comes.

Showing up and walking uphill is not as easy as it sounds. I've attended six colleges and birthed two babies; delivering that B.A. was much more difficult. **As simple as it is in theory, lifestyle self-management it is the hardest thing for students to do, but is essential, in order to succeed.** Lifestyle self-management improves medication's efficacy and, sometimes, even replaces it.

* * *

The emphasis of a college student's journey remains academic; however, an academic journey is anything but. This applies to all college campuses. Academic supporters (advisors, Resident Deans, tutors, etc.) often spend as much time with a student on non-academic and lifestyle-related issues as they do on registration and assignments. Advising meetings may run as therapeutic sessions and entail more nurture than nomenclature. I'd wager that students and their supporters spend more time on these issues, and I'll go one further: lifestyle issues are the main culprits in causing academic issues in the first place.

Several years ago during a training session, academic advisors were advised on how to greet their new students. A PowerPoint slide listed the first three questions to ask:

1. What is your name?
2. What are your goals?
3. What medications are you currently taking?

We were advisors, not psychologists, not counselors, and certainly not psychiatrists. We were not hired or equipped to deal with medical issues or medical management, yet were instructed to inquire our learning-diagnosed students about their medications. Not that we wrote prescriptions; we were academic advisors, after all. But this line of inquiry seemed tenuous, entering a grey area of student monitoring. With each passing year, I felt more like a caseworker without formal credentials than academic advisor. If supporting and monitoring a student's health is expected, then college campuses should be framed as educational hospitals, with appropriate training. This model should be embraced wholeheartedly. Learning is holistic, medications are the norm, and young adult life is volatile; therefore, support should be treated as such.

But, before all that . . . **before inquiring about and monitoring medication . . . before labeling someone as learning-disabled or attention-disordered . . . lifestyle factors must be eliminated as possible causes.** We must first assure that the student is healthy. They need to be well-rested, hydrated, and nourished. They need to be managing their stress with positive coping strategies. (*Wake and Bake* is not considered a positive coping strategy, dude.) They need to be regularly moving their bodies and going outside. They need to have a healthy, supportive circle of friends. They need to practice resolving conflict in healthy, productive ways. They need to be creative—explore their intuition and listen to their callings. They need to give to their community without enabling others. Finally, they need to be motivated to be in an academic institution and believe that they have the capacity to succeed.

They need all this, before taking one single pill.

Lifestyles for Learning

Since college is one of the most volatile times in a young adult's life, and this volatility occurs in the most fragile period in a young adult's brain development, it seems logical that colleges would offer health-challenged students a health-promoting course. Further, such a course should be mandatory to all incoming students at the beginning of their academic journey. **Every college student needs a college**

health course, especially students diagnosed with learning disabilities. Colleges may teach students how to learn, but they must also teach them how to live.

I decided to create a lifestyle curriculum for college students. This course would dive into the real lifestyle issues that affect learning—not how to become a better student, but how to become a better person—more functional, happy, connected, and centered. This would be different than other college health courses that focus on jargon concerning pathology, pharmacology and chemistry. It would not explore cardiovascular health and BMT indexes. This health course would not prepare students for a career in health sciences; instead, it would prepare them for a career in being a college student. Ultimately, it would prepare them for a career in living.

The lifestyle factors I explored were Food, Sleep, Stress, Movement, Environment, Connection, Substances, and "Meta-connection" ("beyond" connection, or how we give). I referred to these lifestyle factors as **"psychonutrients"**: *nutrients*, in that they nourish the body; *psychological,* in how they create chemical changes that affect a person's mental, emotional, and spiritual state. In other words, **people *think and feel* better when they have ample amounts of psychonutrients. With limited psychonutrients, students survive; with ample amounts, students thrive**. Even college students—*especially* college students—may set higher expectations for their quality of life. It is common knowledge that health and learning are inextricably linked. Here was a chance to explore it with the very people who were immersed in it.

Instead of calling this curriculum *Psychonutrient Education*, it seemed more fitting to call it *Lifestyles for Learning*. "Life Skills" connotes established federally-funded educational programs such as *Botvin's Life Skills, Project Northland,* and *Know Your Body*, which are offered to K-12 students. In college, "Life Skills" connotes curriculum offered in Freshmen Orientation classes, such as *On Course, Living on Your Own,* or *Independent Life Skills*. Life skills classes offer practical information, for instance, how to balance a budget. Lifestyle, on the other hand, connotes a person's *style*— the *way and how* of daily living.

Food . . . Sleep . . . Stress . . . Movement . . . Creativity . . . Connections . . . Substances . . . Giving . . . These factors determine a person's ability to function. If they determine one's ability to function, then it would stand to reason that they would affect one's ability to perform academically, and in the more general sense, to learn. In the one area that an LD college student is consistently challenged— the classroom—wouldn't it stand to reason that one's lifestyle would play some role with influencing performance? Then, if something good could improve the learning-disabled person's academic performance, wouldn't it also benefit the "normal" student?

You don't have to be a psychic with a parapsychology degree from Duke University to get that.

BRYN MAWR COLLEGE
BRYN MAWR
PENNA. 19010

OFFICE OF ADMISSIONS

April 14, 1981

Dear Miss Fagelson,

It gives me special pleasure to write you on behalf of the Committee on Admissions that you have been admitted to Bryn Mawr College for the fall 1981. Your admission to the incoming class, conditional of course upon your successful completion of this year's academic work and satisfactory medical records, may be deferred upon written request until the fall of 1982.

A postcard is enclosed for your reply. I hope that you will return it as soon as possible and in any case not later than the Candidates' Reply Date, Friday, May 1. The General Deposit card and fee of $100, to be sent directly to our Comptroller's Office in the envelope provided, are also due by May 1, unless you request an extension.

The faculty and student members of our Committee on Admissions join me in congratulating you on your fine record. We look forward to hearing from you and to welcoming you to Bryn Mawr next fall.

Very sincerely yours,

Jacqueline A. Akins
Acting Director of Admissions

Miss Susan Mary Willowmina Fagelson

cc: Mr. John P. Goss, Director of Guidance

LIFESTYLES FOR LEARNING: A HOLISTIC APPROACH

"Quantum Physics is where science and spirituality actually intersect. The definition of soul is 'an invisible moving force that influences life or matter.' Einstein said. 'The Field is the sole governing agency of the particle.' According to physicists, the Field is defined as exactly the same thing: 'an invisible moving force that influences life or matter.' As it turns out, the Field and Soul are the same. The observer creates reality."
—Bruce Lipton, PhD, recipient of the 2009 Goi Peace Award

"If you are interested in something, you will focus on it, and if you focus attention on anything, it is likely that you will become interested in it. Many of the things we find interesting are not so by nature, but because we took the trouble of paying attention to them."
—Mihaly Csikszentmihalyi, author of *Flow*

"Perhaps the most valuable result of all education is the ability to make yourself do the thing you have to do, when it ought to be done, whether you like it or not."

—Thomas Henry Huxley

THE SOUL, BODY, MIND CONNECTION

If you pick up any college health textbook released in the past few decades, you will notice the term "Mind/Body Connection." Before then, western philosophy separated the two: *I have a mind, and I have a body. Occasionally, they need to interact; otherwise, they go about their business and respect each other's privacy.*

The mind controlled information and was, in itself, segregated. The mind handled two kinds of information: rational (intellectual) and irrational (emotional). The body controlled physical information: physiological functions (blood pressure, breathing) and instincts or impulses (sexual urge, fight-or-flight response).

Then it got messy. People started talking. Researchers began poking around, observing how certain behaviors involved mind and body. For instance, when a subject becomes angry (mind), their blood pressure soars (body). Mind made decisions (behavior) that the body carried out (action). We advanced our understanding of their relationship between the two. "Hark!" the scientific community shrieked, "The mind and the body are connected!"

It took science five hundred years to acknowledge *that* statement? Geez. Not that faith is superior to science, but like mind and body, you can't have one without the other, except that this is still incomplete. **Life is more than a mind-body connection; it's a mind-body-soul connection; and it's not really a mind-body-soul connection; it's a soul-body-mind connection.** We have reached the point in understanding that all living beings are a combination of energy and matter. Living beings are composed of many intertwining layers of energy. This is categorized as "soul-body-mind," based on the "energetic hierarchy"— the order in which energy, particles, and waves influence each other. We experience life first through our souls, then bodies, then minds.

Let's say I encounter a box full of puppies. I happen to love dogs, so this is a good thing. First, my soul perceives the puppies.

Puppy energy flows into my energetic field, and I sense a surge of movement and warmth in my belly and heart. Then, my body perceives puppies. I receive puppy information in my body through my senses: I see, hear, touch, and smell them. Maybe I even employ the sense of taste—chew on one puppy's ear and nibble on his fur (I would totally do that). Next, I have affective, and finally, cognitive reactions. My emotions respond with joy and love, and my mind understands that puppies are sweet and nice and good and make me happy. I identify the puppies as "Labrador," and begin to think about "Labrador stories." I smile and am elated. (Just typing "puppies" here causes me to smile.)

All that started with waves of puppy frequency entering my energetic field, before I had time to make any sense of it all. It's instantaneous and undetectable to our human perceptions, but it happens. It's like that with all things. Take nausea: I am nauseous, then I feel nauseous, then I articulate, "Oh, geez, I'm gonna be sick." Maybe I try a new experience—whitewater rafting or ceramics—and the experience feels "right," like a part of me. I feel more alive, and afterwards, tell my friends about what a great time I had. **First we are, then we feel we are, then we think we are.**

Somewhere along the line, the order got reversed. Thinking got all the credit for knowing, but actually, thinking is not knowing; it is documenting and analyzing. The mind is merely our stenographer, recording what our souls and bodies have experienced. It is the switchboard operator, releasing emotional chemicals based on the stimulus; but, the *experience* of life comes through energetic shifts, bodily senses, and then emotional reactions. Thoughts, themselves, are not experiences, but reflections of these energetic interactions and reactions.

Nowadays, we live as computers—sedentary analytical intellect-producers. We live swimming in an ocean of cognitive information, drifting further from the experiential shores. We are *beings*, experiencing through the senses and energy fields swirling around us.

Until you have biogenetically mutated into an actual computer, you remain human. With humanity comes biology. The game characters on your screen never have to relieve their bladders. You poor thing; you are alive.

When teaching, my mantra is, "Physiology before Cognition." We are bodies before minds. I tell my students, **"I don't care how scintillating my lecture is; if you have to pee, your mind is on pee, not me."** If something is weighing heavily on your mind, you will focus on that, not my lecture. If something is threatening you, well then, I've lost you completely.

This next section takes us through the brain and the mind. We explore our "knowings"—the ways we "know" something to be "true." We begin to understand that the mind is just the tip of the iceberg, and college is the *Titanic*. Without navigating the sea of health, students are doomed to sink.

Three Little Brains

Papa Brain

Once upon a time, there were three little brains: the Papa, Mama, and Baby brain. First came Papa. Papa lives in the primal area of the brain and includes the brainstem, which is the oldest part (creatures without brains have brainstems). Papa brain is commonly known as the "reptilian brain," due to its similarity with reptiles.

Reptiles don't go to college. They don't analyze texts or find critical flaws in philosophical arguments. Reptiles don't write love songs. What reptiles do, and do well, is survive. Therefore, this is where our survival mechanism is located. Papa brain cares about basic functions: heartbeat, breathing, temperature, digestion, and libido. These functions must be met before any other functioning may occur. In other words, first things first. You must first be a living, breathing human before attending class.

This is not as simple as it sounds. Lifestyle factors pounce upon these basic functions. When we are sleep-deprived, we are limited in our ability to remain alert. Students falling asleep in class is so common that it's cliché, but it is because the basic function of sleep is denied. In the game of life, reptilian brain trumps the others. Papa is the boss of his home, king of the castle.

Papa is always concerned about safety. Reptilian brains monitor our fight-or-flight response—the instinctual survival response during a life-threatening experience. In a threatening moment, every animal, from reptile to human, instinctively chooses whether to *fight*—defend, or *flight*—flee the environment. If you are sitting in a classroom, alert and attentive, and someone bursts into the room screaming, Papa brain immediately diverts your attention to this interruption. We don't know if this intruder is a threat to our survival. Once the intruder is deemed innocuous, we may redirect our attention to the classroom.

Mama Brain

Resting on top of Papa is Mama, known as the "mammalian brain." Mammals are distinct from reptiles in many ways, and for our interests, they differ in terms of information. Reptiles react to their environments while mammals discern it. Mammals determine what kind of experience they are having and how they feel about it.

Mama is the workhorse. When you have an experience, Mama processes the information after Papa instinctively reacts to it. Sensory information flows through Papa into Mama (except for smell, the rogue ninja). Mama decides what information is what: verbal, visual, auditory, physical, etc. She sorts it out and then distributes it to areas responsible for processing that particular type of sensory information.

Mama is the housekeeper, organizing different activities in each room in the home: reading rooms, hearing rooms, movement rooms, etc. It's Mama's job to keep the house running properly. We might also think of this part of the brain as the factory with different areas doing different parts of one big production. Experiences come with many sensory experiences, and Mama sees to it that everything is put in its place: I *see* my instructor while I *hear* my instructor while I *touch* the desk and chair while I *taste* some cashews.

Mama also deals with emotional information and body sensations, because experiences travel with feelings and physical reactions. **We feel something about everything we experience in life.** Imagine that you encounter a black bear at the zoo. First, you receive visual information: bear. You may receive auditory information: growl. Hopefully, you do not receive tactile information: maul. The sight and sound of a bear is ample enough to elicit emotional and physical "bear responses." Hot energy rushes through your chest, your stomach clenches and eyes widen. "Whoa, a bear!" you say. You are excited, but not necessarily afraid.

Now let's say you are in your backyard when encountering the bear. Mama brain gets out of the way, and Papa saves the day. Fight-or-flight response kicks in. You don't waste time thinking about the color of its fur or how you might feel about the bear; you get the hell out of that yard.

Mama brain contains the limbic system, where sensory information and emotions are sorted before being sent to the cerebrum or brain factory. The cerebrum is divided into two halves. Generally, each half does different work. The left hemisphere is concerned with words, time, and particular kinds of thinking: linear, logical, and rational. The right hemisphere is unconcerned with these things, preferring to play with the irrational and emotional. It's more visual, spatial, and motor-based, or to think of it simply, what we think of as art—things in relation to other things. The right-side is highly activated during dance, singing (word art), playing music (versus reading music), and playing sports (versus memorizing stats). It's an over-simplification to say that the right side likes music while the left side likes math, but, you might think of it this way: the left side would be more involved with logical linear algebra, while the right side would take over for visual-spatial geometry.

In terms of perception, the left side is concerned with self. It holds an individualistic view of the world. The right side, conversely, sees the world collectively. It identifies connections with others. In a traumatic event, our left side writes in a journal. It reflects on how the event affected itself, while the right side would immediately think of others and how they were affected. The right side would reach out to a friend or participate in some activist response to the event.

Like the mind and body, the two hemispheres are separate but equal, constantly working together, connected through a bridge of nerve fibers, the corpus callosum. The corpus callosum allows each side to share information and communicate. Women or people with higher estrogen levels build bigger bridges. Female (estrogen-dominant) brains more often use their bridges to connect both sides, which creates a more complex view of a situation. The downside is that the more complex a situation is, the more fuel is required to deal with it. Male (testosterone-dominant) minds are more selective, using specified brain areas for tasks. Women tend to be "messier" with their experiences, thinking and feeling in every situation. Men tend to be "cleaner" with their experiences, separating their thoughts from their emotions. If you've ever received a letter (email, text) from a scorned woman (or been one), you understand. If you've ever tried to get a scorned man to open up and spill his guts, you also understand.

In the insightful video trilogy, *Brain Sex* (1991), scans were shown to represent biological differences between male and female brains. The slides illustrated blood flow to specific areas of the brains when performing certain cognitive tasks. They showed three brain slides: language, visual-spatial, and resting. The slides depicted a striking difference: **the resting female brain was as highly activated as when the male brain computed complex algebraic formulations. The woman's brain, it seems, is never at rest.** Basically, we are nuts. (Sorry ladies, but you know it's true).

Near Papa brain is the vital cerebellum, which works with Mama to coordinate thought and movement. A point guard needs his cerebellum in order to drive to the hoop for the winning lay-up. The cerebellum is needed for all sorts of coordination: holding a pencil, raising a fork to one's mouth—any movement that is organized and automated. The cerebellum stores procedural memories such as driving a car or playing video games. Credit the cerebellum for the phrase, "It's just like riding a bike." Automated movements are long-term; once we learn them, we have them. I learned to surf in eighth grade, so even though I haven't surfed since, I should technically retain the ability. (At 51, I'm not sure I want to test that theory.)

Procedural memories are automatic, so we don't need to pay attention while doing them. This frees up our conscious mind to ponder something else. This is a good thing; otherwise, we would swerve off the road and crash into a tree the moment our thoughts began to wander from driving. We rely on our automated skills of listening to the professor while taking notes. Sometimes automatic procedures are unhelpful. Ever drive on the highway, deep in thought, and find you've missed your exit? Ever sit in class thinking about a friend, only to look up and realize the professor's just called on you? Your cerebellum continued driving and listening while you focused elsewhere.

Here's a frightening illustration. Ever go out for a night of partying, only to find yourself at home, in bed, with no recollection of how you got there? Drunks are able to "black out" their conscious minds while their subconscious minds take over. All your procedural memories were intact, independent of attention. You continued to party, dance, text friends, Power Hour on Tinder, hook up, and yes, even drive home afterwards, thanks to the cerebellum.

You don't have to be drunk to do things automatically. If you've ever spaced out, you know what I mean. Ever been reading, only to get to the bottom of the page and have no idea what you just read? Your cerebellum put reading on autopilot, while you obsessed about the fight you had with your roommate. Students report this phenomenon all the time: they read an entire chapter only to discover that they have no idea what it's about. Once a procedure is learned, it becomes automatic. There is no need for our conscious mind to pay attention to it in order to do it. That is, unless we want to make new memories and improve a skill, and that is what this book is about: becoming a better learner. In fact, you may notice that some of the information in this book is repeated. That's because you will likely space out during some of it, and I want your conscious mind to notice the important parts.

The way we make new memories is to be conscious of our experiences. We may know how to ride a bike or read a book, but we haven't been on *this* bike ride or read *this* book. Perhaps we have read this particular book, but we haven't read it in *this* particular moment in our lives. We must remind our conscious minds that this particular moment has never happened. It is a new and novel sensory experience. It may be difficult to convince your brain to pay attention to a commute that you take to work every single day, for years and years. There is a bit of the *Groundhog Day* movie in that philosophy. This moment right now is a unique moment that, while familiar, has never before been experienced. There is always a new opportunity to learn, even in the most familiar of activities. You just have to be a baby about it.

Baby Brain

The final area of learning is the Baby brain, located up front and on top of Mama, in an area known as the pre-frontal cortex or frontal lobes. Picture Mama holding baby in her arms, supported by Papa.

The Baby brain is the last to develop, so for most of our lives, it remains the most immature and vulnerable. "Last to develop" is quite literal. **Baby brain needs to grow up, through building neurons, firing neurotransmitters, and making neural connections—**

brain pathways that become behaviors, skills, and memories.
Ever lived where there was major highway construction? Remember
how it went on for months, maybe years? Remember how many
people were involved in its construction? Remember how inconvenienced everyone was? Remember how great it felt to have the
construction done and how fast you could speed down that new
highway? That highway is Baby brain.

Researchers used to say that Baby matured at around 18 years;
later, the age was extended to 25. Nowadays, college textbooks may
assert pre-frontal cortex maturity between 30 to 40 years of age.
Based on my behavior, my pre-frontal cortex probably reached
maturity when I turned 45. My neurons reached the zenith of
their potential around 2:00 pm, and by that evening, began their
decline. **Ironically, Baby brain, the least mature brain area,
is the area most needed for mature behavior.** Baby houses
the Executive Function (EF), our most sophisticated processing.
The EF deals with organizing, planning, deciding, problem-solving,
creating, activating, and motivating—all these "higher order" skills
needed for higher education.

Executive functioning, while highly coveted in our society, is
the least necessary or most expendable, in an evolutionary sense. We
do not need this area of the brain to survive. Sure, we may need
EF to bring down a six-figure paycheck; but to survive as a living
being on the planet, it is an accessory. This is illustrated all the time.
The eighteen-year-old college student may struggle. They'll be late
for class, blurt out random things in lecture halls, forget homework
assignments, and annoy friends. But they'll live; Papa sees to that.
Their hearts continue beating, their body temperature remains regulated, and automatic body systems persist. Their Mama brains are
mostly secure, as well. Procedures are intact. They have the ability to
receive information; they have the ability to read and write and compute. What is missing is executive function.

For a child's developing years, EF is supplied by parents and other external forces. In college, the responsibility shifts to the student, who is expected to internally monitor. Without some dictating force, many students are unable to sustain the attention and motivation necessary to complete the task of college. Does this kill them? Nope. Failing college is not fatal. If it was, some of you wouldn't be reading this book (and I wouldn't be writing it).

Experts like Dr. Russell Barkley contend that people with ADHD may suffer up to 30 percent developmental delay in pre-frontal development. When you kiss your eighteen-year-old son good-bye, neurologically you may be leaving a thirteen-year-old alone on campus. If you think eighteen-year-olds get into trouble, imagine the damage a thirteen-year-old can devise.

Delayed executive function may prove fatal. Headlines abound with tragedies depicting inebriated students falling off roofs and committing sexual assault. Students drink and drive, killing themselves, passengers, and innocent motorists. Whether fatal, tragic, or inconvenient, a lack of executive function translates to a great deal of suffering and difficulty in achieving the demands of college.

The key in developing our executive function depends upon taming Mama and Papa. **In college, Baby brain learns how to think independently and then learns how to control his thinking.** Baby does this through controlling emotions and desires, both internal and external. Baby must control his own personal feelings and life callings while managing concerns and expectations from those who offer love and support.

Internal control of emotions and desires is different than suppression; it requires validation and expression. External control is trickier and requires Baby to manage the emotions and desires of those who are invested in his college experience.

This delicate managing act *is* possible; it just takes a bit of knowing on your part.

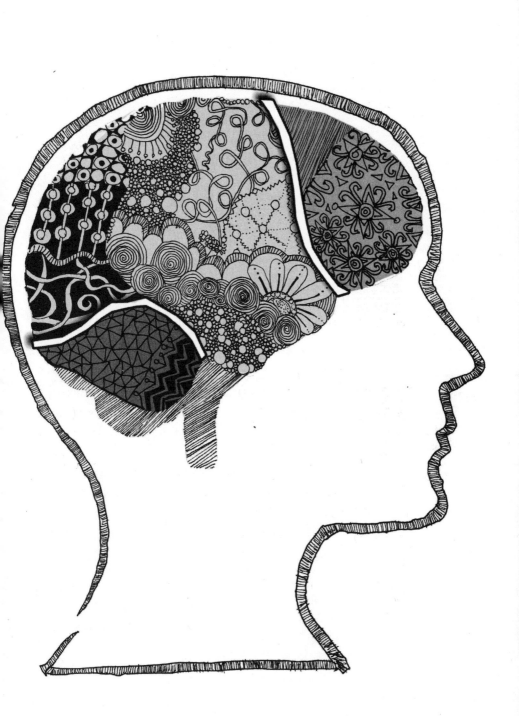

Three Little Knowings

Cognitive Domain: The Rational

You are what you think.

Just as there are three kinds of brains, there are three kinds of knowing: cognitive, affective, and conative. The most valued in our culture is the cognitive domain. Cognition is what we consider thinking and understanding. Cognition is the rational intellect. In academics, it applies to memorizing facts, analyzing texts, and computing mathematical data. Cognition may be thought of as a journalist on assignment, fielding objective questions: who, what, where, when, and how. Traditionally, it is the kind of knowing most utilized and praised in college. Think college; think cognition.

The action of cognition is represented as an information processing system, with an input-output type of mechanism: stuff comes in, the brain does something to it, and then we do something with the stuff. Some information we keep, and some we discard. One popular theory is the **Information Processing Model (IPM).** This model is commonly used to introduce the concept of cognition. It illustrates how we translate experiences into information and information into memories. "Memories" for college purposes is all the cognitive information you are expected to recall for course assessment: quizzes, exams, papers, etc.

As we begin to explore the IPM and later, lifestyle factors, we will consider these key questions:

1. How are academic memories made?
2. How do lifestyle factors affect this memory-making process?
3. What can we do to improve the process, to academically succeed?

Life is a continuous flow of experiences, which we either retain or filter. Retained experiences are memories, and filtered experiences are forgotten. Memories and future plans are unreal. The only real moment is this exact instantaneous moment. Our lives are constantly real, since moments happen in a continuous flow. Our lives are also constantly unreal, since 99.99 percent of life is memories from the past or visions of the future. We make decisions in the exact moment and plan for the future, based on our past memories.

How do we make these memories? It's actually quite mechanical and beautiful. We'll break it down, using IPM. The IPM has three stages: short-term, working, and long-term memory. Information enters through short-term memory, is actively processed with the working memory, and then stored into long-term memory for future use. Basically, stuff enters us, we do something with it, and then store it or discard it. What and how we do all this is dependent upon three factors: sense, meaning, and repetition.

Experiences enter through our five senses, offering us sensory information. This information enters through sensory portals: eyes gather visual stimulus, ears receive auditory stimulus, skin feels tactile stimulus, and so on. Sensory information travels electrically up neural highways into the brainstem via Papa brain, who immediately determines if any of this information is a life-or-death situation and if the fight-or-flight response is needed. If the experience is safe, he sends it to Mama brain who receives and sorts through it all. She sends information to the brain factories: visual information goes there, auditory there, etc. Mama also differentiates between hemispheric preferences: verbal information stays left, spatial stays right, etc.

Before sorting any information, Mama checks the emotional response. Is this information highly emotionally stimulating? In other words, does this experience make us sad, piss us off, or fill us with joy? If there is a strong emotional response to this experience, we first pay attention to the emotions. Emotions also affect how we perceive the experience. If we are filled with joy, colors seem brighter; if we are depressed, food lacks flavor.

Let's say the experience is nonthreatening and emotionally neutral. We may then begin processing this sensory information. We begin to notice the environment around us. What is going on? Are we inside or outside? What sounds are present? Who is with us? What are they wearing? What is the temperature? Dozens of questions are being instantaneously answered by our receiving of all this information.

As quickly as this information enters the brain, most of it exits. The brain filters much more information than it processes. In fact, we only consciously process about 5 percent of all the sensory stimulus that enters our brain in a lifetime. It's a good thing, too. If we processed much more, we'd go mad with over-stimulation. TMI is an acronym that describes a phenomenon called **excitotoxicity**—simply, too much information. *Mama is only one woman, and she needs her rest.* The elite 5 percent that makes the cut is the stuff of potential memories. This experience still needs to run through quality control points, but at this point in the process, we begin memory-making or, as college students would say, "studying."

Please note: we make other kinds of memories. In fact, life-threatening and highly emotionally experiences are more memorable, because they are more stimulating. We don't need to try to remember them; we just do. **We are discussing how to make cognitive memories, which in simpler terms means,** *how do we study in college to remember stuff for exams?*

When you enter college, you already know how to read, write, and compute. These experiences are now skills or procedures, and therefore, coordinated through the cerebellum. If you recall, we do not need to pay attention to procedures to do them. Therein lies the problem. **You don't have to pay attention to study, but you *do* have to pay attention to study *effectively*.** You can read and write without paying attention, but you won't remember what you read or wrote.

Cognitive memory-making occurs when we pay attention to the experience. Mama rattles information in front of Baby: *Look at the pretty girl! Hear that pleasing song! Listen to the interesting lecture given by the professor!* Mama encourages Baby to wake up and pay attention. This is known as the **Active Working Memory**. Whenever you become actively aware of something, you are engaging working memory. It's the point in the ride home where you wake up out of your daydream and remember you are driving a car. "Oops!" you cry, "I just missed my exit!" Now Baby brain is awake. Baby takes control of the procedure from the cerebellum and actively drives the car. With academics, this could be the part of the class where you decide to take notes during the professor's lecture, reread the chapter, or enter answers on an exam.

When it comes to paying attention, Baby brain acts like a baby. How long does a typical baby sustain a solid gaze at something? About 30 seconds. Baby brain is curious and hungry, constantly demanding shiny, squeaky toys—new and novel information.

Let's illustrate memory-making with the experience of attending an Introduction to Psychology lecture. The experience begins with sensory information and Papa brain does a quick check. You walk into the class and are flooded with sensory information: your mind takes in the color of the walls, how many chairs there are, the brightness of the lighting, the room's temperature, the sound of conversations, scuffling shoes, and moving chairs. Once Papa determines there is no threat, then Mama receives and sorts through this information. You notice the outfits people are wearing, how many students are in the room, what time it is, and maybe begin to hear side conversations—topics, laughter, and voice intonation. Most of this information immediately filters out. You don't need to remember it, so the brain jettisons it, making space in the conscious mind. Imagine if you remembered the color of every shirt that everyone wore in every class that you have ever entered . . . since kindergarten? Talk about excitotoxicity.

You have now filtered out most of this experience, but some information creeps in. A few people are wearing similar red shirts. Three chairs are lined up in front of the auditorium. The professor is not yet in the room. You look up at the clock and see that class is starting late, again. You see a stranger in the class seated in the top row of the auditorium. At this point of information processing, new or novel things gain priority, because, if you think about it, they are unknown and may therefore present a threat. We pay attention to them until we determine that they are neutral, and then begin to ignore them.

At this time, we also pay attention to emotionally stimulating information. Your crush is sitting behind you. Someone's ringtone goes off, and it sounds like a quacking duck; you like ducks, so you smile. The idiot who kept raising his hand and asking stupid questions last week is sitting next to you. Your mother texts, reminding you to call your grandmother and wish her a happy birthday. These emotional stimuli command your mind.

As the professor enters the room, conversations subside. Cell phones are turned off. People settle into their seats and open notebooks or laptops for note-taking. The professor begins to talk, and Mama gently nudges Baby brain. *It's time to pay attention, honey,* Mama gently whispers into Baby's active working memory. The academic experience begins.

It's difficult to believe that all this is happening while you are simply trying to pay attention during class. Now maybe you can appreciate how daunting a task school really is. While you are actively trying to pay attention, to control your conscious mind, these other distractions compete for your attention. Ever try to get a baby's attention? It's pretty hard. You have to be pretty entertaining, and even still, you only have that 30-second window.

* * *

The Information Processing Model prioritizes information: *Priority One* is life-threatening information; next is new, novel, and emotional-stimulating information; last is familiar or non-emotionally-stimulating information. Ever hear a student say, "I'm good at a topic if I'm interested"? That's the IPM working. **High-interest information gets priority over stuff we don't care about. For college students, that covers just about everything *but* coursework.** This is the futility of attempting to retain cognitive information. Academic learning, in

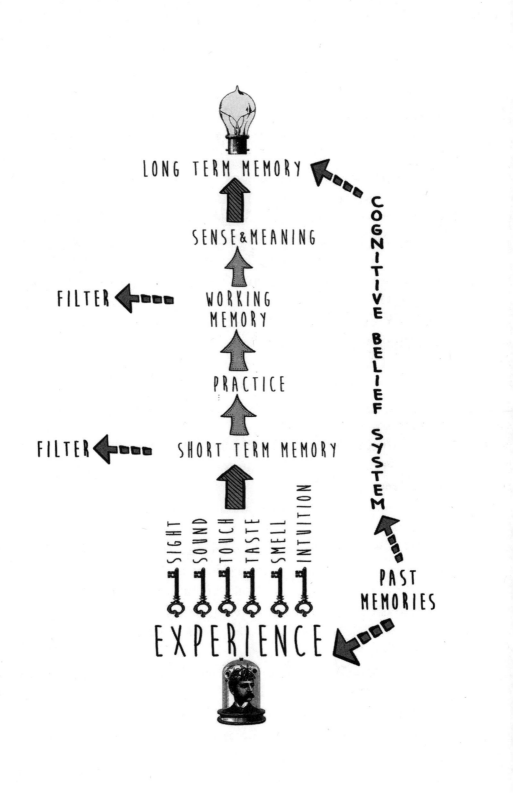

general, is nonthreatening (failing a test won't kill you); nonthreatening stimulating (you don't care about reading the textbook); not new or novel (more reading and writing, snore). Cognition is the least sexy of all information processing and is nearly impossible if one is uninterested in the topic.

Ever find yourself in a classroom, thinking to yourself, *"What is the professor talking about? What's the point? What does this have to do with real life?"* Your mind is reacting to a critical gateway in active working memory: sense and meaning. The experience has to make sense and hold personal meaning for you to remember it, even if you are motivated to learn. Otherwise, the only way you will remember it is with cognitive tricks: rehearsing, discussing, analyzing, applying—in other words, studying the information. **Studying is the academic form of memory-making. It is a series of techniques used to create memories out of information you don't care about, makes no sense, or holds no meaning.** The tragedy in our culture of college is that few students claim to know how to study properly. They don't understand the cognitive challenges and haven't learned how to trick Baby brain into paying attention. This missing link opens the floodgates to lifestyle difficulties, as we will soon see.

Another obstacle to the active working memory is **interference.** Interference is some kind of non-related sensory information that interrupts the memory-making process: you receive a text; a fire alarm goes off; someone sneezes or farts; the professor mentions there will be a major test tomorrow. You are studying in your room and your friend pops in, announcing that you guys are going for pizza *now,* dude. All these cause cognitive interference and when they happen, it's like a bird suddenly flying through the window into a classroom during a lecture. Whoa! Whatever it was you were actively working on, pre-bird, is lost.

One added layer of active working difficulty resides in sensory modality. College relies primarily on eyes and ears for sensory delivery; we see and hear information. College is a word world. Professors talk and write on the board. Students take notes, answer questions, write essays, and take exams. College is slightly tactile; science, art, and technology courses are hands-on, but the primary realm of college is verbal information presented in visual and auditory ways. Interestingly, these two ways are the least effective in creating long-term memories. Touch, taste, and smell rule the memory files. The writer, Albert Camus, eloquently observed, "Some people talk in their sleep. Lecturers talk while other people sleep."

Taste and smell are not considered cognitive, unless you happen to be enrolled in culinary school. When is the last time you had an olfactory exam? That would be kind of cool, but it's never happened on my watch. It's unfortunate, as smell is the most effective way to make memories. Smell bypasses both Mama and Baby brain. Papa receives olfactory information and immediately processes the smelly memory. Doctors use aromas to initiate memory in Alzheimer's patients. Smell is the most easily stored and most readily available memory, and yet smell and taste continue to be ignored in academia.

Some studies are conducted where students study for an exam while exposed to taste and smell stimuli, for example, sucking on peppermints. When they take the test, they are given a mint, which supposedly helps to recall information. These studies explore a concept known as **State Dependent Learning.** Recall is enhanced when we return to the particular state in which we originally studied the information. In State Dependent Learning, learning is enhanced when we are in a particular state. It's why teachers suggest that students adopt a study routine at the same time and place each day. The brain begins to recognize the state of being there, and will "reboot" to "study mode." Boarding schools use this strategy; students have "study hours" from, say, 8:00–10:00 on weekdays at the same location, such as the library or lounge. If you happen to eat a particular type of food when studying, this theory recommends you eat that same food when you need to recall the information—for instance, when taking a test. Some studies reported mint-suckers demonstrating a 20 percent increased recall. Translated into grades, that means sucking on a mint increases your C to an A. That's one sweet strategy.

The act of paying attention in class is a precise, methodical, and extremely difficult act. One must constantly be monitoring distractions and regulating motivation to notice potential interference. While feeling threatened, we must remain open-minded and attentive. How we pay attention and what we pay attention to, consciously or unconsciously, is greatly affected by value, sense, and meaning: information is important and we believe it (value); we may apply it to our lives (meaning); we understand what the heck the teacher is talking about (sense). College disequilibrium challenges all three areas, constantly. If these are missing, we must trick the mind into thinking that information is valuable (studying).

Blame it on biology; as a college student, you are doomed the minute you enter the classroom. No amount of mints may help.

Affective Domain: The Irrational

You are what you feel.

The IPM is critical as we begin to comprehend just how we process sensory information—literally, how we process life. We are more than thinking machines; we also feel. Quantum physics challenges outmoded ideas about feelings. Emotions are no longer airy-fairy things of which we have no control. Emotions are chemical reactions to stimuli just as a sound stimulus elicits a chemical reaction. Just as we perceive information, we perceive emotions. These emotions inhabit the Affective Domain.

In terms of attention, emotions trump reason. Scholars may pout, insisting that intellectual thought is more important, but Affective Domain doesn't buy it. If it's Thirsty Thursday, you know where attention resides.

The Affective Domain may be considered the "female" side of information processing, complementing Cognitive Domain's "male" side. This domain rules how we react to information versus how we memorize and recall it. The Affective Domain creates our interests, values, and beliefs. Basically, if something makes us feel good, we like it, and it becomes an interest. If something makes us feel bad, we don't like it, and it becomes something to avoid.

I use this activity to introduce this concept. Students fill out a simple questionnaire:

Affective Domain activity

LIKES List a few activities/academic subjects/hobbies you enjoy doing OR consider a strength.	DISLIKES List a few activities/ academic subjects/hobbies you don't like doing OR consider a challenge.

Select one from each column and answer the following questions about it.

LIKE _____ DISLIKE _____

1. How long have you done (been interested in) this activity?
2. How often do you do it?
3. With whom do you do it?
4. How do you feel when you're doing it?

1. How long have you done (been interested in) this activity?
2. How often do you do it?
3. With whom do you do it?
4. How do you feel when you're doing it?

Affective Domain pervades our assignments. When given the opportunity to choose the topic, we'll choose one we care about or that affected us. We will research bullying, psychoactive substances, or diseases we and family members suffer. We may reflect on defining moments, such as a car accident or moving from our home town. People who write books on cancer have either had cancer or have been deeply affected by it. I write books on how to stay healthy and avoid college failure. It is in our human nature for passions to emerge through significant transformative experiences.

Emotions are regulated by Mama but ruled by Papa; this is an appropriate self-defense mechanism. If someone screams during a scintillating lecture, you will divert your attention to the scream. You are a human being designed for survival, so a potential threat overrides a scintillating lecture. In fact, an activity doesn't have to be life-threatening to feel threatening. If we don't like doing something or don't like how we feel when doing it, then we avoid it.

In college, students are expected to do many activities regardless of how they feel about them. Parents of learning-disabled students lament how their kids only do well in subjects they like and struggle with things that hold no interest for them. This excuse is unacceptable, because everybody functions that way! Unless you are a masochist who derives intense pleasure out of pain, you will instinctively avoid unpleasant experiences. That is a natural act of self-preservation.

Self-preservation is one thing, however, and college is a completely different thing. As Thomas Henry Huxley aptly put it, "Perhaps the most valuable result of all education is the ability to make yourself do the thing you have to do, when it ought to be done, whether you like it or not." **An essential function of college is to suspend our emotional reactions in order to pay attention to the information in front of us.**

We also have to be open-minded. Because of Papa brain, new concepts are often met with suspicion, rejected before comprehended. As Temple Grandin says, "You don't get interested in stuff you're not exposed to." When you enter an environment whose very goal is to knock you off balance by introducing you to new experiences, you must be in a constant state of suspending assumptions.

What about that Bryn Mawr essay? As a writer, writing held great meaning, but as a writing assignment, the essay did not make sense. Completing the assignment became threatening. Entering class without completing the assignment also felt threatening, and I began to skip class in order to feel safe. In order to feel justified about this behavior, I had to reject both the assignment and the class as meaningless.

Because safety trumps interest, learning must feel safe in order for students to be able to pay attention. This is a major feat. Consider all the factors needing to be in place:

These are just a few examples, but you can see how having a safe environment can be such a huge factor, yet so elusive. We haven't even mentioned psychonutrients! Even if all these safety factors are in place, a student needs to be in a balanced, healthy state to reap the

---

Safety Requirements for Optimal Academic Success

Physical Environment:
- Spacious classroom with proper ventilation
- Ample full-spectrum lighting and natural sunlight
- Comfortable chairs and tables
- Comfortable room temperature—heat or AC, depending on climate
- Mold and dust-free rooms, equipment, rugs, etc.
- Suitable time of day to study—not too early or late
- Reasonable class length—not too short or long a time period
- Classroom is accessible—student can arrive on time, in all kinds of weather, with parking, etc.

Social–Emotional Environment:
- Positive rapport with the professor
- Accepted among other students
- Comfortable class structure—lecture hall or small-group seminar
- "Drama-free" classroom—free from psycho ex-partners, stalkers, or dysfunctional friends
- "Drama-free" life—students' minds are free from obsessing over fights with romantic partners, roommates, parents, friends, professors, or any other conflict that may divert one's cognitive attention
- Interest in the topic
- Control—voluntarily taking this class (versus it being a required class, taken against their will)
- Confidence—believing they are capable of doing the work in the class
- Clarity—assignments are clear and the student believes there is an appropriate amount of time to accomplish the assignments.

full benefits of a classroom experience. It's a wonder students can pay any attention at all, in any classroom.

Conative Domain: The Calling

You are what you desire.

It's always been fascinating to watch highly intelligent, emotionally stable college students go up in flames. Of course, each case is unique and no two people are alike, but **I've wondered if there might be a common thread connecting all their failures. After over**

a decade of observation, my money landed on the soul. I believe that these students' souls were stalled and just going through the motions, but how do you communicate this to a student in your class or to their parents who are desperate for their child's success? How do you sell soul in higher education? The predicament eluded me, until I began writing this book. Once again, writing saved the day and reminded me of a favorite quote by Flannery O'Connor, "I write to discover what I know." I discovered the Conative Domain.

Conation derives from the Latin *conatus*, meaning any natural tendency, impulse, striving, or directed effort. It is one of three parts of the mind, along with the Affective and Cognitive Domain. **The cognitive part of the brain measures intelligence, the affective deals with emotions, and the conative drives how one acts upon those thoughts and feelings.**

Conation is defined by Funk & Wagnall's Standard Comprehensive International Dictionary as "the aspect of mental process directed by change and including impulse, desire, volition and striving," and by the Living Webster Encyclopedia Dictionary of the English Language as "one of the three modes, together with cognition and affection, of mental function; a conscious effort to carry out seemingly volitional acts." Volition is the act of deciding and committing to a particular course of action. The Encyclopedia of Psychology, "Motivation: Philosophical Theories" says, "Some mental states seem capable of triggering action, while others—such as cognitive states—apparently have a more subordinate role [in terms of motivation]."

The term conation is pretty obscure. Conation is, in fact, listed in *The 1,000 Most Obscure Words in the English Language* (Schur, 1990) defined as "the area of one's active mentality that has to do with desire, volition, and striving." **The Conative Domain is the final frontier of knowing, but may be the most integral to success.** Survival controls emotions and emotions control cognition, but desire also controls emotion. Emotions are simply a reaction, while desire is the intention. In some cases, our desires are as strong as our survival instincts. Many people have died or destroyed their health in the name of desire. Crimes of passion push our physical safety aside to pursue our treasonous goal.

Does college reside in your conative domain? Let's rephrase the question.

What are some collegial desires?

- Go to college
- Maintain good grades
- Graduate
- Secure a job in the field I studied
- Earn good money
- Find a life partner
- Live happily ever after

Are these your desires or your parents'? Who's driving your conation train? If they are your intentions in college, are they your *only* intentions? Maybe you have some competing passion? **We may have the ability to think and reason and we may feel safe in our academic environments, but we must be driven to learn, or we won't.** Conversely, little will deter the truly determined learner from reaching his goal.

Sometimes we meet students who seem improperly suited to college. For whatever reason—immaturity, lack of motivation, or conflicting commitment—these students seem to be actively unengaged in their academic experience. As one colleague famously remarked, **"If a student is determined to fail, they will succeed."** The answer may lie in the Conative Domain; their mind and heart may be into school, but their soul is not. Sometimes the way to help a college student succeed is to help them transition out of college, until their desire ignites. Despite societal pressure, college is not the answer for everybody. Many people need to be out of college in order to continue on their paths, and college may very well be blocking them, at least in that moment of their lives.

Simon

One student from my past comes to mind, a young man named Simon: medium brown hair, slight build, very sweet, shy, and respectful. Simon was failing my class, so we met one day to discuss the situation. We began discussing strategies to improve his grade. Simon knew exactly what to say. There was no trace of joy or enthusiasm in his voice. There was also no trace of anger or indignation. His voice and tone were . . . *void* is the way I remember it. Very politely robotically responding to my questions.

I suddenly stopped myself in mid-sentence and, uncharacteristically, asked him a question.
"Simon, are you happy?"
"Huh?" he looked up for the first time.
"Are you happy here?"
"What do you mean?"
"What I mean is . . ."
I asked him the question we are never to ask college students.
"Simon, why are you here?"
"Uh. What? What do you mean, Mrs. C?"
"Simon, why are you here?"
"Uhm. I'm here. To. You know. Go to college."
"Hmm. Yes, I get that. But, do you want to be here?"
"Uh. Well, my dad thinks–"
"Simon, I'm not asking you what your dad thinks. Let me ask it another way. What do you love?"

Simon straightened up and his eyes shone. He looked right at me. "Music. I love music. I play the drums. I love playing the drums. I wanna go to Los Angeles and join this band that my friend started up. I've always wanted to be a musician and I love playing music, but my dad says there's no money in that, and that I should go to school and get my bachelor's degree first, and then I can pursue music, cuz since it's really unlikely that I'll make it, then I'll have a backup plan to fall back on."

Maybe it was all the books I had been reading—*Life 101* and *Do it! Let's Get Off Our Buts!* Maybe Martha Beck had been *Steering my Starlight* for too long. Maybe Carolyn Myss prodded my fourth chakra a bit too vigorously. I never said this to a student, before. I looked directly at him.

"Simon, I like you. You're a nice boy, but you're shit as a student. I've never met someone who wanted to be here less. I'm going to tell you something that we are never supposed to tell a student. If I were you, I'd get the hell out of here. Leave college and go play the drums. If you don't want to be in school, then don't be in school.

"Simon, there are only so many hours in a week. You got about 40-60 hours a week to devote to your work. You can spend that working on Plan A or Plan B. So, what are you gonna do—bust your ass at school for the next five years, getting your Bachelor's degree, and then, when you're twenty-seven, *then* go try to make it as a musician? Compete with a bunch of twenty-two-year-olds, then? Life is short, Simon. We can always settle for Plan B.

"There is always an opportunity to do the thing we don't want to do. Do yourself a favor, and get the hell out now. Go play your drums, Simon. And, if your dad freaks out, give him my email."

> Simon did leave college, after that semester. He emailed me
> a few months later, telling me he moved to Los Angeles and
> joined his friend's band.
>
> You may be wondering, "Did he make it?" And, my reply to
> you is, who cares? He went to Los Angeles to play the drums.
>
> He made it.
>
> P.S. Simon and I recently connected. Read what happens, in the
> Epilogue.

Cognitive Belief System: The Assumption

You are what you believe.

All these diverse brain functions culminate in what David Sousa refers to as the Cognitive Belief System (*How the Brain Learns,* 2002). The Cognitive Belief System (CBS) is the sum of all your long-term memories. This system runs *your* system, driven by conative domain, motivated by affective domain, and executed by cognitive domain. It rules Papa, Mama, and Baby. You think, feel, act, and are driven by what you believe. The cognitive belief system transforms as a result of your experiences. The cortex or "filing cabinet" grows as we gather long-term memories. These memories become our life stories. Baby brain grows up learning who he or she is, based upon these memories.

Even though we have new experiences all the time, we constantly rely on previously stored memories to perceive our new experiences. This is a clever brain trick called "transfer," and thank goodness we do this. Imagine waking up every morning forgetting everything you learned the previous day. You'd have to re-learn how to speak, read, write, etc. **Transfer** operates between the cerebellum and the pre–frontal cortex, transferring automated procedures to navigate new similar experiences. If you already know how to drive an automatic vehicle, learning to drive a manual one is much easier. If you know how to speak one foreign language, it is easier to learn another one.

Sometimes transfer is unhelpful or downright hurtful. If you've been told all your life that you are a bad writer, and every writing assignment receives an F, you believe it. You save "bad writer" memories. Every time you enter a classroom, you transfer in the "bad writer" perspective. The phrases, "seeing the world through rose-colored glasses" and "self-fulfilling prophecy" refer to the power of transfer. Our experiences color our world. Even though I am entering this particular classroom for the first time, I am pre-programmed to believe who I am in that class, and consequently, my belief helps manifest the outcome.

In my previous book, *The No Recipe Cookbook*, I discussed the most important aspect of cooking: *Mise en place*. *Mise en place* is a French term, meaning "everything in its place." This may seem like an odd place to discuss *Mise en place*, but the culinary term also applies to conation, belief, and the art of academic success.

The No Recipe Cookbook Excerpt: Mise en Place

Mise en place means knowing what you are creating.
Visualize it as you go along. Picture the dish completed and ready to serve, the kitchen is clean, and you, the calm, happy, loving chef, ready to enjoy your meal.
Mise en place relates to a theory called psycho-cybernetics (Maxwell Maltz, 1960), an offshoot of cybernetics, which was originally devised for technology and by mathematician Norbert Weiner:

Cybernetics appeared such a breakthrough to Maltz because its implication was that achievement was a matter of choice. Most important to the dynamic of achieving was the "what" (the target), rather than the "how" (the path). The frontal lobes or conscious thinking part of the brain could devise the goal, or create the image of the person you wanted to be, and the subconscious mind would deliver its attainment.

The "set and forget" mechanism of guided missiles would also work for our deepest desires. (www.butler-bowdon.com/psychocybernets). Psycho-cybernetics gained popularity in the sports world, adopted by coaches to improve athletic performance. The experiment involved basketball players picturing themselves at the free throw line. They visualized sinking ten shots in a row—nothing but net. The players who could achieve this (and oddly, it is more difficult than one might think) improved their accuracy.

Cybernetics theory asserts that when one "clearly fixes" upon a target or goal and repeatedly focuses clearly or creates a "constant feedback loop," it sets in motion an "automaticity" that self-propels the fixation into fruition. This theory eventually found its way into our psyches and culture, emanating into the self-help genre. Books such as *Do What You Love and the Money Will Follow* and *The Secret* are by-products of cybernetics.

Even with ignited desire, clear vision, and powerful transfer, the imbalance of disequilibrium may be too much for a student to handle. I entered that Bryn Mawr English class full of confidence in my ability as a writer, but lacked confidence in understanding how to clarify an assignment. The disequilibrium involved learning how to ask for help, and it blindsided me, as it does many students. When parents complain to their children, "You know how to write! Just *do* it!" It may not be that simple. Something is blocking their belief that they can succeed in that moment, and that needs to be validated before it snowballs. Sometimes the smallest thing can knock a student off balance, sometimes for good.

Transfer's influence on our CBSs results in not only disequilibrium but another staple of college, cognitive dissonance. **Cognitive dissonance is a conflict or disconnect between the way we think something should be and the way it really is.** This happens a bazillion times in college. My son Sam, the straight-A high school student, lamented, "I thought college would be like high school." It's a legitimate complaint; after all, high school is expected to prepare students for higher learning. Sam transferred his expectations and was blindsided. His downfall was not in *experiencing* cognitive dissonance, but in *dealing* with that dissonance. If students understand that this is a natural part of the college process, they may be able to shift their perspective and move into problem solving. If they refuse to accept the new reality, then lifestyle factors begin to collapse.

College may feel like one major cognitive transfer from high school, but so much is different. Academic skills may be the same, but the quality and quantity vastly increase. Additionally, college is never static: each class, roommate, relationship, teacher, and semester are different, requiring their own particular transfer and dissonant balance. Transitions can be a piece of cake; you just don't know if the cake is angel's food or devil's food.

Students must picture themselves as successful students. They need to have experienced moments of success and happiness before stepping foot on campus. If they haven't, they need to override the urge to perceive themselves as failures. They must transfer in belief and confidence. I had already failed Bryn Mawr the moment I stepped on campus, because I had already been rejected from Duke. I may have told myself and the college president that I was something special, but my subconscious thought otherwise.

The Soul Body Mind Connection: The Whole Package

You are how you be.

We don't just believe in our minds; we also believe with our bodies and souls. I toss around "soul" and "spirit" liberally. Please note, we are discussing energy, not spirituality or religion. If this makes you uncomfortable, allow your Cognitive Belief System to disagree and your cerebellum to activate the motor response in your arm, and then hurl this book against the wall and return to skimming that Reddit page. If you're still here, let's clarify what I mean. **"Soul" is defined as one's individual energetic field, while "spirit" is the universe's energetic field. Soul is I; spirit is all.**

Soul and spirit love talking with each other. The way they communicate, the smartphone, if you will, is through the subconscious. The subconscious is the portal connecting your individual self to the great and powerful Oz. Your soul dictates who you are—your purpose in life, what you believe, and how you live—in short, your conative domain. Spirit is the messenger to your soul, offering subtle suggestions on how to feed and activate your conative domain— how to follow your bliss, achieve your goals, *get 'er done*. You'd think something this important would be known to our conscious minds, but most often we are unaware of what's going on, subconsciously. It is "sub" or beneath our attentive state. Papa notices this inter-galactic communication, and Mama feels ruffled by it, but Baby, bless his heart, remains clueless.

So, like, wow. The soul is our individual energetic field, which flows and swirls into spirit, our universal energetic field. That is intensely groovy. Now, let's reel it back to the college campus. **If you believe something about yourself subconsciously, you**

will behave that way, consciously. If you want to change how you behave consciously, you have to change how you believe subconsciously. The way you change how you believe subconsciously is not through the conscious mind. You do not intellectualize change. If rational thought initiated change, we would change every time someone pointed something out and we respond with, *"Yeah, I know, I know. I really should* _____ [drink less, study more, call my mother on her birthday, eat vegetables, etc.]."

This may explain why change can be so difficult. Some people complain how positive affirmations don't work. Baby brain repeats, "I am special. I am worthy. I am successful." Still, Baby feels like crap and nothing good happens. Baby's parents tell him, "You can succeed in college! Just work hard and you'll be all right." Baby wants to work hard and succeed, but still fails. It's because the subconscious doesn't believe a word of it.

Our subconscious minds are programmed through experiences, not affirmations, intentions, or praise. If you have failed, you will believe failure. If you give up trying, you believe you are garbage, worthless, and weak. Every time the conscious mind chants, "I am worthy," the subconscious mind replies, "Who are you kidding? That's not how you are behaving."

This is something extremely difficult for modern parents to swallow. Incessantly praising their Precious Flower on how wonderful they are will not make their flower bloom. Kids have to live their own experiences, which include making many mistakes and failing many times. Modern parents hate seeing their children fail. Western society abhors **The Privilege of Hardship** (see "Connect" chapter). Parents tell kids, "You can do it!" while actually doing it for them. All the child learns is that they are incapable of doing something, and the subconscious is paying close attention. No gold stars, no pats on the head, no shrieks of "Good Effort!!!" take the place of experience. Nothing else but life makes Baby brain grow.

In order to make change, you have to convince the subconscious that you're serious. You don't convince the subconscious mind with positive affirmations. You don't just tell the universe you're different; you have to prove it. If you want to be worthy and special and successful, then accomplish something. Go out and challenge yourself to complete a goal. Don't just say you are special. Go out and *be* special.

When people say, "God is watching," or "Do your best, and God does the rest," this is a way to interpret what they mean. Your subconscious—the entire universal energetic flow—is watching. When you truly commit and take action is when the subconscious responds, lending a mystical hand with serendipity and synchronicity. When you commit, magic happens.

* * *

As we now begin to explore lifestyle factors, remember that these "factors" are experiences in your life you have saved as long-term memories. Your lifestyle is based on your Cognitive Belief System. You behave based on sense, meaning, and repetition: how you eat, sleep, move, have relationships, spend your free time, and react to things. You believe who you are based on what you've done and how you feel about it. But you are in college (or soon will be), so it's time to change what you believe.

You are reading this book because someone—either you, your parents, or some supporter—is curious about how your lifestyle factors are affecting your academic success. As a reminder, these are our key questions:

1. How are academic memories made?
2. How do lifestyle factors affect this memory-making process?
3. What can we do to improve the process, to academically succeed?

We'll now explore these answers in our next section. **This book is not designed to teach you how to study effectively, but rather, how to prepare your soul, body, and mind so that you are *able* to study effectively.** It teaches you how to *be,* in college. The rest is up to you.

How do you change? How do you navigate this iceberg-infested, landmine-riddled place called college? How do you develop your mind, regulate your emotions, and honor your calling? How do you manage your psychonutrient factors? How do you defend your health and education at the same time? How do you connect soul to spirit and activate your subconscious, in order to succeed?

Lifestyle reveals the answers. Health is the difference between being present and being absent. Regulating health balances soul-body-mind, which allows you to see clearly through murky waters. Health keeps you alert and agile through the precarious steps and missteps, the crisis and chaos of college.

* * *

How do you begin? Breathe.

Breath is the first step toward transformation, the immediate way to connect the conscious with the subconscious. Breath is our smartphone calling the universe, and there is always a clear signal.

With each inhalation, you breathe in a bit of spirit. With each exhalation, you breathe out a bit of soul. Breathing activates the parasympathetic system—the calming system of the body. Breathing increases intuition, relieves stress, soothes the mind and emotions, and eases the body. Breathing is the physiological version of stopping to smell the roses.

Breathing is the pause button in the crazybusy, offering insight and guidance. We are layers of energy: solid body, fluid thoughts and emotions, and ethereal auric field. Breathing allows all energetic fields to "sync up," and when we do, soul and spirit are in sync.

You'll learn more about this process as we explore stress. For now, as you begin your journey into lifestyles for learning, breathe. Take a slow and deep breath, filling your belly up into your lungs.

Hold it for a moment.

Slowly release.

Let's begin.

PSYCHONUTRIENT FACTORS AFFECTING ACADEMIC SUCCESS

An old Cherokee told his grandson: "My son, there is a battle between two wolves inside us all. One is Evil. It is anger, jealousy, greed, resentment, inferiority, lies and ego. The other is Good. It is joy, peace, love, hope, humility, kindness, empathy and truth."
The boy thought about it, and asked: "Grandfather, which wolf wins?"
The old man quietly replied: "The one you feed."

—Traditional Cherokee Folklore

STRESS

"Stress may be the number one health problem in America today. And it is getting worse. Depression, hypertension, Type 2 diabetes, obesity, cardiovascular and gastrointestinal distress have all been directly linked to excessive stress. Wellness programs that target stress reduction are far more likely to impact other high-risk behaviors, resulting in cumulative cost savings. To ignore stress in the workplace is to ignore millions of dollars paid in medical and disability claims and in lost production."

—HeartMath Institute

"With fifty trillion cells in your body, the human body is the equivalent of a skin-covered petri dish. Moving your body from one environment to another alters the composition of the 'culture medium,' the blood. The chemistry of the body's culture medium determines the nature of the cell's environment within you. The blood's chemistry is largely impacted by the chemicals emitted from your brain. Brain chemistry adjusts the composition of the blood based upon your perceptions of life. So this means that your perception of any given thing, at any given moment, can influence the brain chemistry, which, in turn, affects the environment where your cells reside and controls their rate. In other words, your thoughts and perceptions have a direct and overwhelmingly significant effect on cells."

—Bruce Lipton, PhD

You are how you perceive.

We can live a few weeks without food, a week or two without sleep, maybe a few days without water, but only a few minutes without breath. Healthy breathing is crucial to a healthy lifestyle. Breathing is a constant supply of energy flowing in and filtering out. Your job as a college student is to regulate what comes in and what comes out. This applies to your thoughts, especially. We may manage our lifestyle, but if we cannot manage our thoughts, our health is doomed to suffer.

We don't just breathe air, drink water, and eat food; we also consume thoughts. We eat three times a day, but think about 50,000 thoughts per day! That's a lot of thoughts. These thoughts, like an IV drop, flow through our SBM (soul-body-mind) most waking moments and some when asleep. Dr. Ted Morter, the late renowned chiropractor and author, wrote about the Six Essentials for Life: how you breathe, exercise, and rest; and what you eat, drink, and think. Dr. Morter, like many holistic practitioners, believed that the last one—what you think—has the strongest influence upon one's health.

When we think a positive thought, we receive a drop of nourishment. When we think a negative thought, we receive a drop of poison. Thoughts fill every moment of the college student's career. Overflowing academic information holds the mind captive, while disequilibrium constantly wracks emotions and beliefs.

It's not enough to simply say positive thoughts, either; you have to believe them. Remember the subconscious spirit and Cognitive Belief System? By the time you are a college student, Mama and Papa brains are firmly established. Baby brain believes all the things that have happened to you and most of what you've been told. If you have had experiences of being a good athlete or a bad writer, you will believe these to be truths. If, all your life, you've been told you're good-for-nothing or can do anything you set your mind to, you may also fall prey to these beliefs.

By the time you arrive at college, others have navigated your identity. College is your turn to steer the ship. It's why college is so shattering: young people are expected to shatter their perceptions of themselves and re-create them, based on their own beliefs. This is traumatic, not only for the young adult, but also to the parents and guardians who have nurtured a particular value system unto their baby.

College does not prepare you for "what you are going to do" with your life. These days, people wear so many professional hats and engage in so many relationships that the myths of a linear career and single monogamous relationship have disintegrated. With choice comes opportunity, economic turmoil, and transitions. **College prepares you for "who are you going to be" with your life,** so that, no matter what happens, you remain yourself: where you live, who you date, how you work, and all the thousands of decisions that add up to you.

A young adult has the developmental task of redefining who they are. It's their job. *"Isn't it enough to do well academically? Do I have to find myself in college?"* Yes, you do, or else it finds you. You either consciously choose who you are going to be, or others will decide for you. As you discover who you are, it may be very different from who you once were.

Hans Selye "Discovers" Stress

As you might imagine, that causes a lot of stress. **Stress may be considered *the* number one lifestyle factor affecting academic success.** How a student perceives, reacts, and responds to stress will make or break his academic success and, maybe, save his life.

What is stress, anyway? It's such an overused word, tossed around so often that it doesn't hold any particular meaning. Stress is change. In terms of lifestyle, stress is a change in soul, body, or mind, due to an experience. This change is a physiological change: functions alter in response to a stressor, which is the thing that causes the change. The stress response is the way we respond to the stress. The coping strategy is how we deal with the stress response in order to regain balance. The whole experience is what we simply refer to as "stress."

Although stress has been around as long as life itself, it wasn't formally recognized as a lifestyle factor until the 1950s. Dr. Hans Selye is regarded as the founder of stress research and pioneered the field of **psychoneuroimmunology**—the interaction between psychological processes. Psychoneuroimmunology is the in-depth study of the interaction of the mind, the central nervous system, and the immune system, and their impact on our health and well-being. Psychoneuroimmunology is generally referred to as the mind-body connection and what I refer to as the soul-body-mind connection or SBM.

The story of how Hans Selye discovered stress is stressful. Dr. Selye conducted experiments with mice and needed to inject a select group with a chemical. He may have been a good scientist, but he was an awful animal handler. The mice would continually escape, and he would have a heck of a time trying to get them back into their cages. They'd be scrambling all over the counters and floor, while he'd be "sweeping" at them with a broom, in a pathetic attempt to corral them together. What he discovered was that he had, in fact, created another variable in his "controlled" experiments. There was a new factor to be measured: stress.

The mice exposed to stress developed significant health issues, particularly in three systems: immune, digestive, and adrenal. These three areas are responsible for keeping one well, energetic, and nourished. When stress attacks, one becomes sick, tired, and starved.

Stress affects the SBM, but not all stress is created equally; rather, not all stress affects in the same way. Stressors used to be classified as *distress* (negative) and *eustress* (positive). New studies reveal that it's not the stressor but your reaction to a stressor that determines if it's good or bad. In other words, **your attitude about the stressor determines how it will affect you.** If you see the stressor as a reasonable challenge and opportunity to grow, then you respond positively, as eustress. If you see the stressor as an unrealistic challenge that you are unable to handle, then you respond negatively, with distress. This is immediately illustrated when introducing a group of kindergarteners to a tarantula.

We witness this all the time (not with tarantulas, hopefully). Twenty-five students take the same academic course. They are exposed to the same stressors: professor, class, assignments, and exams. By the end of a semester, they will have twenty-five unique experiences. Like a bell curve for academic performance, students will report different perceptions of the class. Some insist it was life-altering. Some might remark how it helped them to see things in a new way. Some will hate the teacher. Some may dismiss the course as a waste of time. Some have no opinion, whatsoever. It's as if they were all enrolled in their own solitary classroom.

Perception is created completely based on our own beliefs. The stressor may be "bad," such as a car crash or failed assignment. It could be "good," such as rooming with your best friend or acing a final exam. On the other hand, the car crash might result in a new, better car. Rooming with your BFF may fail miserably and you become enemies. Thus, determining if stress is good or bad ultimately depends upon your *perception* of the events unfolding and your *reaction* to them. This perception, in turn, affects how your body responds to that stressor.

It can become more complicated. Let's say you are planning a long-term project with a group of students. You might consider this *eustress* while your classmates consider it *distress*. Some people thrive in chaos and last-minute deadlines, while other people thrive in routine and discipline. If you were to poll most of my Bryn Mawr classmates, most would shake their heads, asserting, "All she had to do was ask someone about the essay!" This stressor could have been transformed into eustress in seconds. Instead, it became the catalyst for failure. Stress is definitely in the eye of the beholder.

How do you know if the stress is good or bad? Here is where the energetic order of SBM enters. Discernment is as simple as how you feel. Check in, honestly. If the experience affects you in a good way—if you feel calm, happy, excited, or ready, it is likely the *bing* of eustress. On the other hand, if you feel lousy—angry, sad, confused, thrown off balance, and "not yourself," it is likely the *thud* of distress.

When determining if stress is a bing or thud, check in with the soul and body, because they never lie. Papa brain doesn't think; he responds to Mama's emotions and Baby's tantrums. Papa just nods his head and says, "Yes, dear." In the movie *My Big Fat Greek Wedding*, Maria Portokalos claimed, "The man is the head, but the woman is the neck . . . and she can turn the head . . . *any-way-she-wants.*" Only Baby and Mama lie; Papa is pure response. The mind lies all the time. Emotions mask true feelings. "I'm *fine!*" we shriek to our partner after they've mistreated us. Oh, really? You don't seem fine. If words could kill, that "fine" would have cut someone's head off.

We are in constant denial of our true feelings. *Whatever. I'm over it. I don't care.* These throwaway lines are akin to shoving a drowning person's head under the water in order to stop them from making such a commotion. Baby's denial masks Mama and Papa's true message, and until we face the message, it remains. **When we bury our feelings, we bury them alive.** This is especially true of young adults. Forget self-management. Baby brain is still experiencing some emotions for the first time.

Baby doesn't always lie intentionally; sometimes, he's hijacked. You ever see one of those action movies where the main character is trying to talk a killer into relinquishing his weapon? In that calm, hypnotic voice, he will gently repeat, "Give me the gun. Give me the gun." The killer is under siege, held captive by his own brain. In the cognitive industry, we call this an **amygdala hijack**. This image illustrates where emotional stress stimulates the brain. Teenagers show more activation in the amygdala, the part of Mama brain that receives and processes emotion. The amygdala has the ability to shut down the frontal cortex while Mama protects Baby.

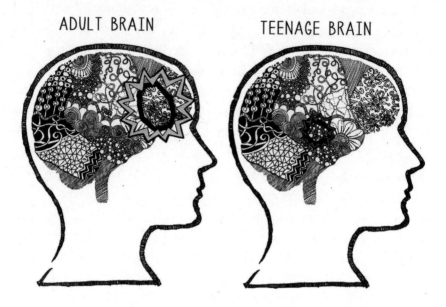

ADULT BRAIN   TEENAGE BRAIN

As Baby matures, he has more emotional experiences: more romantic relationships, more jobs, and more life. We come to realize that we will not die of a broken heart or failed career. We begin to recognize strong emotional responses and stop ourselves, reflecting on the experience. Our frontal cortexes observe, "Gosh, I sure am feeling sad and angry; however, if I drive my car into my ex-girlfriend's front porch, there may be dire consequences to deal with." We employ our higher-order civilized mind to analyze the situation and inhibit dangerously strong reactions; in short, Baby grows up.

Allostatic Stress: Daily Hassles

Stress is not just a state of mind, but a state of being. Duration and intensity influence our stress response. In terms of duration, there are two kinds of stress: acute and allostatic. Acute stress is fast and furious: earthquakes and break-ups. Acute doesn't necessarily mean catastrophic. An acute stress could be a pop quiz (or failing one). Acute stress is an isolated type of event, while allostatic stress lasts longer. It is referred to as the "daily hassle" type of stress. If you are managing an illness, monitoring medication, or handling an unhealthy relationship, these types of stressors inject a more "timed-release" type of stress response.

Intensity is not directly related to duration, but we tend to perceive things that way. If you are in an abusive relationship, you will find strategies to survive it. If you are in a loving relationship and your partner suddenly attacks you, it will feel quite intense. The attack is new and unexpected, so you pay close attention to it. Long-standing abuse may be just as intense, but you become desensitized and see it less as a direct threat. **Coping with long-standing stress becomes a "procedure" of sorts, and we become automated in our response.**

Allostatic stress may feel less stressful, due to its predictability. When something is unpredictable, like an earthquake or a newly abusive partner, it may cause significant stress. If something is predictable, it brings a sense of control, which lessens stress response. On the other hand, if you know you're having a test four times a semester, this may cause added stress. Adversity is another factor. Even if a stressor is perceived as highly stressful, if someone is able to bounce back quickly from an incident, they are less likely to suffer stressful consequences. Duration, intensity, predictability, and adversity are key factors, which together, influence our perception. **Consider the power that you yield. You may determine your life story, simply by how you perceive and respond.**

Let's say I abruptly pull out in front of your car and cut you off. Let's say you live in the city. This kind of thing happens all the time, so you quickly forget about it. But let's say you live in the country, raised to be a polite and defensive driver. My offensive maneuver may deeply offend your core values of decency and fair play. You may become incensed by my car swerving in front of yours. You may even perseverate on this incident for weeks, maybe months! Your acute stress evolved into allostatic stress, solely due to how you chose to perceive the event. You are feeding the Evil Wolf, from this section's Cherokee folklore quote:

An old Cherokee told his grandson: "My son, there is a battle between two wolves inside us all. One is Evil. It is anger, jealousy, greed, resentment, inferiority, lies and ego. The other is Good. It is joy, peace, love, hope, humility, kindness, empathy and truth." The boy thought about it, and asked: "Grandfather, which wolf wins?"

The old man quietly replied: "The one you feed."

***

Which do you think is worse, "fast and furious" or "slow and low"? Research has shown allostatic stress to be more detrimental; slow trickles of poison seem more deadly than major oil spills. Major oil spills make front page news; they are novel and controversial, so we pay attention. But the daily hassles? A snoring roommate, alcoholic father, or menacing professor? Like living in a city, we filter out stimuli, unconscious of the stress it is causing; but like toxic chemicals dumped in a river, the damage doesn't stop just because we stop paying attention.

How would you categorize college? Well, it consists of a multitude of small, non-life-threatening stressors, continuously administered into your soul, body, and mind for an indeterminate amount of time. Earthquakes are bad, but I've never known one to last four years.

Stretch Zone: The Goldilocks Law

Another way to monitor stress response is to notice where you land. We live in three stress zones: comfort, stretch, and panic. Too little stress creates a comfort zone where life feels familiar and easy. There is little growth in our comfort zones, but there is opportunity to practice things we've learned, to rest and rejuvenate before our next round of learning happens. Panic zones are high-stress situations, when life feels alien and hard. There is also little growth

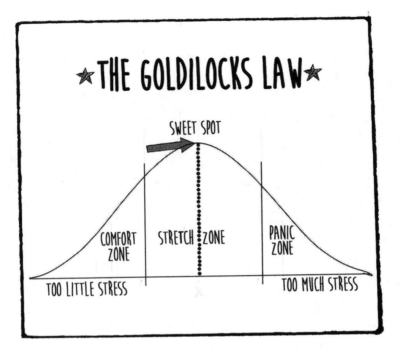

in panic zones, as energy focuses on survival. Panic zones occur during injury and trauma and often during new experiences. The stretch zone lives in between, categorized as the **Sweet Spot** by researchers Yerkes and Dodson. The Sweet Spot respects The Goldilocks Law (categorized by Crowther). Stress is not too easy and not too hard . . . it's just right. That is how you want your college experience to be. **If tasks are too boring, you will avoid them. If they are too daunting, you will avoid them. College has to be just right.**

The Sweet Spot may help explain why some people lose interest in a new partner after a few months of dating. The thrill of pursuit is gone, replaced by the comfort of companionship. To shake up the comfort zone, we break up with the partner, throw ourselves and our partner into the panic zone, and then desperately seek new companionship in an effort to regain the stimulating stretch zone of a new partner.

Stress Causes GAS

Dr. Selye also developed the GAS theory or **General Adaptation Syndrome**, which is funny, due to the digestive turmoil caused by stress. Selye plotted the journey of a typical stressful experience: the Alarm phase is when you first encounter the stress. The Resistance phase deals with the stressor. You are basically resisting or managing the stress, followed by the Exhaustion phase, when the stress experience ends.

In the Alarm phase, you immediately react to the stressor, which is like an alarm going off in your body. The stress is new and surprising and knocks you off balance. This could be as minor as someone making an offhand comment or something more complicated, such as wrecking your car. Your response depends upon the several factors, which create your perception.

Interestingly, someone's offhand comment may sting more than wrecking a car. We mustn't judge perception. If you're wealthy, totaling your car may result in your parents simply buying you a brand new one. It's all good. What if, however, you earned the money for your car by working all summer at some crappy job? You sacrificed a great deal, and a totaled vehicle may cause great alarm.

Consider the stress of a college semester. You enroll in a class and on the first day (acute), you realize it's going to be more challenging than you bargained for (allostatic). This is a required class, eliminating control. Intensity and duration are high (you hate it, and it lasts all semester). Predictability is low (Moody professor gives pop quizzes. Panic zone is high.) Assessing all the stress elements, you deduce that this class is going be a bitch. You remain in Resistance phase for the entire semester. Each and every day, you have to wake up, remember you are attending this class, feel the stress response, and prepare to engage with this stressor. This stupid class stresses every waking *and* sleeping minute of your life.

The final exam arrives. You hand in your exam and, wait . . . still resisting . . . until finally you receive your grade. You passed! Huzzah!

Congratulations. Your reward is to immediately enter the Exhaustion phase. After months of successful management, the stressor is eliminated. All the resistant energy suddenly frees up, and the body collapses into a sea of exhaustion. You've run a marathon, and at the end, you collapse. GAS explains why students become sick on weekends, holiday breaks, and during exams. These "crescendo" moments are culminating in maintaining the stress for so long that every resource is depleted.

You may notice a slight dip in the chart just after the Alarm phase. A drop in energy often occurs at the beginning of a stress journey, due to issues of resistance and denial. If the stressor persists, however, then we must roll up our physiological sleeves and get down to the business of dealing with the stress.

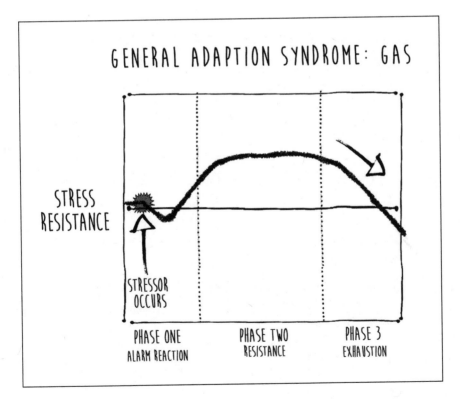

GENERAL ADAPTION SYNDROME: GAS

STRESS
RESISTANCE

STRESSOR
OCCURS

PHASE ONE
ALARM REACTION

PHASE TWO
RESISTANCE

PHASE 3
EXHAUSTION

Kenneth

I was a pretty stressed out guy in college. I didn't want to be there for the first year and it was incredibly stressful being in a place that 1. I didn't want to be and 2. I still had trouble believing I needed to be. I didn't fit in all that well because I hadn't been tagged with the LD label for years. My LD was caused by an injury during childhood. I faked my way through school with a higher than average verbal IQ and the ability to talk my way through most any situation. I found out at the end of high school that I had a learning disability, difference, difficulty, or whatever it is that you want to call dysgraphia.

I resented the implication that I was anything other than normal. I wanted to blame someone for not catching it sooner. I wanted to blame my teachers for letting me get by with sub-par work. I wanted to blame my parents for not checking my work more closely or for not making sure I did more than the bare minimum. I wanted to blame everybody but myself. I was headed for a college that was my mother's choice and I didn't know if I really belonged there.

The nature of my learning difference added stress because when I first got to college, I was still learning coping strategies that others had had years to perfect. My work suffered because I couldn't fake my way through anymore— I actually had to do work instead of pretending to work and then wowing teachers with my ability to verbally express my thoughts in a way that I never could on paper. I started to stress because I wasn't getting work done. I was stressing when I did get work done because the grades I was getting on the work were not what thought I should be capable of. I was stressing myself to the point of failing classes.

When I was in college I handled stress by hiding from it. I had what, in the beginning, was a legitimate excuse for missing classes, the occasional migraine. When I first got to college I didn't realize that one of the things that triggered my migraines was stress. Once I realized that stress caused my migraines I thought I had a ready-made excuse to skip classes. Professors accepted it without question and I began to realize that I could use the migraines as an excuse to miss classes even if I didn't have one, and soon I was in a vicious cycle of skipping classes either because of stress-induced migraines or because I was close to failing and using a migraine as an excuse to not look the teacher in the eye.

It took the patient urging of my academic advisor to get me to go to the professors whose classes I was failing and ask for help. It took professors who understood the nature of my situation and were willing to let me clear the backlog of past-due assignments. In one case it took the complete and total use of a bonus points system in one class that let me go from an average of about 27 to an average of close to 94 in a week. With the improving grades, the frequency of real migraines went back to what it was in high school, about one every one to two months, instead of the weekly frequency that I was dealing with at the height of my class skipping cycle. I survived college by managing stress and by extension managing my migraines. That stress and migraine management would not have been possible without the patience and guidance of the academic professionals involved in my first college semester.

Stress: A Full-Time Job

What happens to your SBM when you encounter a stress? Oy. So much, it could take a book. Basically, everything. That sounds like a cop-out, but stress gets its naughty little mitts into every nook and cranny of our being. Remember Hans Selye and his poor mice? Stress employs all non-essential energy to be directed toward fighting off the stressor. Stress's chemical responses deplete the "non-essential" body systems, starting with immune, digestive, and adrenal.

Stress hinders digestion. When we are under attack, digestion stops. We need fuel and blood for our limbs, so we can fight or flee. Allostatic stress means digestion chronically shutting down. Under stress, people don't stop eating, they just stop digesting their food properly. The food ferments, rots, and turns toxic, and we become gassy, constipated, or diarrheic.

Normally, nutrients are absorbed into our bloodstreams through portals in the small intestines. From the bloodstream, they are distributed to various ports to maintain and rebuild the body. If digestion is disrupted, nutrient absorption stops. Think of digestive stress as an embargo—nutritional supplies are cut off. Stress causes us to literally starve ourselves, no matter how much we eat. You'll see how this is extremely bad news when we explore food, but for now, let's just say that, in college, we are not at our "nutritional peak."

Stress attacks the immune system, whose role is our defense. You may consider defending illness an "essential" body system, but in the bigger picture, it makes sense. For which would you rather have energy: fighting a cold or running away from a bear? **Stressed-out people are often sick. In fact, if someone is sick, ask them, "How is your stress level?"** I'll bet next year's tuition they've been knocked off their sweet spots.

The final system neglected during stress is the adrenal, which regulates energy and blood sugar levels. Glucose, our bodies' main fuel, is essential for brain function and mental maintenance. Stress viciously disturbs glucose maintenance. **Thanks to stress, you are now sick, malnourished, exhausted, crazy, and unable to study.** Game over.

* * *

When teaching stress management, I was surprised to learn that 90 percent of all emergency room visits are stress-related. Stress-related issues such as running late, emotional distraction, and sleep-deprivation are involved in more than half of all vehicular accidents. That is a helluva lot of stress. Most health practitioners validate how every disease relates to stress. Either the stress caused it, the disease worsens from stress, or the stress inhibits the immune system, delaying healing. Even genetic diseases are affected by stress; many autoimmune diseases express their genetic mapping after a traumatic event.

Most modern deaths are stress-related. Thanks to modern science and hygiene, westernized countries rarely die from cholera, polio, or salmonella. Water treatment systems, pasteurization, vaccination, and other regulatory devices reduce these once-epidemic adversaries. Despite all these modern advances, we still die of unnatural causes. We may live longer lives, but are sicker, longer. **Instead of dying from germs, we now die from lifestyle factors: cardiovascular diseases, cancers, autoimmune disorders, addictions, and obesity.** We smoke cigarettes, drink alcohol, eat junk food, lead sedentary lives, and are inundated with carcinogenic influences, including cell phones and power lines. Conventional foods commonly contain pesticides, preservatives, bleaches, antibiotics, carcinogens, neurotoxins, endocrine disruptors, and undergo genetic modification. We constantly marinate in so many stress hormones that we poison ourselves to death.

Genetics play a role, and it's tempting to blame one's nature, but genes are also strongly influenced by our nurturing lifestyles. **Epigenetics** supports this surprising revelation. Epigenetics involves genetic control by factors other than an individual's DNA sequence.

Stress has been directly linked to lupus, rheumatoid arthritis, Bell's palsy, fibromyalgia, and other autoimmune genetic expressions. **Our current lifestyle manipulates our future generation's DNA.** (Hey, it's another opportunity to blame your parents.) Our quantity of life has increased, but our quality has not. Stress-related symptoms are now so commonplace, we just consider them part of life:

Stress!

Physical symptoms: increased and irregular heart rate, tightness of chest, sweating, TMJ/grinding of teeth, sleep deprivation and insomnia, tinnitus, blurred vision, fatigue, headache, pain, tightness in neck and back, muscle tension, nausea, vomiting, urinary frequency, indigestion, missed menstrual cycle, diarrhea, reduced interest in sex, slumped posture, trembling, twitching, and accident proneness.

Emotional symptoms: emotional irritability, tendency to cry easily, depression, nightmares, angry outbursts, suspiciousness, emotional instability, jealousy, poor concentration, decreased social involvement, disinterest in activities, bickering, withdrawal, complaining, criticizing, restlessness, tendency to be easily startled, anxiety, increased smoking, increased use of sarcasm, and use of drugs or alcohol.

Intellectual symptoms: forgetfulness, errors in arithmetic and grammar, poor judgment, preoccupation, poor concentration, inattention to detail, reduced creativity, reduced productivity.

Productivity symptoms: increased lateness, absenteeism, low morale, depersonalization, avoidance of contact with coworkers, excessive breaks, resistance to change, impatience,

---

negative attitude, reluctance to assist others, carelessness, verbal or physical abuse, poor quality and quantity of work, threats to resign, resignation.

Source: Eliopoulos, C. Nursing Administration Manual for Long-Term Care Facilities, 7th ed., Health Education Network, 2008.

Study that list for a moment. How many of these symptoms relate to the work of being a college student? Yep. When is the most volatile time in a person's life? College? Yep. **Managing a full-load of courses is only the beginning. College students also manage the full-time job of stress.** You can see why stress is listed first; it affects every other lifestyle factor.

Stress-related diseases produce a list as long and insidious as the symptoms: cardiovascular issues such as stroke, heart attacks, and hypertension; increased rate of cancers; greater risk for chronic auto-immune diseases, such as asthma, rheumatoid arthritis, Crohn's and celiac disease, lupus, and skin disorders like shingles, psoriasis and eczema; mental disorders in all categories, including schizophrenia and migraines; insomnia and other sleep disorders; increased vulnerability to bacterial and viral diseases, such as ulcers, colds, flu, and greater risk of becoming infected, such as staff, strep, E.coli and salmonella; worsened symptoms in learning disorders, such as dyslexia and ADHD; eating disorders; infertility. The list is exhaustive, yet constantly growing.

Some studies even cite stress as the biological cause of homosexuality. The film series *Brain Sex* explored this theory. Researchers were curious about the reasons for the sudden spike in homosexual behavior with Baby Boomer children immediately following World War II. The theory involves hormonal development during gestation.

During its 9-month journey, an embryo travels through three distinct periods or trimesters. In each trimester, there is a hormonal "flooding" that relates to gender and sexuality. Sex is determined in the first trimester. Chromosomes do not determine the sex; hormones do. If a genetically pre-determined male (XY) receives a flooding of estrogen during the first trimester, he will develop female genitalia. The same applies to chromosomal females (XX), with testosterone flooding. Second trimester hormonal flooding determines sexual preference. In a "normal" flooding, a male receives more testosterone, and he becomes attracted to females. If he receives too much estrogen, he will be attracted to males. The amount of attraction is dependent on the amount of hormone released. Equal sexual orientation or bisexual preference would be attributed to an equal estrogen-testosterone flooding. The third trimester determines behavior. Once again, hormones regulate the outcome. Typically, a male receives testosterone and acts masculine. Girls receive estrogen and act feminine. Tweak the hormones, and boys become effeminate while girls act like tomboys.

Each flooding is independent. Three separate floodings of two contrasting hormones provide several combinations and continuums. A male could be attracted to females, but act feminine. A male could possess XY chromosomes, become a female, be attracted to males, and act masculine. If you really consider the scenarios, it seems hard to believe that nature could nail it, every time. An XY chromosome male develops as a male, is attracted to females, and behaves as a male? I mean, what are the odds?

What is responsible for this hormonal abnormality? The theory claims that another hormone is involved in these gestational floodings ... a hormone that directly influences the outcome, causing imbalance. Want to wager a guess? That hormone is ... cortisol. Yes, **cortisol**, the stress hormone, released during times of stress. Cortisol floods the system during emotional responses of anxiety, worry, frustration, anger, and fear.

Here's how it plays out. World War II broke out. Men were called to war. Men impregnated their new blushing brides. Men went off to war. Women experienced increased stress, anxiety, worry, frustration, anger, and fear during their gestational periods. Cortisol ambushed the delicate hormonal floodings in each trimester, upsetting the meticulous balance of testosterone and estrogen. Homosexuality exploded. Since these young people came of age during the civil rights era, a previously sexual taboo was now freely expressed and cultural awareness raised.

Managing stress is a full-time job, in addition to your already full-time schedule. If you answer, "crazybusy," when someone asks you how you are, then your life force is being used up to deal with the constant clean-up of physiological flooding of stress hormones. If stress can turn a boy into a girl, it can easily turn an A into an F.

Dances with Stress

Since stress is a fundamental part of our lives, it's vital to develop a relationship with it—learn the dance. The dance steps are coping strategies.

Coping Strategy # 1: Breathe

The primary dance step is to breathe. Like food, we need air to survive. Breathing is the handiest coping strategy. You may retort, "I breathe all the time, so I shouldn't have any stress." Not so. Stress-reducing breathing is belly breathing: slow, steady breaths, filling our lungs from the diaphragm (bellow the belly) upward. Deep breathing relaxes, increasing attention and reducing anxiety. Shallow quick breaths arouse, when energy is needed.

Coping Strategy # 2: Alter State

Smile. Right now. Go ahead, I'll wait. Even better, I'll smile along with you. ☺

Keep smiling. Why rush, for gosh sake? Allow the smile to spread out from your lips, down your chin, up into the corners of your eyes, and over your head. Smile down your back, smile over your butt and legs, down to your smiling toes. Hug yourself with a smile.

Smile!

How do you feel? A tiny wee bit better? Well, you do, whether or not you want to admit it. Science proves it, so there! One little study proved what millions of anecdotes reveal. The soul and body lead the way, so when we smile, our minds respond obediently. Our minds, in turn, release happy chemicals, bathing the body and soul in happy hormones. We don't actually need to be happy; we simply need to arrange our body into a "happy shape," and then the chemicals respond accordingly. Just thinking about or "air-petting" those little Labrador puppies reduces anxiety. Cool, isn't it?

One of the easiest ways to reduce stress is to alter your state. Even the tiniest change—one smile or deep breath—nudges the body's focus. Another simple way to alter one's state is to shift your position. If you're sitting down, stand up (and vice versa). This simple shift causes significant physiological changes and can dramatically shift moods. Similar to distracting a crying baby with a shiny toy or gentle swaying, the altered state distracts the body from hyper-focusing on the stressor.

Stand up, stretch, and smile! Don't you feel better, already?

Coping Strategy #3: Relax

The Relaxation Response is a process coined by Dr. Herbert Benson, co-founder of The Benson-Henry Institute for Mind Body Medicine, affiliated with Harvard University. Benson identifies four dance steps of the **Relaxation Response**:

- A quiet environment
- A comfortable position
- A mental device, such as a repeated word or phrase
- A passive attitude

The Relaxation Response is instant meditation that immediately alters one's state. Using a "mental device" keeps Baby brain busy, so he doesn't return to obsessing over some problem. It also helps train the mind to stop the incessant flow of thoughts, our "monkey mind," giving your mind a cognitive rest.

Coping Strategy #4: Act

Cognitive researcher William Glasser suggests that we need to *do* something before we *feel* like doing it, and then, finally, we *believe* that we can do it. It's an odd reversal of logic, but one that supports the idea of the subconscious ruling our behavior. We typically wait until we feel ready to do something and believe we can do it, but Glasser argues, if we do that, we wait forever.

Action comes first. Most people feel better *after* they finish writing a research paper. This strategy is a vicious catch-22 in most situations. Take depression. The way to immediately feel better is to alter one's state. A longer-term strategy is to change one's behavior, but depressed people *wait until they feel better* before they change. This also happens with exercise; almost no one wants to work out, yet most people feel better afterwards.

Action may feel like acting, but after a while, your actions become real. Remember Kurt Vonnegut's advice? *"We are what we pretend to be."* If you are stressed out, "pretend" to be happy. Act relaxed and calm; chemicals don't know the difference. Your body and soul will convince your mind to play along.

Coping Strategy #5: Reframe

One of my favorite classroom activities is to show a clip of the classic 80s movie, *The Karate Kid*. After getting beat up by the mean bullies, Daniel asks Mr. Miyagi for help in learning karate. The next few scenes show Daniel doing a bunch of meaningless activities that have absolutely nothing whatsoever to do with karate: painting, washing, and waxing Mr. Miyagi's home, fences, and automobiles. Daniel does these chores willingly, due to a pact they initially made at the beginning of the training—he will do whatever his instructor says, without questioning.

Around the fifth day, Daniel snaps. As he finishes painting the house, he confronts Mr. Miyagi, who is returning from a leisurely day of fishing. His mentor retorts, "You are learning plenty." Daniel, facing extreme disequilibrium and cognitive dissonance, rudely screams, "Screw you. I've had enough of this! I'm going home!"

Mr. Miyagi takes control. He demands Daniel show him the techniques needed to do all the "housework." Each one of these chores had specific movements designed for blocking and attacking an opponent. As Mr. Miyagi repeats each technique now with their proper labels, he then proceeds to attack Daniel with full force. The master throws punches and violently kicks at Daniel who, unbeknownst to himself, begins responding automatically (thanks to his cerebellum!). After the attack has been successfully defended against, Mr. Miyagi and Daniel bow to each other.

This scene so deftly illustrates reframing, I used it for every class, each semester. I love when the students sense that magic moment of reframing—when Daniel abruptly shifts from anger to humility, from feeling betrayed to being empowered.

Reframing is altering one's state of perception. Like the name suggests, we reframe or put a different frame on the "picture"—the experience we are seeing. When you are confronted with a stressor, take a moment and stop. Ask yourself, "Is there another way to see this? What lesson am I missing?" By reframing the perspective, you may diffuse the stress response.

Coping Strategy #6: Ask

You have the choice to ask for help. Call it asking, praying, or surrendering, you are simply having your conscious mind ask your subconscious mind for help, and it works magically. Had I followed my own advice at Bryn Mawr, I would be off gallivanting the world doing famous brain doctor things. Instead, I refused to ask anyone for help and failed my first year in college.

It can take remarkably little to fail. This Achilles heel curses so many college students. Teaching a predominantly male demographic, I've observed how the typical male student abhors asking for help. It's as if asking for help immediately reassigns his sexual preference (the stress itself is doing enough endocrine disruption).

It doesn't matter who or how you ask. Let your soul decide. Your mind is excused from this strategy. Feel it in your gut and heart, and then let your mind execute. Don't let the mind decide what to ask for; it cannot be trusted under stress. Take a quick moment, breathe through your gut and heart, and the message will come.

Coping Strategy # 7: Stuff

Props help. There are a variety of herbs, supplements, and food stuffs one can take to help offset stress. A few include:

- Consume stuff:
  - Water
  - Lemon water—fresh lemon juice and water

- ○ Raw, undistilled apple cider vinegar and water
- ○ Water-soluble vitamins B & C from products like *Emergen-C*
- ○ *Kombucha*, a fermented tea
- ○ Green tea
- ○ Miso
- ○ Herbal teas: Lemongrass, Passionflower or Kava Kava (visit a health food store and inform them that you are stressed. You can practice Coping Strategy #6, too.)
- • Apply stuff:
  - ○ Aromatherapy
  - ○ Bath salts
  - ○ Lotions and balms with lavender, orange, geranium, rosemary, passionflower or lemongrass

Coping Strategy # 8: Laughter, the Best Medicine

Children laugh about 200 times a day; adults laugh about 15. Wow. That's not so funny.

You may think that stress is no laughing matter. It is *exactly* that. **Laughter is the greatest coping strategy of all.** What's so great about it? Laughter, for its efficacy, ease, and lack of negative side effects (other than expulsion from libraries and public snot-snorting), may well be the best medicine. One of the most effective coping strategies in reducing stress is in altering one's state. There are multiple ways to do this discussed in this book: food, drink, sleep, exercise, creativity, substances (over and under the counter), and company. But, **the hands-down most fun way to alter one's state is to laugh. Just one little giggle initiates so much change in a person's physiological state, it ought to be regulated by the FDA.**

Laughter is the father, son, and holy ghost of coping strategies. It combines all of the others: breathe, alter states, relax, act, reframe, ask, and stuff. It is physical action that connects us outside of ourselves, into seeing perspectives. In this way, laughter connects soul to spirit, which is probably why it feels so fulfilling.

Laughter is the antidote to stress. Laughter has clear and direct biochemical effects on the SBM, reducing serum cortisol, dopamine, epinephrine, and growth hormone—chemicals related to the classical stress response. People think of dopamine as the "happy hormone," but as we'll see in the "Control" chapter, too much dopamine is a bad thing. If laughter reduces serum cortisol and other stress hormones, it may diminish the chemical effects of stress on the immune, digestive, and adrenal system. That means we are less sick and tired. In college terms, that means we attend class and turn in our assignments. Laughter alone may be the "good kryptonite" that shields us from the biochemical warfare.

Health Benefits of Laughter

- Stimulation of the production of catecholamines and hormones, which enhance feelings of well-being and pain tolerance
- A decrease in anxiety and increase in endorphins (natural narcotic-like substances produced in the brain)
- An increase in cardiac and respiratory rates
- Enhancement of metabolism; an improvement of muscle tone
- Perception of the relief of stress and tension with increased relaxation, which may last up to 45 minutes following laughter
- Increased numbers of natural killer cells, which fight viral infections of cells and some cancer cells
- Increased T cells (T lymphocytes) that fight infection; increased antibody immunoglobulin A, which fights upper-respiratory infections
- Laughter exercises the breathing muscles, benefits the cardiovascular system by increasing oxygenation, and promotes relaxation.

- Laughter helps control pain by distracting one's attention, reducing tension, and changing or reframing one's perspective.
- During episodes of laughter, the blood pressure increases, but then it lowers below the initial rate. Dr. William Fry, a researcher of the physiology of laughter, has called laughter "internal jogging," giving our internal organs a workout.

Eliopoulos, C. Nursing Administration Manual for Long-Term Care Facilities, 7th ed., Health Education Network, 2008.

Start with yourself. Laugh. Laugh out loud. Laugh often. Laugh at yourself. Give yourself permission to be human. Pay attention to your own self-talk. Replace negative actions with positive ones. Change your behavior, and the subconscious will notice.

Coping Strategies Gone Wild

When is a strategy not a strategy? When it causes more problems than it solves. If, by doing something, you feel less balanced—sick, hung over, injured, more stressed, or find you've wasted the day in doing it—then it is a negative coping strategy.

The Bryn Mawr essay was a stressor; or rather, lack of clarity in an assignment was a stressor. Because I began to feel threatened in attending class, my coping strategy was to avoid class and prevent the threat. In order to feel justified in this strategy, I reframed my perspective about the essay. The assignment was stupid and the class a waste of time. Denial now became a coping strategy, and it worked, temporarily; I did feel better. After the first semester, the problem remained and the coping strategies became an obstacle to solving the problem. **The coping strategies, themselves, became a bigger problem than the original problem.**

When does a negative coping strategy become an addiction? When it causes more problems *and* you cannot stop doing it. We'll discuss this in depth in the "Control" chapter, but for now, heed one college student's tale:

Andy

I value this (video) game because it lets me escape from reality and it helps me deal with stress. When I am feeling stressed I can sit down with this game, and the freedom it gives to let the player do anything they want helps me to relax. I enjoy being able to create large structures block by block—I'm not as good as most of the people on the internet who build things but since no one is judging my creations or critiquing them, it feels relaxing. The sheer number of things you can do in the game is in complete contrast to real life where you are constantly being told what you should do and what you can't do. In Minecraft you are allowed to create incredibly complex machines in order to do a simple task such as opening a door, and it is considered normal.

Sounds great. Video games helped this student cope with the stresses of everyday life, but video games were his only release. What happens when he doesn't have access to his coping strategy? What happens when he's stressed out and can't play video games? **We need strategies that we can use anytime and anywhere.** You may not be able to play a video game or smoke weed in a classroom, but you may always breathe deeply and smile. Breathing, smiling, shifting . . . the illusion is that they are too simple to be so effective, but they work as well as your favorite distraction. It's important to have coping strategies that are accessible.

The Dark Side of Humor

Sarcasm. Cynicism. Defense Mechanisms. Bullying. Not all laughter is created equally. Laughter has a dark side, used as a weapon to deflect our own feelings. Misaligned humor causes as much damage as any allostatic stressor. Studies monitoring Kirlian photography reveal how sarcastic thoughts "cut" one's auric energy—our souls, if you will. In metaphysical circles, it is believed that negative communications like sarcasm interrupt one's auric energetic field. Masaru Emoto's water crystal research, documented in *The Hidden Messages in Water*, offered us a glimpse into the world of energy. Well-formed water crystals mutated by simply thinking negative thoughts toward the containers or writing negative messages on them. We use terms such as "cuts like a knife" and "barbs" when referring to sarcasm. Metaphor may be reality in this case.

Balance: Don't Be Dexter

Ever watch the show *Dexter*? (I don't dare, but my son insists I'm missing out.) It's about a serial killer employed as a serial killer detective. Talk about taking your work home. How about the introvert who works from home, then spends every evening alone with their nose in a book? Balancing work and play is key to surviving stress. It aligns us in our Sweet Spot.

College life is a sedentary life. Students sit in class. They sit doing assignments. They sit during exams. They sit during office hours. Even extracurricular activities are often sedentary: school newspaper, clubs. Free time is often *veg* time, screens. Sometimes students will rally for a round of Ultimate frisbee, but often, default mode is *sit and stare*. Add substances to the mix, and you have a hyper-sedentary mess on your hands. Pot is a comfy person's dream companion. Booze may

get you up on the dance floor, but too much booze will land you back in bed. Students need coping strategies that involve non-screen, creative movement. Arts and sports are life-changing, keeping the student unplugged and alive.

Balancing the *quality* of stressors is as important as the quantity. College immerses students with short, product-driven assignments that often hold little personal meaning. Balance these stressors with creative play that includes food for your soul; hobbies where the process is as important as the product: sing, hike, cook, and bike. Try new art skills with low risk (it doesn't matter how things turn out): take a pottery or video class. You may feel overwhelmed by the amount of cognition and socialization at college. Spend time with yourself, quietly walking through nature, away from screaming words and crowds.

College is a job that hurls you square on your butt about 75 percent of the time. Make sure that the remainder of your time is spent actively, screen-free. Honor your energy and allocate wisely. Don't be a Dexter.

Stressed Out on the Memory Highway

The four-year earthquake of college is basically a four-year job in a memory factory. Your job is to manufacture facts, data, and information you may perceive as meaningless. Therefore, we must revisit the Information Processing System. As we are human beings, we are pre-programmed, in terms of attention. **Humans have an attentional hierarchy, when it comes to paying attention.** It's pretty simple: first things first.

First is survival—Papa brain. All animals have a Papa brain, and it rules. Anything that threatens our survival commands our attention, first. You are seated in biology class watching a film on metabolism. Suddenly, a fire alarm rings out in the hallway. What happens? Attention is immediately diverted from the movie to the threatening sound, as well it should. After all, an alarm is more threatening to your survival than watching a movie on cellular repair. **As a living being concerned with staying alive, you are programmed to pay attention to potential threats.**

Let's say no alarms go off; it's a quiet day on campus. The next category to receive attention is emotional stimuli—like, omg, the drama of being a college student: cheating boyfriends, crazy girlfriends, stupid parents, psychotic roommates, smelly laundry, boring work-study, unfair parking tickets, no money, drug deals, good grades, bad food, bad gas, and on and on . . .

If something weighs heavily on your mind, you pay attention to it. **Emotions rule our mental kingdoms. Further, negative emotions receive more attention than positive experiences.** It makes sense; negative emotions are more threatening than positive ones. A fight with a roommate is more threatening than receiving a B- grade on a quiz; therefore, we invest more of our mental energy paying attention to it.

If nothing is threatening our survival and nothing is overstimulating our emotional centers, then we may finally allocate energy and attention to cognitive processes: reading, writing, speaking, computing—in short, academics. This is a key concept of the book. **Learning academic information is last on our list of attentional priorities, as it should be, because it is the least relevant to survival.** We are designed to stay alive, and emotions are always more interesting than information. This is why studying is so difficult and why you obsess on social media when you need to write that essay. Papa's safety and Mama's love overrides Baby's homework assignment.

There's another way to consider this, however. Not only do we pay more attention to our survival and emotions, but we need to feel safe and emotionally secure in order to learn. This is a relatively new concept for teachers to embrace, whose training traditionally focused on content; but the truth is, if a student feels uncomfortable in your classroom, they are going to be absent. If they do attend class, they will likely shut down (and shut up).

"Uncomfortable" takes many forms in the classroom. Papa brain scans the situation: Are you hungry or thirsty? Have you slept? Are you hung over, or worse, drunk or stoned in class? Then Mama checks it out: Any former stalkers or sketchy kids in this class? Prior to class, did you receive good or bad news? What about the class itself? Do you hate it or the teacher? Is this a morning class and have you been up all night gaming? All of these things count in "physical and emotional safety."

***

If the physical and emotional environment is safe, you may still be threatened by your stressors. Did you ever study all night for an exam, only to enter the classroom and have your mind go blank? Did you ever sit there mulling over a test, not being able to recall a vocabulary word—a word that you have used in class for weeks? This is due to the body's stress response and Cognitive Belief System. Let's say you have a history of scoring poorly on tests. You now believe that you are a poor test taker. You enter the new environment, and today the sensory experience is "taking a test." Like the puppies, your body immediately reacts, but unlike the puppies, this is not cute. Your body immediately reacts, and cortisol floods your system. Now your soul, body, and mind are all threatened. You boot up your perception of yourself: *I suck at tests, and I'm gonna fail.*

What just happened? The "memory highway"—a system of intricate neural pathways involved in memory consolidation—is vulnerable to stress hormones that can inhibit cognitive functioning and long-term memory. The weigh station in the middle of this highway is the memory maker, the **hippocampus**. Think of the hippocampus as a town with one main road. The road leading into town brings information to make memories. The road heading out of town sends memories to storage facilities. When we need to recall information, the directions are reversed: information is retrieved from the storage areas, passes through town, then heads back into the frontal lobes, where we pay attention.

Stress hits the town and highway like a hurricane. Cortisol causes major flooding, roads wash out, and the town becomes stranded. **During stressful moments, we are unable to store cognitive information (study for a test) and unable to retrieve memories (take a test).** You arrive to take the test, and it's as if you never studied, at all. You continue to be a poor test taker, and your self-fulfilling prophecy has been reinforced. The next time a test is scheduled, another storm hits. You might consider studying in college to be like living in Tornado Alley. (We'll discuss the hippocampus with more depth in the "Sleep" section.)

This phenomenon also occurs without warning. Let's say you're in a bar hanging out with friends. Your girlfriend comes in, hanging off the arm of some jock-like turd. You go ballistic, and the next thing you know, he's on the floor, while you pummel his head with savage fists. "I dunno what happened. My mind went blank. I just saw red." These common terms accurately describe the automatic response to this highly emotional stimuli, the amygdala hijack. Baby brain, our area of rational and inhibited thought, shuts down when emotions threaten. We rely on automatic procedures and behaviors coordinated by our cerebellum. Papa and Mama take over and protect Baby.

Once you learn a procedure—ride a bike or play the piano—you do it without thinking. Once you learn a behavior—pretend to pay attention in class—it's also automated. You can sit and stare at the professor, smiling pleasantly like a model student, while planning your weekend. **Automatic behaviors can come in handy, but they also can wreak havoc. This happens all the time in college.** You read to the bottom of a page and realize that you have no idea what the section is about. Your mom nags you for the gazillionth time. You hear her and have no idea what she just said. You can even respond automatically, interjecting, "Yeah, you're right, got it," while mom continues her tirade. We automatize behaviors so efficiently that we often don't know we've shut down. When enlightened people refer to "waking up," they refer to focusing your attention—your conscious attentive state—on the immediate moment you are experiencing. In hippie terms, this means "being present."

There is a creepy side to automating behavior. Let's say you deliberately shut down your frontal lobes. The fastest way to do this is with substances, the most popular being alcohol. Alcohol is the "social lubricant," because it inhibits inhibition. The second round of drinks warms us right up . . . we delight in that candid, engaging conversation. This is the "What do you *really* think of our philosophy professor?" part of the evening. Baby has low tolerance, and he quickly acts less civilized. Stay for a few more rounds, and things really heat up. . . . all those dirty secrets are revealed: "I never liked that jerk," and "My folks don't know I buy booze on my gas card."

If we continue drinking, we may reach that point known as the "**blackout**." The frontal lobe completely shuts down. It's like a temporary lobotomy. "Lobotomy" is science's fancy way of saying "No Baby brain." Papa manages black outs on pure instinct. Even emotions become automatized, expressed without regulation: think drunk dialing. Ever wake up in your (or someone else's) bed, having no idea what happened? After a few drinks, Baby brain was tucked in, fast asleep, while you continued the party, automatically. Heavy partiers who "can handle their booze" have had more practice running on auto-pilot. "Handling" one's booze is not something to brag about; you are closer to being alcoholic than your floundering friend.

Auto-pilot happens all the time. We pay attention to new procedures until we learn them, then stop paying attention and do them automatically. The frontal lobe hands the procedure over to the cerebellum and is again freed up to pay attention to new information. It's why you can text and drive. It's how Denzel Washington, a pilot in the movie, *Flight*, skillfully landed the plane while coked up and hung over.

An upside to having procedures automated is that we perform them better. Thinking, oddly enough, interferes with coordination. Automation is what sports players refer to as **"being in the zone."** The moment we think about the activity, we interrupt that flow of movement and coordination. If we pay attention, the mind thinks we are trying to learn something new. We cannot be thinking about how to do something when we are in the act of doing it. In the middle of a pitch, we are not trying to improve our swing. The time to improve your swing is during batting practice, where the mind can be fully alert, thinking about how your body is positioned and what the coach is saying. You can practice this new skill dozens of times until your cerebellum gets it, then move onto new skills. Studying works the same way. You need to actively practice the information, so that when you take the test, recall is automatic, even in the face of a cortisol storm.

Another way to think about it is to imagine how chaotic life is for Mama and Papa when Baby appears. All of our regular physiological maintenance is disrupted by taking care of the screaming nocturnal newborn. Ask your mother how her emotional state was when you were born, and she will be too glad to tell you (only if you have a few hours to spare). **The act of thinking significantly disrupts natural functions and balanced emotional states.** College mandates disequilibrium; part of its purpose is to transform your entire way of thinking, and that diverts extreme amounts of energy. Energy normally delegated to maintaining health is now used up for memorizing excessive loads of cognitive information. In the next section, we'll see just how much body fuel is used for the academic rigors of college.

Stress can help us remember or forget, depending on the amount of stress and how you perceive it. Stress impairs our ability to concentrate and to make good decisions, and yet, stress helps to focus our attention. Like the Yerkes-Dodson Sweet Spot, just the right amount of stress—not too much or too little—will strengthen the ability to make memories. If you are bored, you're likely to space out. If you are panicking, you are likely to blank out. Either way, you are not there. Your attention is elsewhere, other than on the task at hand, and you are unlikely to remember it. There is no information to deliver to the hippocampus. It's the same as being absent, and in college, that's a complete waste of time, resources, and money.

Sometimes emotions *can* increase memory. While Baby brain sleeps, we may still process information subconsciously. We may not select the things we want to remember, however. For instance, if you are stressed out over a fight with your boyfriend, you may not remember anything about the lecture, but you may remember that it was raining outside—something you wouldn't consciously care about, but relates to your sad state.

This is where the soul plays an integral role in college. **The more stressed we are, the less reliable our minds and emotions become. In automated states, we rely on our conative domain—our subconscious desires and drives. These overrule the obligation to focus on the professor's data and derivatives. Desire always takes better notes.**

* * *

What does all this have to do with getting a better grade in your humanities class? The answer lies in your emotional state in the classroom. How do you feel about the class? Do you like the teacher? Do you believe the teacher likes you? Do you feel prepared to do the work? Do you like the topic? Do you feel confident in your abilities? Does this feel like a waste of your time, a diversion to your ultimate purpose in life? Do you feel that you are on your path, in your passionate pursuit? All of these feelings enter the classroom with you, whether or not you are consciously aware of them.

Once you realize this, you have some power. You may then say to yourself, *Wow. This class holds no interest for me. Class starts at 8:00 am, which totally blows. The professor is a jerk. I hate the reading and the assignments are long, boring, and irrelevant. But, gosh. Now I know all this! I know that my emotions and instincts are resisting every step of the way. I now understand that my fight-or-flight response is activated every time I step into this classroom.*

That is the moment the soul awakens. It's the moment everyone agrees to be in college. We engage our frontal lobes and say, "*Instincts, I hear you. Emotions, noted. But, I need to pass this class in order to take more classes in order to graduate, which is my goal. So, Mama and Papa, you both need to chill the eff out, and let Baby pass this class.*"

They mean well, bless their hearts. But, Baby brain is actually in control, now that you are in college. Papa may be the head and Mama the neck, but Baby brain is the neck of the neck, controlling all movement. **You have the power to decide how you will respond to any stimulus.** Your identity is unique and involves breaking away from your tribal family. Recall at the beginning of the book,

From the nanosecond parents say goodbye, they are fired. Suddenly the child is in charge, but the promotion comes with two hats: employer *and* employee. The college student is the CEO of their life. Every decision is their own. This may sound empowering, and it is, but it is also devastating. At the same time they become their own boss, they lose their office manager and personal assistant—the great and powerful Mommy. Every single task of their daily lives, managed until that kiss goodbye, is now up to them. That kiss changes everything.

The frontal lobe is the last to develop, because first things develop first: first we learn to function as human beings; then we learn how to manage emotions; next, we learn our community's values and beliefs; and finally, we discover our personal identity. When younger, we learn in a parroted way, mimicking our models. College is disequilibrium, the Baby Awakening. We acquire our own values, beliefs, skills, and behaviors in order to be functioning, happy adults, separate from our parents. If parents don't want to let go in college, you have to be the adult.

FOOD

"It is true that local and organic food costs more. It is worth more, too."
—Michael Pollen, author of *Fresh*

"The typical American child's diet has changed greatly over the last few decades and does not remotely resemble what children ate 60 years ago. A meal then did not consist of a bowl of multicolored cereal for breakfast, chicken nuggets loaded with synthetic chemicals and fillers for lunch, and a dinner of macaroni and cheese so brightly dyed that it almost glows in the dark. What's more, snacks are often now so full of preservatives that they can be as old as a child and still look fresh!"
—Jane Hersey, National Director of the Feingold Association
and author of *Why Can't My Child Behave?*

"What's good for the heart is good for the brain."
—Dr. Charles DeCarli, Director of Alzheimer's Disease Center

You are what you eat.

Other than stress, the most important lifestyle factor in one's academic success is food.

First things first. Let's keep you alive. You'll need food. I'm sorry to break the news, but you are a living thing. You may entertain the romantic notion that you are an extension of your computer, subsisting on video games and soda. Mom or Dad, if you're reading this, you may romantically believe you can subsist on work and lattes.

Nope. You are alive, and living beings require certain things in order to stay alive. They need air, water, food, and sleep; without these things, they die. The body's job is to consume, digest, assimilate, and excrete food. Food is converted into every single body part you have. Where else did you think you got your bones, muscles, organs, and blood?

You are a college student. You need a lot of nutrition, probably more than you'll ever need, beyond the age of two. Being in college is one of the most cognitively demanding times of your life. You are learning thousands of facts and analyzing thousands of pieces of information. This is higher-order thinking, and it uses more fuel than any other activity, including something strenuous like marathon running.

Food is made up of things called **nutrients**, which manage the body: run systems, rebuild parts, and provide fuel to move and think. Nutrients are crucial in college, as the brain needs a constant level of fuel, chemicals, and electricity to function. **Brains are the biggest consumers, burning about 20 percent of your total fuel intake. In college, that percentage rises to 30 percent.** Almost half of all the calories you eat go to learning new information! Yikes. Ever see a baby? They move nonstop, until they collapse. A baby's growth rate is faster than in any other time in their life, and in college, your brain is a baby.

Think of yourself as a car: the better the fuel, the better the performance. If you run out of gas, your car stops. If you don't refill your fluids, you won't be able to see, steer, or brake. If you don't change your filters, the car chokes, knocks, and stops. If you use bad gasoline, the engine stutters and stalls. If you burn up your oil, the engine seizes and stops. If you put sugar in the gas tank, you instantly kill the engine.

The brain is like a shark; it has to be constantly moving, or else it dies. Moving, in terms of college, relates to a constant steady stream of quality nutrients. Your grades are only as good as your brain, so feed it well. The better the food, the better the SBM.

Still resisting? This may be a hard concept to swallow in our current economic society, because you are raised in a *cheaper is better and size matters* mentality. In order to thrive, you need smaller portions and larger nutrition. You also need food that is *actual* food, not plastic, poison, or petroleum.

College kids subsist on dead foods like ramen noodles and mac and cheese. Why? Is it because these provide maximum nutrient density? No, it's because these are cheap and filling. Students believe "full" is "nourished" or even if they don't believe that, they don't care. They'd rather *feel* full. Eating junk food is also seen as an activity, something to do when we're bored or watching screens.

I can smell the, "So what? It tastes good." Sigh. Okay, I won't bore you with mundane facts about how nutrients will keep you alive. Heaven forbid. Maybe we could jazz it up a bit? If you eat junk food, that's like living in a war zone with constant bombing. If you eat healthy food, that's like moving into a unicorn palace, surrounded by scantily-clad virgins on sunny beaches with bags of money. Too far-fetched? Sorry, I'll give you more credit. Let's talk business. Eating is studying; the better your food, the better your GPA. After you graduate, eating is salary; the better your food, the more money you make.

Consider the *Paycheck Principle*: Say you work some job 40 hours a week. At the end of the week, your boss approaches you with two paycheck options: one is a check for $1,000, and the other, a check for $50. Which check would you take for your work? I hope you said the thousand. Please tell me you did. That wasn't a trick question. In college, the Paycheck Principle translates to academic success. At the end of the semester, which would you prefer, a 3.7 or 1.7 GPA? Again, not a trick question. It's the same thing with food. Your nutritional job is to eat, digest, assimilate, rebuild, and excrete. Why not earn every single grade point and dollar that's coming to you?

What to Eat: Food and Water

Water

The most important nutrient is water. You must consume more of it than any food. Water is essential for all things college: thinking, reasoning, reading, computing, writing, planning, presenting, analyzing, and examining. Water is the ideal tutor, as it stimulates the brain. Water activates neurons and activates the corpus callosum, the neural fiber bridge connecting our two hemispheres, for more complex (higher order) thinking. **Water increases brain function by 20 percent. For those who struggle with math, that's the difference between a C and an A.** That's a pretty cheap way to improve your GPA, right there. Water is so important that I grade students on it. They are required to bring water to class and drink it; a daily check-in confirms their water bottles. Students are expected to consume water in class, just as they are expected to pay attention and take notes. (You can finally stop reading this! Just drink water and tell your folks you finished the book. Watch their delight, as your grades come sailing through with flying letters.)

Water is the fountain of youth, the delta of intelligence, and the ocean of awesomeness. No single ingestible product is more valuable to the academic experience than water. Ironically, no single ingestible product is less consumed by the typical college student than water. It is not sweet, bubbly, or blue enough to gain their attention. (If you do drink water, never mind. I love you.)

Water!

- Hydrates the cells
- Stimulates neurogenesis
- Increases energy
- Connects corpus callosum—increases cognition, whole brain activity
- Regulates mood
- Increases concentration
- Stimulates immune system
- Stimulates digestion
- Reduces stress
- Improves memory
- Repairs muscle tissue
- Removes toxins, wastes, and dead cells

You are a human being. Human beings are comprised of 50–90 percent water, depending on age and health. In your current state, let's settle on approximately 75 percent. Biologically, that translates to more watery body composition. The more water you consume, the more watery you become. The more watery you are, the healthier you are. Healthy people are more watery in their quality of life, more flexible, adaptable, and resilient in SBM.

Note: Overconsumption of any substance, including healthy substances like water, may be hazardous to your health. The general guideline is to consume approximately eight cups of water per day.

Put any positive health attribute on that list, because water contributes to it. It also puts out fires, wakes you up for class, cures a hangover, and silences the annoying roommate. Water is the only beverage you ever need to drink, in and out of college.

Water vs. "Water"

Please. Make it *good* water. Clean well water or spring water are best, since they are naturally purified and most nutritious. Being in college, those options may not exist, but you may still defend your health. Use a water filter. Avoid tap water and "purified" water manufactured by soda corporations (pop, for you Midwesterners). These products use waste water that's been "chemically purified." Translation: cleaned up piss, poop, and toxic ponds. Drink water treated by nature; she knows what she's doing. Look for brands labeled, "Bottled at the source," like Poland Springs and Crystal Springs.

For water on the go, use a Nalgene or stainless steel bottle. Never refill plastic water bottles that have the # 1 in their recycling logo, only the #2HDPE. The "1" implies one use. Reusing these containers leeches plastic into the water, right into your body. Want to drink plastic? Of course you don't. Stick to approved metal, ceramic, or #2-rated recyclables.

Forget trendy accessorized beverages that *contain* water, like coffee, tea, Gatorade, Red Bull, or soda (pop). Avoid "designer" water, such as Vitamin Water. Many of these brands contain synthetic sugar, the devil's playground. Plus, they are expensive, and you are a poor college student. Better to invest in a water filter and good water bottle, and call it a day. What's that? You're not poor? Dude, you will be after you graduate.

Starting today, never purchase another bottled drink, ever again. I'm serious! There is no legitimate reason. Sodas, bottled juices, aseptic packages, etc. create a constant need for aluminum, glass, and plastic containers. Externally, they stuff our landfills, pollute our environment, and waste energy in manufacturing and recycling. Internally, bottled drinks create as much pollution and congestion. Sodas contain carbonic and phosphoric acids, which weaken blood vessels and rot teeth, but mostly, they ruin the body's pH (acid/alkaline) balance.

The pH scale runs from 0-14. Zero is highly acidic, 14 is highly alkaline, and 7 is neutral. The human body has a normal pH of around 7.4, slightly alkaline. Pure water's pH is around 7. Most bottled drinks contain sugar, and sugar is acidic. Excessive consumption of acidic products causes the pH to lower, which creates an acidic biological environment. This weakens blood vessels, organs, and tissues, raises blood pressure, increases cholesterol, and irritates liver function. If you add alcohol into the mix, your liver becomes severely taxed. Acidic environments cause headaches, lethargy, irritability, and depression. Academically, this translates to reduced attention and increased absences.

If left alone, our bodies are smart and adaptable. One way the body attempts to dilute the acidic state is through retaining water. Here the madness ensues. College students gain weight, due to all the junk food they're cramming and toxic drinks they're glugging. **Freshman Fifteen**—the dreaded weight gain plaguing many incoming students—rears its evil head, and students resort to diet sodas as an aid to weight loss. These contain all that nasty acid, so the body retains water (gains weight) to compensate for the acidity. Our smart body dilutes itself to re-establish its slightly alkaline state. It chooses weight gain over death, and what do you do? Drink more diet drinks, and the cycle continues.

The simplest way to stop this weight gain cycle and regain balance is to drink pure water. It's no accident that our bodies and water have about the same pH, as we're mostly water. So, drink up, already.

Food

The best foods FARE WELL: Fresh, Ripe, Whole, and Local. "Fresh, ripe, and whole" mean raw and unprocessed: fruits, vegetables, nuts, seeds, sprouts, and fresh juices. They are the most valuable foods in terms of nutrient density. Raw foods contain live enzymes, which aid in digestion and regulate body systems. FARE WELL foods are A+, high-octane fuel that aces the exam. For optimal academic performance, FARE WELL foods must be the major part of your diet.

Eighty percent of the immune system resides in the digestive tract. In order to stay healthy, you'll need foods that contain live enzymes, which nourish the immune system. Fermented live foods like sauerkraut, yogurt, and kimchi are remarkable super-heroes, rich in enzymes and probiotics or friendly bacteria. These bacteria perform thousands of functions, including killing germs that cause diseases. Koreans claim that kimchi cures everything from colds to cancer, due to kimchi's remarkable probiotic qualities.

Always choose organic foods when possible, including meat options. Conventional foods commonly use carcinogens, neurotoxins, and endocrine disruptors in their production. To the college student, think "sick and crazy." Ever encounter a woman with PMS? Ever been one? Imagine feeling that way, every day, in class. Neurotoxins destroy mental activity and cause nerve damage, and that's bad enough; but "endocrine disruptors" are treacherous, affecting every bodily system. Tiny residues of the endocrine disruptor atrazine have have been shown to turn normal male frogs into hermaphrodites. Hormonal imbalance may be linked to increases in early onset puberty (kindergarten girls getting their periods) and gender-identity disorders. Our food did not used to be poison. It used to be food.

Unfortunately, it may be nearly impossible to FARE WELL and eat organically in today's college cafeterias. Colleges are profit-driven and motivated to cut costs. Dining services rely on canned, refined, and processed foods, mistakenly believing that fresh foods are expensive to buy and time-consuming to prepare. Regardless, it is up to you to defend your education, and that begins with feeding your SBM. Eat "clean" food, which is the least processed and chemically altered: local, organic, and GMO-free (Genetically Modified Organism-free). When eating in campus dining halls, focus on food choices: whole foods like fruits, vegetables, nuts, and seeds; vegetarian foods like salads and soups; ethnic foods that are rich in grains, veggies, and beans; whole grains like brown rice and whole grain products like whole wheat bread.

If you're cooking for yourself, you'll have some freedom to defend your health. Shop at health foods stores, local farm stands, and farmer's markets. They provide food that thrives in your geographical area. If these are unavailable, shop the natural food sections in traditional supermarkets. Buying locally supports your local economy and saves on fuel costs, reducing carbon footprint. Save the planet and save yourself. FARE WELL provides you with the richest health benefits.

What and how much should you eat?

Answering these food questions is simple, because in college, food is served on plates. Imagine the plate is a pie chart: half of your food is vegetables and fruit; one quarter is protein—beans, nuts, seeds, and legumes (lentils and peas); one quarter is whole carbohydrates from whole grains and whole grain pastas, breads, and crackers.

Where's the beef? Where's the sugar? **Animal protein and sugar are meant only as flavoring, rather than the main components of a meal.** Does this contradict everything you've ever been told or eaten? Have you lived on a diet of meat, white bread, and pasta, and fatty foods like fries, pizza, and doughnuts? Good. Following my advice will allow you to experience disequilibrium, and college is where paradigms are shattered. Some may challenge this advice, touting high-protein diets like the Paleo, Atkins, or gluten-free diets that include sugar. You may choose to follow these diets, but what I am suggesting is a basic major step toward your health.

You don't need to consume meat or white sugar and are better off without them. Meat and sugar industries need you to consume them in order to profit, so these foods are heavily promoted. Corporate executives and soulless physicians want you to eat them so you can develop heart attacks, diabetes, and cancer. Treating you pays for their yachting and golfing habits. (Doctors in China were commonly compensated for healthy patients, but that is a dying practice.) Meat and sugar taste good, so use them for flavor, instead of your main source of food. No more burgers or Meat Lover's pizza. No more Super Big Gulps. No more Wing Night. Sayonara, candy and ice cream. Say goodbye to your little friends.

This nutritional advice may shock and aggravate you, but bear with the disequilibrium for a moment. Breathe in. Release. The typical college student's diet is jammed with meat, refined grains, dairy, sugar, soda, and coffee. These foods are entirely unnecessary and, in fact, destroy your health. Bad food in college equals bad grades.

Another delicious benefit to eating healthfully is a beautiful body. It is nearly impossible to gain the dreaded Freshman Fifteen when you FARE WELL. Another sneaky benefit is that you will begin to feel . . . good. You will have an unusual amount of energy. Your moods will be smooth and calm. You may find yourself able to attend class and pay attention. Health is elusive; because it is not threatening, we pay less attention to the positive feelings of balance. We notice the absence of health (disease, illness) more than the presence.

Buy healthy snacks at natural food stores like food co-ops, Whole Foods, and Wild Oats Markets. Mainstream supermarkets also have natural food sections, where you can buy healthy fuel:

- Nuts: tamari-roasted almonds, pumpkin seeds, cashews, etc.
- Organic fruit and veggies

- Dried fruits: apples, raisins, figs, etc.
- Cheese
- Popcorn
- Whole grain products: bagels, crackers, etc.
- Miso and other healthy soups

Comprehensive lists and ways to prepare healthy foods are included in *The No Recipe Cookbook: A Beginner's Guide to the Art of Cooking* (www.norecipecookbook.com).

No matter what you consume, be grateful. Thank your food and feed it messages like Masaru Emoto did with his water crystals. Masaru Emoto's fantastic discoveries in *The Hidden Messages in Water* offered us a glimpse into the world of energy, how thoughts and feelings may affect our energetic fields. He researched how thoughts transmit energy waves that may affect water crystal formation, both positively and negatively. Negative messages such as "I hate you," "You make me sick," and, "I will kill you" significantly deranged the crystals, whereas compassionate messages, such as "Thank you" and "I love you" produced symmetric, clear, and lovely crystals. Since college students are so watery, they may benefit from feeling gratitude. Merely repeating positive affirmations may not change your physical appearance immediately, but choosing healthier foods and feeling grateful will benefit your water's energetic structure. Spiritual energy does affect one's constitution, and you will notice a difference in how you look and feel.

College students complain about college food so often that it's become cliché. Applying Emoto's theory on intentions affecting energy, thinking "This food sucks" and "The dining hall food blows" has the power to transform water crystal composition in the food. You are a super-hero, able to transform your food into poison with a single thought. With great power comes great responsibility, Spidey. Appreciate your food. Take time to thank it. The gratitude will resonate into the food and make it healthier with your good-intentioned laser beams.

Sugar in the Gas Tank

Let's look under your hood. After all, you need more energy in college than in any other time in your life, right? If you were drinking water while reading that last section, you'd know this. What is energy? What's the best kind? In other words, what kind of fuel will get you the best grades?

Glucose is the body's main fuel. It is the burnable form of sugar we receive from food nutrients called carbohydrates—sugars and starches from grains, beans, vegetables, and fruits. Carbohydrates are "simple" and "complex." Simple carbohydrates are pure fuel—sugar only, devoid of everything else. Complex carbohydrates contain starch, which supplies other nutrients and takes longer to burn. FARE WELL foods offer complex carbohydrates, but tend to be rare in a college student's diet. Three fuels most likely abundant in college are protein, simple sugar, and fat.

One of the reasons you are still alive is because the human body has the ability to convert protein into fuel. In fact, the first thing the body burns is protein, mainly because protein cannot be stored. Protein is building material for the body. It is not meant to be an energy source, but we can't leave building materials lying around the construction site. We have to use all our materials delivered each day, or else they clutter everything up, obstruct the building site, and then rats get into every-thing, and the rain destroys them all. Too much protein lying around your body is like that. Excessive protein becomes toxic in the body by creating a buildup of uric acid, which exacerbates inflammatory diseases like arthritis and gout. Excessive protein is biological hoarding.

Protein is highly acidic, like those sugary carbonated drinks. Animal protein is too high in fat and acidity to sustain the human body. **Another major problem in eating excess protein is brain star-vation.** The brain cannot utilize protein as an energy source. Glucose is the brain's only fuel. The brain is starved when glucose is missing, and in our modern diets, it often is. High protein diets starve the brain. Protein is essential, but was never meant to be the major diet staple.

Because excess protein is so dangerous, we quickly eliminate it. Proteins from alcohol are burned first, followed by other proteins (helping to explain why alcoholics, as well as high-protein gorgers, don't drop dead of malnutrition). Proteins are filtered through the body. Too much protein taxes the liver and kidneys. Instead of detoxifying the body of its daily waste and poison, these filters now must deal with great oil spills like that double cheeseburger. If we become too acidic, we may even die of acidosis. Instead of using energy to study, the body has to divert energetic funds into clearing out these toxic pools. This exorbitant waste of resources could have been used to take notes in class and study tonight.

After excess protein is burned off and filtered out, the body can focus on its real energy: carbohydrates. The body can burn only a certain amount of glucose at a time, like a woodstove. Excess glucose is stored and used as needed. Think of glucose as the logs in the fire and stored carbohydrates as the woodpile. The woodpile is called glycogen.

Complex carbohydrates from vegetables, fruits, whole grains, and beans are the main fuel source in the human diet, comprising half of all food consumed. Carbohydrates are to the body what gasoline is to an engine. A car runs on gasoline, but gasoline cannot burn by itself; it needs a spark of nutrients to burn. A body, too, cannot burn carbohydrate without sparks. It needs protein, minerals, vitamins, enzymes, oxygen, and other nutrients to properly convert the carbohydrate into usable energy.

Complex carbohydrates release steadily as the body carefully monitors its sugar level and converts starch to sugar as needed. Complex carbohydrates supply the other nutrients needed to burn its sugar, keeping the fire burning at a steady pace. You experience this as a steady energy level, stable mood, and focused attention.

Simple carbohydrates, or simple sugars, are lighter fluid for the campfire. Imagine trying to sustain a fire in this way. You'd spend the entire day holding the tin can over the fire. That's why people who eat junk foods are often hungry. Whatever sugar you can use burns fast, but then the rest is stored. You can only burn so much with the few nutrients you have. This leads to being hungry again. It's ironic, as there may be ample energy stored, but without the nutrients to facilitate burning, you cannot access the fuel source. It's like losing your ATM card with $5,000 in your bank account.

Simple sugars are fast and furious, raging rampantly, flooding the bloodstream, and dangerously raising blood sugar levels. Picture a dam bursting. Your body is the small town in the valley below. Simple sugar is acidic—highly acidic. Too much sugar in the blood can cause acidosis. If you have any doubts as to its potential health hazard, ask any diabetic about acidosis; it can be fatal.

Assuming you are eating complex carbohydrates and burning them effectively, once glycogen is used up—when the woodpile is depleted—the body then turns to fat, breaking it down into smaller units to be absorbed in the bloodstream. Fat represents the big log stumps and must be chopped up before using. People love the taste of fat, but fat is the hardest fuel to burn. Wood stumps don't burn easily; you need a great bonfire to get them going. Athletes may burn fat, but for most students, college is sedentary. Think little campfire. A person has to be super-active to use fat as fuel. The rest of us use fat as fat.

We need some fat in most cells, for self-regulation. Fat offers essential fatty acids (EFAs), essential for brain function. These EFAs create our **myelin sheath,** the coating that insulates neurons. Myelin sheaths function similarly to electrical wire. Without insulation, the wire is unable to transmit energy waves. Cognitively speaking, "transmitting energy waves" means thinking and feeling. Insulation is also required for nerve health and without it, nervous systems perish. Some studies link low levels of EFAs with cognitive disorders, such as ADHD and Parkinson's disease. Cigarettes and stimulant substances erode myelin sheaths. People using stimulant medication may experience neurotoxicity from deteriorating sheaths and should monitor medication through brain scans.

Essential fatty acids come from quality fat. Considered the most nutritious, olive oil is your best bet. Olive oil contains *squalene*, a powerful antioxidant highly beneficial to the immune system. Olive oil offers a rare vegetarian source of squalene. The only other common source is found in shark's liver. In general, choose unrefined, organic oils. Their tastes and smells are more pungent due to healthier processing, which retains more nutrients. Store healthy oils in cool dark places, as heat and light can destroy their nutrients. Store your bottle of olive oil next to your bottle of good vodka.

The last fuel source we burn is, interestingly, muscle. We actually burn our own muscles as fuel, in times of nutritional crisis. Gross, huh? We burn muscle when we deprive ourselves of nutrition.

Brandon

Brandon was a poster child for ADHD: wiry, fidgety, wildly smart, but also wildly random, blurting out comments and connections at a rapid-fire pace. Students were encouraged to bring food and water to class, and Brandon made great use of this invitation. Every day, he'd sit down and unpack his meal: several candy bars, a few sodas, a triple espresso latte, and two pints of Ben & Jerry's ice cream. Every day. He'd spread the food and beverages out and calmly consume all of the sugar and caffeine, and a funny thing happened. Nothing. Rather, nothing different. Brandon maintained that he was always hungry and needed to eat huge amounts of sugar in order to be able to pay attention in class. His behavior did not worsen with this caffeine and sugar, but it may have actually begun because of it.

Let's see what's going on under Brandon's hood.

When do we "deprive ourselves of nutrition?" When we eat a typical *UnitedStatesian* diet loaded with protein, junk food, and empty calories. It's ironic and tragic that we eat so much food and consume so few nutrients. We'll explore this odd phenomenon in the next section. For now, consider that **people with poor diets, eating disorders, heavy drinkers, and partiers are overconsuming and starving themselves. Unfortunately, college students comprise a major segment of these populations.**

Live by the *Paycheck Principle*. Your job is to be alive and healthy. Part of that job description requires you to eat a few meals every day. You get paid for the amount of nutrition you receive. If you don't receive nutrients in your food, you're not doing your job and you don't get paid. Sooner or later, you will get fired.

What Not To Eat: Unnatural Born Killers

Caffeine: Your Bipolar BFF

Caffeine is required drinking for college students. There are more coffee shops than libraries on campuses. Red Bull and Monster drinks pump up workouts and alcohol, keeping the party rocking. All-nighters wouldn't be all-nighters without these cognitive cattle prods. Caffeine is not the friend you think he is; there lurks a dark side of drama. It has to do with the way you burn fuel.

Let's say you've decided to eat well. You read my section on complex carbohydrates, and you're committed to defending your health. You are enjoying a diet rich in whole foods, but being in college, you consume several caffeinated beverages per day. Applying the paycheck principle, caffeine is the co-worker who wants to party all the time. You may be earning a solid nutritional paycheck, but if you hang out with this manic amigo, you'll be hitting the ATM and paying for his dastardly adventures. Your nutritional savings gets used up before you earn more.

Let's break it down, starting with sugar. Our bodies are homes with wood stoves, and sugars are the logs. The best logs to burn in your stove are the medium-sized ones that take a few hours to burn slowly and steadily: vegetables, grains, and beans. Smaller logs act as kindling to get the fire started: fruits and fruit juices. Bigger logs keep the fire burning longer and are helpful while we sleep or if we have an active life (mentally and physically): nuts, seeds, oils, meat, fish, and dairy. White sugar is the lighter fluid, giving immediate energy that burns out quickly. Artificial sugars and synthetic fats are plastic, burning toxic fumes into the air (we'll discuss these next).

We can only burn so much at a time. You can't put ten logs into a stove that holds five. We often eat more logs than we can burn at a time. When we do that, the body stores the logs in our muscles and liver. The carbohydrates (logs) are stored as glycogen (woodpile) in our muscles and liver. It's the liver's job to convert these sugars—stack the woodpile. The liver also converts the glycogen back to glucose—fetch logs to burn in the wood stove.

How do we know when we need more sugar? Our body has chemicals that communicate this. When we utilize our sugar—as we burn through our logs—the adrenal glands and pancreas notice the fire going out. When the drop is significant enough, the pancreas releases glucagon, a hormonal secretion, into the blood. Glucagon cues the liver to convert glycogen into glucose, and the blood sugar safely returns to normal levels. Think of the pancreas as the nagging girlfriend, and glucagon is her nag. The liver is the nagged boyfriend who has to go out into the cold and get more firewood to stoke the fire. As we deplete our glycogen storage (burn our logs), we experience hunger (the house gets cold), and the nagging cycle continues.

We retrieve logs from our muscles. If we don't have enough glycogen stored, we become hungry and consume more food. If we eat too much, we must store the glycogen. White sugar and fat are stored as fat, which you may recall from the last section is the hardest and last food product to burn. White sugar or fat stores permanently as fat, unless you exercise daily.

How are you doing? With me so far? Okay, here comes the party.

Enter caffeine. Caffeine is an aggressive stimulant, bullying the adrenal glands and conning the pancreas into releasing glucagon, which causes a flood of sugar whether or not it is needed. This high blood sugar level stimulates the release of an opposing hormone, insulin, which is the glucose watchdog; it whisks glucose quickly out of the bloodstream, so we don't suffer from acidosis. Once again, blood sugar lowers, signaling the pancreas to release more glucagon, which once again cues the liver to begin converting glycogen to glucose, dumping more sugar into the bloodstream. The "jolt" we feel from caffeine comes primarily from excess sugar in the blood—sugar that was meant to be stored and released slowly over time, sustaining us steadily for many hours. The more caffeine we drink, the more the madness ensues.

You may ask, "What's so bad about a sugar party? It sounds fun."

Well, play it out. Think of sugar as money. Sugar in the bloodstream is money in your pocket, and stored sugar is money in the bank. **Burning sugar too quickly is like spending money too quickly. When you use up your stored sugar, you've withdrawn all your funds**. Now you're out of money. That money in the bank was meant to pay for bills throughout the week. Caffeine is your convincing friend who loves to party. This friend convinces you to go to the ATM and withdraw $500. You blow a week of wages in one night. This stored glucose was meant to sustain you while attending class, studying, and managing your hectic college life.

Imagine a bonfire in your backyard. For an hour you're nice and toasty with a roaring fire blazing. After that, you're freezing and your fuel is gone. Since the brain needs a constant supply of glucose, this creates a problem. Denying your brain glucose is like losing cell reception, but it's a bit worse. You don't die from losing cell reception connection (I know, you may *feel* like you're going to die, but Snapchat is not glucose). The way we burn sugar affects our behaviors. We either have "sustainable" or "rave party" personalities. Observe your friends who eat and drink a lot of sugar and caffeine. They have a bipolar temperament. It's very stressful on them and on you.

Caffeine enables. We'll discuss enabling in the Connect chapter, but for now note that while "enable" sounds positive, it is quite damaging. The more caffeine one drinks, the more the body begins to rely upon it to initiate glucagon and insulin release, like the chronically sick patient who becomes dependent upon antibiotics to stimulate his immune system. When people say they cannot function without coffee, they are correct.

When the wood stove breaks, malfunctioning develops with fuel-related imbalances such as diabetes, hypoglycemia, and Addison's disease. Some health practitioners assert a correlation with compromised blood sugar regulation to cancer and autoimmune diseases. At the very least, you are continually exhausted and unable to regulate your energy. If you want to maintain a reasonable GPA with a crazybusy lifestyle, you better have a properly functioning furnace. Fortunately, the body is smart and adaptable, and this dependence is reversible for most people.

* * *

Consuming caffeine and white sugar will make you crazy and fat, and that is just the beginning. You may be dismantling yourself. First, by depleting your stored glycogen, you are constantly hungry. Caffeine will continue stressing your adrenal glands and pancreas, forcing your liver to use up your glucose. Constant consumption also signals the release of stress hormones such as cortisol and adrenaline. These chemicals cause riots in your system. The body is tricked into feeling "energized" when, in fact, it is experiencing a stress response—same as a fight or flight response. Basically, your body is under attack, inundated with chemical warfare. Exciting? Sure. Balanced? Not on your life. The problem multiples when people consume simple sugars with their caffeine. Before you know what hit you, you've burned all your stored sugar and replaced it with a bunch of stored fat. You just spent that $500, and now you've gotten a speeding ticket.

Here's where it gets weird. Let's say you want to keep the party going, but you are broke. What do you do? You might borrow some money, but your friends are broke. If desperate, you might resort to stealing. Your body thinks in the same way. It must receive sugar from *somewhere*. If outside sources (food) and internal sources (glycogen) are depleted, where does the energy come from? From fat, you may guess? Seems logical, but remember, fat is the last energy source to burn. We burn sugar, starch, and even protein before fat. Unless we have high metabolisms, most of us die with most of our fat.

Where, then, does your desperate body derive its energy supply? Think protein . . . building blocks of our bodies. If you run out of firewood, you start burning what is available: chairs, tables, walls, floors . . . in short, your home. The liver initiates self-cannibalism and begins tearing down the house, converting the body's muscle and tissue into usable sugar so that the body can survive. Then it gets worse.

Worse than self-cannibalism? Yep.

We're talking about burning sugar, right? Carbohydrates are macronutrients—nutrients that the body needs in macro—or large— amounts. Proteins and fats are also macronutrients. Micronutrients are nutrients that the body needs in smaller amounts, such as vitamins, minerals, and enzymes. Macronutrients require micronutrients to be assimilated, just as gasoline needs nutrients for it to burn. Without oxygen and fire, gasoline is just a smelly useless liquid.

Without micronutrients, carbohydrates cannot be burned and must be stored as fat. **When you eat meals with only simple carbohydrates (white sugar and starches), the body extracts micronutrients from its own muscles and tissues in order to metabolize the meal.** More self-cannibalism occurs in an attempt to utilize this excess sugar dumped into your blood. It's either auto-cannibalism or death by acidosis. Bodies tend to choose death as a last resort. If someone held a gun up to your head and said, "Death or diabetes. You choose." What would you choose? Exactly. So does your body.

If we do not supply the necessary micronutrients every time we ingest caffeine or white sugar, we continue to borrow them. Some micronutrients are water-soluble, meaning un-storable; they must be used promptly or else eliminated. If you've ever taken a vitamin B supplement and experienced the bright-yellow stinky urine, you've witnessed water-soluble B vitamins flushing down the drain. Burning fuel requires B vitamins, so we extract them from our body. B vitamins are mandatory for brain regulation. One of the first signs of B vitamin deficiency and auto-cannibalism is mental irregularity.

Unfortunately, caffeine is just the beginning of this horror flick. Alcohol contains loads of lighter fluid—simple sugars. During the day, we auto-cannibalize with caffeine and junk food. At night, we continue cannibalizing with alcohol. The poor liver, needed to regulate all this sugar conversion, is now also busy dealing with the excessive toxins produced by caffeine and alcohol. Forget partying and speeding tickets; we are now spending our nutritional paychecks on bail bondsmen and lawyers. People with poor diets who consume caffeine and sugar are self-cannibals, consuming themselves to stay alive. People who eat junk food are storing fat and eating their own muscle. Who needs zombies and mutant bacteria? You are your own flesh-eating horror fantasy.

Caffeine, like sugar, is insidious, and coffee is just the beginning. Most energy and sports drinks contain it. Chocolate contains caffeine, as do some common herbs: tea, Maté, Kola nut, and Guarana, to name a few. Oddly, cigarettes contain caffeine. Some medicines contain it, like *Excedrin* aspirin. Excessive sugar and caffeine consumption is a major cause of malnutrition in first world countries. The US overproduces food and struggles with an obesity epidemic, while its citizens suffer from malnutrition. This crazy consumption also accounts for the tragic irony of the anorexic physique: severely underweight people consume their own muscle and tissue in order to survive, while unburnable fat remains amassed. Malnutrition is not caste dependent; it is lifestyle dependent.

College may be the worst of these circumstances, since no one is monitoring the independent student. Junk food and sedentary lifestyle account for the Freshman Fifteen, the dreaded ailment plaguing most incoming students. They don't understand the concept of maintaining a healthy woodstove. The emancipated CEO is free to eat whatever they want, and without understanding the mechanics of sugar burning, they eat what tastes good. College means staying up all night, whether it's for the non-stop partying or for cramming the night before a big test, due to all the partying. All-nighters mean caffeine, then more caffeine to muster some attempt at remaining awake in class. Even for the immortal young adult, there are limits to what the body can endure.

Empty Calories: Fat White Death

A calorie is a food unit of energy, and "empty" implies that it contains few to no nutrients along with that supplied energy. An empty calorie is the opposite of nutrient density, offering nothing but lighter fluid to the fire. White sugar is an example of an empty calorie food. White foods are heavily processed, stripped of all micronutrients: vitamins, minerals, fiber, protein, enzymes, and essential fatty acids. All that remains is the lighter fluid, the sugar.

In a diet rich in empty calories, whatever micronutrients we *do* eat are first spent on burning and storing this volatile fuel instead of serving physiological functions. Refined grains supply the fuel, but not a way to burn it; thus, Doritos and saltines do not qualify as fuel.

Imagine filling a syringe with thick, solid fat, like lard or Crisco. Now inject that syringe into your leg. Go on, keep pressing. That's right. Inject the entire syringe of fat into your thigh muscle. That's the same thing you're doing when you eat ramen. Ramen noodles have no nutritional value. Empty calories fill you up and never nourish. I used to tell my students that "white" foods like Ramen noodles, saltine crackers, white bread, pasta, and rice are the devil: pretty and tempting treats filled with salt, sugar, fat, bleach, preservatives, and plastic. They look fun and taste creamy and sweet and salty and never spoil. They are advertised heavily to marinate your mind into thinking they are food. The truth is, they are fat white death.

Trans-fats: Nutritional Con Artists

Refined oils are stripped of nutrients, bleached, and loaded with preservatives. Bad enough, right? Almost. Hydrogenated oils win the prize for most damaging, as they have the additional problem of not even being food. Hydrogenated or trans-fat oils are oils that go through chemical manipulation: extra hydrogen atoms are forced onto the long fatty molecular chains. The new *isomer* (similar chemical compound but restructured) becomes twisted through a process called "trans-isomerization"—thus the name, "trans-fats." What's the benefit in doing this? This twisted trans-isomerization and hydrogenation procedure is performed because people like to spread things on bread. Settle in, kiddies, and Mama will read you a bedtime story.

* * *

Once upon a time, back in the beginning of the twentieth century, there lived a wicked food named Butter and its villainous cousin, Lard. Butter and Lard were evildoers, causing heart attacks, obesity, and other cardiovascular problems. Good Puritan villagers needed something to replace these monsters.

A logical alternative would have been to switch to olive and other vegetable oils. But, no . . . civilized Puritan people liked *spreading* something on their bread. *Dip* one's bread in oil? What are you, some kind of Mediterranean savage? Oh dear, no. The refined villagers preferred pies and cookies to those ruffian puff pastry concoctions like *Baklava*, which nicely tolerate liquid oil. Pies require solid fat to create those delicate, flaky crusts. One's bread must have *spread,* and one's crusts must *flake.*

In order to satisfy public demand and avoid killing people, the villagers needed a non-animal miracle: a vegetable oil that remained solid at room temperature. Economists and marketers responded the way they always did: employing wizards to solve the problem. *Create a magic solution,* the desperate villagers implored.

Those crafty wizards did just that, inventing hydrogenation. Like spinning straw into gold, vegetable oil stayed solid at room temperature! Huzzah! This changed everything. Suddenly margarine and Crisco were available at every market. Sweet advertisements besieged the townspeople, displaying lovely young homemakers wearing brightly colored aprons, proudly spreading wonder-fats on breads, frying foods, and creating flaky pie crusts. This dandy, fatty miracle could do everything butter did, but since it was vegetarian, all would be spared their nasty little heart attacks! Everyone lived happily and healthily ever after! The end.

Except that this didn't happen.

What happened was that no one considered that, in hydrogenating an oil, it stops being an edible oil. Consider its name: trans-fat. You may not know what trans-fat means, but you know what transplant, transformer, and transgendered mean. Fat has transformed and is no longer food. It becomes something more like plastic and burns in a similar way. Ever try burning plastic? What happens? Mhm. Now picture that effect in your body. The "fat" molecules in hydrogenated products break down less efficiently than their non-manipulated counterparts. Globules of this plastic fat remain in your blood vessels and intestines where they cause blockages, stick to walls, and contribute to stroke, heart attack, and digestive diseases, such as diverticulitis and Irritable Bowel Syndrome (IBS). This atrocious practice is not revolutionary. It is common in our culture to create first and consider the implications later. If you don't believe me, watch *Jurassic Park*.

One more horrid revelation regarding hydrogenated oils: food that is advertised as "zero trans-fats" or "trans-fat-free" is most likely anything but. Current USFDA laws allow a product to list hydrogenated fats in increments of .5 grams per serving size. If a product contains .49 grams of hydrogenated fat per serving, it could be legally listed as 0 grams of fat per serving. If you're porking away on a bag of "trans-free" potato chips, you may be swallowing a few grams of plastic poison.

How harmful can a few grams of trans-fat be? Several respected mainstream authorities have strong opinions about this and have issued warnings:

- The US government's recommendation in its *Dietary Guidelines for Americans 2005* is "keep trans-fatty acid consumption as low as possible."
- In June 2006, the American Heart Association (AHA) issued its "2006 Diet and Lifestyle Recommendations." The AHA recommends that your daily intake of trans-fats be limited to 1 percent of total calories, which is equivalent to roughly 2 to 2.5 grams of trans-fat per day.
- The Institute of Medicine recommends we keep our intake of trans-fats to "as near zero as possible." (http://pubs.cas.psu.edu/freepubs/pdfs/uk093.pdf).

In terms of empty calories, hydrogenated plastics are turbo-empty. Hydrogenated substances have been used in nutritional research to *induce EFA deficiencies* in both animal and human volunteers. Consider that for a moment. This plastic is used *specifically* and *intentionally* to create a nutritional deficiency! For all you malnourished minds, let's dumb that down: **Hydrogenated fats steal nutrients from your mind and body.** Add that to your auto-cannibalistic over-caffeinated lifestyle, and your mind is a mess.

Studies show that trans-fats delay neurogenesis, the re-growing of brain nerves and cells. Hydrogenated fats damage one step further; they are *anti*-calories. They steal from your nutritional bank account, and you are paying to be robbed.

When both subversive health nuts and mainstream experts agree, you know you have a nasty product. Someone has to be stupid to eat these plastic monsters. You are no dummy; you are in college! The vote is in. Avoid hydrogenated fats.

Olestra: "Hey Apu, you got any of those potato chips that cause diarrhea?"

When a company who manufactures toiletries decides to branch out into food products, expect trouble. Olestra is manufactured by Procter & Gamble. That's like saying Satan manufactures Christmas toys.

Olestra is another monster of chemical engineering. Sugar molecules are artificially forced to bind with fatty acids, creating a polymer, yet another plastic. This polymer creates a creamy sensation on the tongue, fooling you into thinking you are eating something yummy when, in fact, you've just consumed a large wad of plastic. This sugar/fat/plastic polymer is too big to break down and so complicated that digestive enzymes are unable to deal with it. Once again, this is what we get when we allow chemists to invent food. (All you chemical engineering majors, take note!)

The other problem with these plastic disasters is that they don't leave the party alone. They drag vital nutrients with them. When you suffer food poisoning, your body doesn't take the time to sort the edible food from the poisoned parts. The body is in such a hurry to bounce these poisons out the door that valuable nutrients become lost in the shuffle.

Artificial sweeteners and fats are treated like poisons in the body and eliminated in that same swift fashion, also dragging valuable nutrients. Like a toxic magnet, Olestra traps fat-soluble vitamins: A, D, E, plus fatty acids and other fat-soluble nutrients. It blocks anti-oxidants like beta-carotene, lycopene, and lutein. Antioxidants are nutrients that help regulate body functions and detoxify the body. These antioxidants are critical for eye health and maintaining vision. You might consider whether your eyesight is more important than a creamy-tasting chip.

Most Olestra products were yanked off the market due to the alarming rate of distressing bouts of diarrhea that occurred a few hours after consumption. Homer Simpson concretized this dilemma in the infamous *Simpsons* episode when he asks the store clerk, "Hey Apu, you got any of those potato chips that cause diarrhea?"

Sugar Substitutes: Nutritional Psychos
Aspartame: Not Tame

Aspartame, sold as *NutraSweet* and *Equal*, is a synthetic sugar intro-duced in the early 1980s. Aspartame is created from the amino acids phenylalanine and aspartic acid. Amino acids are the building blocks of protein. Phenylalanine is an essential amno acid; it is *essential* that we consume this in our diet, because our bodies do not manufacture it. Conversely, *non-essential amino acids* are manufactured in our bodies. When we eat a healthy diet, it is *non-essential* that we consume them. Aspartic acid may be manufactured in our bodies and is therefore considered a non-essential amino acid.

Aspartic acid is a vital regulating neurotransmitter. In college terms, aspartic acid is the Resident Dean who watches over you and keeps you on the right track. Phenylalanine, known as the "brain protein," coordinates brain function in a process similar to the way insulin regulates blood sugar levels. It's like the roommate who gets you out of bed and into class, so you don't drop out. You might think that aspartame would be good for you, right? Wrong. Aspartame is pure trouble. In order to create it, natural substances are, once again, converted into non-food. Aspartame converts into two substances: *methanol* and a synthetic form of phenylalanine.

Aspartame on the Brain

The brain is a sacred space, protected by a border known as the **blood brain barrier**. Our brain is the Pentagon; as such, it needs strict security. Certain chemicals have clearance: glucose for energy, and select amino acids for function. Phenylalanine has been granted diplomatic immunity, readily crossing the blood brain barrier and converting into the excitatory neurotransmitters norepinephrine and epinephrine.

If the blood delivers more phenylalanine than other amino acids, the natural balance of neurotransmitters is upset. Calming and stabilizing neurotransmitters serotonin and Gamma-Aminobutyric acid (GABA) are crowded out. Phenylalanine stimulates certain neurotransmitters, dopamine being one. Dopamine is a special hormone, considered both excitatory and calming, giving an inhibitory effect on the mind. Dopamine plays with Baby brain, teaches him new skills, and then tucks him in for his nap.

Due to its versatility, excess phenylalanine may create brain imbalance, and synthetic phenylalanine creates major imbalance. Like hydrogenated fats, aspartame damages the systems a real nutrient would be regulating, in an Incredible Hulk-Dr. Bruce Banner manner. Synthetic phenylalanine over-excites the brain, causing erratic thoughts and behaviors. As a result, symptoms include short attention span, impulsivity, hyperactivity, moodiness, irritability, insomnia, decreased agility, and seizures. Recognize these symptoms? They mimic the DSM's definition of Attention Deficit Hyperactivity Disorder! In fact, some alternative health theorists attribute synthetic sugars to the upswing in ADHD diagnosis. It's interesting to consider, as aspartame hit the market around 1981, which correlates with the emergence of ADD as a clinical diagnosis.

In addition to synthetic phenylalanine, aspartame contains methanol, or wood alcohol, a toxic non-food grade alcohol. Our livers are Poison Control. They neutralize (detoxify) and metabolize (break down) toxins and alcohol. The college student's liver is often busy metabolizing ethanol, the alcohol found in wine, beer, and spirits. When aspartame is consumed, the liver also needs to deal with methanol, ethanol's evil twin. Ethanol is potable, but methanol is poison. A cocktail of diet Red Bull and vodka causes your liver to work a double shift throughout the night, instead of attending to normal body repair.

Aspartame, a tasteless sweetener with no calories that could be safely used by those who react to sugar, seemed too good to be true . . . and it was. Shortly after its introduction, the Center for Disease Control published the results of a 1983 study they conducted on consumer-based complaints associated with food products containing aspartame. Complaints involved central nervous system malfunctions, digestive upsets, and gynecological problems. Symptoms included irritability, insomnia, and seizures. Gastrointestinal complaints included abdominal pain, nausea, and diarrhea. Some hormonal issues included migraines, erratic mood changes, and irregular menses.

In many documented studies spanning decades, aspartame has been linked to various neuropsychiatric disorders, including panic attacks, mood changes, visual hallucinations, manic episodes, and isolated dizziness. Aspartame has been linked to brain diseases such as migraines, tumors, Parkinson's, seizures, mental illness, and autoimmune diseases, such as lupus and shingles. If aspartame is so damaging, why is it used? You may guess: economics. Synthetic sugars are less expensive than sugar. Money talks and health walks.

Aspartame might have been the original gang leader, but now many accomplices have joined.

Acesulfame K: Not OK

Acesulfame K (acesulfame potassium or AK) is an artificial sweetener 200 times sweeter than sucrose or table sugar. AK is used in foods, beverages, gums, candies, tabletop sweeteners, pharmaceuticals, dietary supplements including protein powders and nutrition bars, and cosmetics requiring a sweet taste. There are even sugar-free edible underpants made with this stuff. Like aspartame, AK is not metabolized as sugar. In fact, it's not metabolized at all, but passes through the body, unchanged. While the tongue perceives it as intensely sweet, the digestive system doesn't recognize it and therefore cannot break it down. Plus, it has zero calories! You would think this little chemical would be the Holy Grail of sweeteners, eh?

Once again, nope. Due to its intensely sweet flavor, acesulfame K deceives the body into thinking that fuel is on the way. In anticipation of the sugar, the pancreas releases insulin. Too much insulin in the blood causes a need for sugar, so we eat more. Thus, consuming products with AK encourages weight gain and low blood sugar.

In fact, AK has been shown to instigate and aggravate hypoglycemia or low blood sugar, a "broken woodstove" disease. Low blood sugar causes irritability, mood swings, and inattentiveness—all symptoms that make it difficult to focus in class. Too much insulin also hinders neurotransmitter release, which further reduces our mental capacity.

Acesulfame K is the creepy micromanaging boss or overzealous texting mother who causes you performance anxiety and unproductive work habits. Imagine sucking on a diet soda laced with AK while trying to take notes in a lecture hall. The soda is an IV drip of brain poison, reducing your ability to concentrate and regulate emotions.

Acesulfame K has also been linked to causing many kinds of tumors. In several rodent studies when even less than maximum doses were given, tumors manifested everywhere: brain tumors, breast tumors, lung tumors, several forms of leukemia, rare types of tumors of other organs (such as the thymus gland), and chronic respiratory disease.

Remember grandma's Tab? It contained saccharin. In a word: cancer. We no longer see saccharin on the market. A few decades of protest and boycott finally shifted mindsets, but aspartame and acesulfame K—and more artificial sweeteners to come—are still in the transitional stages of being concurrently challenged and distributed.

Splenda: Not Splendid

Sucralose, marketed as *Splenda*, began to grace our presence around the turn of the twenty-first century. Heating artificial sweeteners had been a problem. Aspartame was unable to withstand heat. Acesulfame K could tolerate heat, but was unstable. Sucralose solved the problem. It tolerates heat well, and is therefore used commonly in processed foods.

Sucralose was invented by chemists who combined sugar with chlorine gas. It produced a chemical much sweeter than simple sugar. Cool for chemistry, but not for biology. Chemists are not necessarily nutritionists, so it didn't matter if the stuff was healthy or even edible; that was for the FDA to sort out. Sucralose happens to taste sweet, but is yet another poison the liver has to deal with, because we refuse to eat sensibly.

Every time the liver has to deal with some poison, it wastes valuable enzymes that ought to be used for maximizing our health. Eating poison is like living in Tornado Alley. The town has to allocate a majority of its funds for damage control, instead of paying salaries, building new buildings, repairing roads, and other basic essential functions. The healthier you are, the less of a problem this is; but you are a college student, whose liver is, by definition, severely compromised. You don't need a tornado blowing into town after a hurricane has already decimated Main Street. You've got enough stress on your plate.

High Fructose Corn Syrup: Slipping Papa a Rufie

How about high fructose corn syrup? That's from real food, right? Well, it originates from food. High Fructose Corn Syrup (HFCS) is a simple sugar, so it does all those nasty lighter fluid things. Then it does something weird; it slips Papa brain a rufie during the rave party. HFCS inebriates the hypothalamus, a part of Papa brain responsible for signaling fullness. While Papa is knocked out, HFCS swipes his wallet and steals his car. HFCS dopes up the hypothalamus' satiation signal. Without Papa telling you when to stop, you just don't recognize when you're full, so you continue to crave and eat more sugar and fat. These flood the bloodstream system too quickly, and the cycle continues. This time, Papa wakes up in prison, wondering what the hell happened during his last meal.

* * *

Long ago, before you were born, food contained sugar and fat. Sugar would make you crazy and fat and rot your teeth, but at least sugar burned as fuel. Fat would make you fat, but it wouldn't poison. Unfortunately, modern values play by the credo that anything worth doing is worth overdoing. People eat so much sugar that it acts more like a poison and drug in their bodies, creating manic highs and depressive lows, dangerously acidic pH levels, and self-cannibalism. Sugar turns our bloodstreams into acidic rivers, dumping all kind of neurobiological nightmares onto our shores. But—and again, it's a big but—at least white sugar and fat are actual food products, and if you move your body enough and eat them in moderation, you can burn them.

With fake sugars and fats being cheaper and lasting forever, their presence is pervasive. They are now the rule, with real sugar and fat the exception. Pick up any processed food product in the grocery store, and you will likely see one of these nutritionally psychotic replacements. Since fatty acids are vital for cognitive processing, neurological health, and hormonal regulation, eating nutritious fat like olive oil will never be replaceable by trans-fats. Since glucose is the only fuel our brains burn, one has to actively choose to feed their brain.

In conclusion . . . just don't eat any of this poison! Just don't.

The Required Taboo

"Don't get me started on how coddled the American anus is."
—Dwight Shrute, from the television series, *The Office*

Fuel burns. You're in college, so you have legally passed some basic science. You may understand that burning things leaves stuff behind. So too, this happens in our bodies. Food has nutrients, water, and fiber. Nutrients rebuild the body. Water rehydrates, makes connections, and flushes toxins. Healthy cells die constantly and need replacing. Illness and disease must be healed with new cells. Fiber is a nutritional sponge, absorbing cells, toxins, and debris that the water flushes. All this garbage is collected and delivered to your waste site.

It's funny. **We may talk about cognitive filtering in front of a lecture hall of 500 students and no one bats an eye, but mention rectal filtering, and everybody starts to squirm and giggle**. Elimination may be a taboo topic, but is a biologically required taboo, so here we go.

Our intestinal tracts are about 24 feet long, and it takes about 24 hours for food to pass through. Nature is kind to our math sensibilities. In each 24-hour day, we experience three biorhythmic cycles: Cycle One begins our day, from 4:00 a.m. to noon, with elimination. We sweat through our skin, accumulate sleepy seeds in our eyes, and awaken needing to pee and poop. We slough off dead skin cells on our sheets and partners. Eeew, right? Thank goodness we do this. As every Jewish grandmother used to say, "Better out than in."

By noon, Papa is hungry. The hypothalamus activates, ready to fuel up, and Cycle Two begins. Health lore may champion breakfast being the most important meal of the day, but lunch is the body's primary fueling time. Southerners refer to lunch as "dinner" or "supper." Whatever you call it, the noon meal is the most important meal of the day. Between 12:00 and 8:00 p.m., your body's mission involves *intake*—taking information, in all sensory modalities. We eat food, attend class, and study. Intake involves a well-stoked woodstove, so the body's fuel is directed toward these tasks. Digestive juices run vigorously in Cycle Two to efficiently burn fuel.

Around 8:00 p.m., intake stops, and Cycle Three completes the daily rhythm. We begin assimilating. **All food should be in the small intestines by now, which means no eating after 8:00 pm.** Forget fast food slogans; there shall be *no* fourth meal, no 3:00 a.m. post-club binging at Denny's, and no ingestion of alcohol or other psychoactive substances. There shall be no consumption, with the exception of water or non-caffeinated herbal tea.

Say whaaahht?

After that last paragraph, some of you have now officially used this book for toilet paper or Frisbee. Don't blame me; blame biology. From 8:00 p.m. to 4:00 a.m., your body's job is to assimilate all the input it's received throughout the day, all the food, liquid, and information: sights, sounds, tastes, touches, smells—all of it. You break it all down, absorb nutrients, collect all the damaged and dead cells, filter information that you don't want or need, and by 4:00 a.m., you are ready to eliminate and start again.

Let's examine this biological cycle in the culture of college. **College culture navigates in direct oppositional currents against our bodies' natural flow. Just when the body wants to cease all intake and shut down, most college students are gearing up.** Students are sleepy zombies, staggering throughout their day. It takes some until 8:00 p.m. to *begin* waking up and feeling hungry. Consumption involves large sugary-protein laden dinners followed by binge drinking.

Food consumption is Priority #1 on physiological hierarchy. Consumed food, if left undigested, may quickly ferment and rot in our intestinal tracts. Trapped gas and rotting foods quickly turn toxic and can even be fatal. Papa brain understands this and intervenes. Anything you were doing before eating stops, so that the body can take care of the food, so that you don't become sick or dead. It's why you don't swim after eating or move off the couch after Thanksgiving feasts. It's also why so many cultures embrace the afternoon siesta. Not we productive US Americans, though, eh?

Every time food enters the stomach, the body has to stop its current process. In the middle of the night, when we need assimilation, the college body must instead digest an onslaught of food and booze. Late consumption puts a pause button on all repairing and regenerating, which starts a backlog of elimination. The delay continues each time we interfere with the cycles. This interference also occurs with late night studying. Pulling all-nighters for last minute assignments forces the brain to use up glucose for information-processing, rather than tending to the immediate tasks of Cycle Three.

There's an old saying, "Every hour of sleep before midnight is worth two, after." The quality of sleep before midnight is deeper, more restorative. During the early hours, the sleep cycle performs its heavy lifting of digestion, assimilation, and cleansing. It can't perform these vital functions if you're out there on the dance floor chugging down *Cubra Libres*, gorging on wings, or cramming away for tomorrow's exam.

Think of it this way. You live in a small room. Every night, you receive a box of stuff that you need to sort. Some of the stuff you keep, and some you throw away. You need to go through this box every night. While you begin sorting the box, someone comes in with a box and says, "Let's party." You leave both boxes and hit the town. In the morning, you have two boxes to deal with, which takes you twice as long.

You may not think this is a big problem. Two boxes isn't a big deal. But let's say you consume after 8:00 p.m. most nights. Every night, while you are going through a box, someone interrupts and convinces you to go out. Your body is designed to go through one box per night, but every night you have at least two, plus all the other accumulating boxes that you didn't get through the previous nights. By the end of the month, you have over fifty boxes piled up in your room. You may think, *Who cares? That's not so bad.* Extend that throughout a semester. Over one hundred boxes are stacked in your room and there is no more room to move. Now you have a problem. Imagine trying to function around them and how much allostatic stress it causes to have to live with them. If your roommate has a similar lifestyle, add their boxes to the picture.

No wonder you are exhausted and unable to concentrate. Even if you are blessed with a strong conative domain, your motivation is squelched by your lifestyle. You are consuming when you need to be sleeping and assimilating. You are sleeping when you need to be eliminating. And you are eliminating when you need to be consuming. In college, you consume more information than any other time of your life. So in effect, two boxes are delivered each day, before your interrupting box-dropping buddy knocks on the door every night.

You are one boxed-in mess, dear one.

MOVE

"To keep the body in good health is a duty.
Otherwise we shall not be able to keep our minds strong and clear. "
—Buddha

"I call exercise 'Miracle-Gro' for the brain. Exercise keeps brain cells
healthy in a way that playing chess and other highly cognitive activities
do not."
—John Ratey, author of *Spark*

"All truly great thoughts are conceived while walking."
—Friedrich Nietzsche

"A body at rest stays at rest."
—Newton's First Law of Motion

You are how you move.

Other than stress and food, the most important lifestyle factor to one's academic success is movement.

Sitting in classrooms, confined to a concrete box with four walls, listening in lecture halls, studying in libraries, taking exams, attending presentations, conferences, and meetings. Attending interest groups, governance councils, community meetings, club meetings, advisor meetings, office hours, therapy sessions, support groups. Hanging out with friends on beds and couches and lawns. Surfing, gaming, binge-watching, Instagramming, video chatting, Snapchatting, Tinder Power-Houring. The academic life is a sedentary life.

This is unfortunate, as human bodies are designed to move. If we were meant to sit and stare all day, we wouldn't have arms and legs. Maybe in 50,000 years, evolution will erode our extremities, mutating us for perfect alignment with a sedentary lifestyle. We will have morphed into a bio-computer. Until then, you are stuck with this body that requires a great deal of motion. In college, it may be extremely difficult to achieve the amount of movement required by the body to maintain optimum academic performance.

College is a Physical Activity

Now that you've fueled your body, let's move it! Academia, despite what it seems, actually requires a great deal of movement. Some movement is obvious. Students travel miles over campus from building to building. Students move through their extracurricular activities. Some movement is less obvious. Studying actually requires movement. Student brains are in constant electrical motion, thinking, feeling, and monitoring.

The body is designed to move. As you read this page, your heart is pumping. Blood is coursing through hundreds of miles of the cardiovascular network. Your lungs are expanding and contracting. Your eyes are moving. Your eardrums are vibrating, and neurons are firing. Thousands of processes are transpiring to promote the essence of your being ... and you have not even lifted a finger to turn a page. The body is not intended to be stagnant. Every movement, each effort of the muscles to pump blood brings the life force to every cell and flushes or removes from the body all that is no longer needed.

—Charlotte-Eliopoulos, *Invitation to Holistic Health*

"Writing is a physical activity," says Keith Hjortshoj in his groundbreaking book, *Understanding Writing Blocks* (Oxford University Press, 2001). Back in 2001, I studied the relationship between writing and health in a doctoral program. Reading that passage, I was struck by that revolutionary concept: *Writing is a physical activity.* Hjortshoj explored the physical writing body, how we maintain a posture during writing, constantly engaging hands, arms, neck, and shoulders. Writing demands steady hands, constricting muscles for great lengths. Reading is also a physical activity. Eyes are in constant motion, rotating back and forth and held steady, focusing.

It's tempting to think how these academic tasks are completely mental; but once again, we must respect our minds living in a body, surrounded by spiritual energy. Writing and reading, like every activity on the planet, requires SBM coordination. That includes every other classroom activity, such as note-taking, classroom discussion, organizing, time management, self-regulation, and emotional management.

We tend to perceive the pursuit of academia to be solely intellectual. Imagine talking heads floating around campuses, rationally conversing with like minds, logically deducing. The raw truth is that when we attend college, the entire being is accepted, not just the mind. You may possess a high intellect, but if you are emotionally stunted, lacking self-care or life purpose, you are likely to fail. Academic management requires monitoring motivation, which is ruled by the conative domain. If we are interested in an activity, we say that we put our hearts and souls into it. If we are uninterested or forced to do something, our souls feel compromised and we resist the process. This drains our emotions and attention. **The mind may get you into school, but the soul and body navigate you through it.**

* * *

Even when we move, we seldom move freely. People move within a culturally scripted language. There are socially acceptable ways to move our bodies and socially rejected ways that are discouraged. There are acceptable ways to walk. Monty Python illustrated our kinesthetic rigidity with the "silly walk." Running is reserved for kids and escaped convicts, unless you are wearing sneakers and training for a 10K. Socialized movement builds certain muscles and disregards others.

There are conventional ways to communicate non-verbally, too. When emphasizing a dramatic conversation, people have particular ways of holding their bodies, gesticulating their arms, and exposing their facial expressions. There are established ways to exercise: yoga, aerobics, free weights, and nautilus machines, and these exercise modalities require specific, controlled movements in a syncopated fashion. There are even appropriate ways to dance and make love. All these "synchronized movement melodies" restrict holistic muscle development. Free, uninhibited movement is rarely seen in our society in humans beyond the age of three. A toddler dancing around freely in a bank line is seen as adorable; at 33, he is labeled psychotic.

This section is not referring to exercise, merely *movement*. **There was a time when people led physically active lives *and* required exercise for optimal vitality. Nowadays, our hyper-sedentary lifestyle requires movement just to maintain a basic level of existence.**

Move It or Lose It

Let's see what happens every time you put down the screen, arise from the couch, and activate that "brain shell" known as a body.

Back to the classroom. Movement makes you smarter. I claimed that drinking water was the single best lifestyle factor you could do to improve your GPA. Movement is next. Movement is brain aerobics, pumping

---

Move!

Movement improves metabolism—the way we burn fuel:

- Utilizes fat for fuel, instead of storing it—think "Better Butter Burner" (*Fit or Fat*, C. Bailey)
- Regulates blood sugar or glucose levels (wood burns steadily)
- Increases demand for oxygen, which manages insulin (clean-burning stove)
- Stabilizes body's blood sugar levels (efficient wood stove)

Movement transforms body image:

- Improves muscle strength and tone
- Improves appearance, posture, and body image
- Increases confidence
- Improves outlook on life

Movement makes us better machines:

- Increases blood flow and grows and repairs blood vessels
- Prevents cardiovascular diseases, such as adult-onset diabetes, heart disease, and atherosclerosis
- Causes muscles to grow
- Supports bone strength
- Increases lung capacity, reducing stress and stimulating the immune system (cleaning the wood stove)

Movement creates three major benefits for the brain:
- Stimulates production of nerve growth factor
- Manages stress
- Enhances neuronal metabolism

---

blood, oxygen, and glucose into your head. It literally awakens the brain. What good is a body present in a classroom if the mind is unconscious? Ever see a coma patient raise her hand with the correct answer?

In college, the brain consumes more glucose, due to the cognitive taxing. Cognition is the most difficult kind of memory-making, because we have to actively work at it. Daily glucose consumption may rise to 30 percent in college students. LD students, who have neural developmental delays, require more glucose, as well. The brain has to send and receive messages every second of the day. It doesn't get breaks, like the spleen or stomach do. Therefore, the brain requires constant access to our blood and oxygen supply.

A wonder drug for the brain, **Neural Growth Factor** (NGF) is a hormone involved in regulating nerve health. NGF replaces and repairs brain cells and the nervous system. Daily stress and physical demands destroy cells. NGF is the super glue, and its production is stimulated when the body is physically active.

NGF repairs all brain and nerve cells. NGF greatly affects Mama brain and her memory maker, the hippocampus. The hippocampus is the part of the brain responsible for consolidating data and creating memories for long-term storage. It is directly stimulated by NGF and movement. Some studies reveal how movement increases hippocampal size. That's like increasing your computer's RAM and processing speed. In academic terms, increasing hippocampal size increases your ability to make memories, which in turn increases your ability to graduate.

You may recall that stress attacks the SBM. Cortisol destroys NGF as well as a myriad of other health-promoting hormones and chemicals. Cortisol creates the highway pile-up, and NGF works as the police and fire departments. Since movement produces NGF, consider movement the budget paying for these civil servants who are hired to protect and repair our infrastructures. Movement keeps all departments running smoothly.

In stress management, one highly effective way to alter your state is to move. Movement quickly escorts stress hormones, dead cells, and toxic chemicals out of the body. Think of movement as a great toilet, flushing toxins down the drain. (Think of a sedentary life as a toilet in the middle of your dorm room. Pretty smelly.) You must constantly flush these toxins out of your vital blood, glands, and organs in order to remain healthy. Interestingly, the most effective way to expel toxins is through your breath. Movement increases oxygen, stimulating breath. Breathing eliminates more waste than sweat, urine, and feces combined.

Movement also helps reactions to future stressors. It seems to improve perception. Ever talk to someone who's started an exercise regimen? Notice how annoyingly positive they are? That's a body and soul free of stress hormone build-up! Movement does more than just perk up our perception. It also markedly enhances mood, creating a feeling of tranquility. This well-documented "tranquilizer effect" continues after we move, much like the way eating carbohydrates burns for hours, without refueling.

Movement stimulates pleasure chemicals like serotonin and opiates known as endorphins, while reducing cravings by decreasing "wanting" chemicals like dopamine (see "Control" chapter). Endorphins are about two hundred times more potent than morphine. When we move vigorously, production skyrockets and in college, that's the difference between finishing your homework and falling asleep in mid-sentence.

If you've ever stayed awake in a challenging class, you may recall how effective movement is on attention. The natural tendency after class is to rise and stretch. Movement also decreases depression and increases motivation. These chemical magic tricks are linked; many studies compare movement to psychotherapy and medication, in terms of effectiveness. Movement is also an effective substitute for talking or crying, so when no one's around, get up and move! Alter that state, and give your friends a break from all the free psychotherapy they are supplying you.

Movement-based or experiential programs such as Outward Bound, SOAR, Semester-at-Sea, and certain Gap Year programs are designed to get students moving. They understand the powerful health benefits, but also respect that the student is developing neural pathways, cognitive power, and mood regulation that give them a competitive edge in managing college life. These programs also offer healthy risk-taking in a supportive environment, which are essential to improving academic success, as we will explore in the upcoming chapters.

Daily movement reduces anxiety and tires us physically, which brings better sleep. We reach restorative delta states that are necessary to make memories. Movement also reduces phobias and feelings of fear. Talk about a magical strategy! Since so much is new and unsettling, college supplies a bevy of fearful challenges: dating, classroom participation, non-stop assignments, and the pressure to succeed. Anxious thoughts destroy REM sleep, bringing nightmares, less restorative sleep, and fewer memories. Students awake just as tired as when they went to bed. College will stop anyone in their tracks, and movement gets you back on, safely.

Healthy movement, like smiling and breathing, makes us happier, and that happiness is infectious. When we are happy, we are confident. Just as movement improves blood and oxygen flow and eliminates toxic chemicals, it allows energy to flow more freely into our souls, expanding social experiences by improving self-esteem. We like ourselves more, and are more likely to believe that others could like us, too. Movement creates better relationships. We feel better about our bodies when we're moving, and that reflects in how we interact with people. Want a romantic partner? Want some friends? Get moving!

The Sweet Spot of movement involves enough movement to keep us attentive during the day and tired at night. How much movement is that? It depends on you. Health textbooks advocate a regimen of 30 minutes per day, three to five times per week. Some people find daily exercise does the trick, but you know yourself better than anyone. If you are overweight or out of shape, simply walking to class may be sufficient. The key is to engage in enough activity to keep you in the stretch zone.

One of the best things movement does is prevent aging. If you like being alive, move your effin' body! My recommendation is to simply move your body a bit more today than you did yesterday. Repeat until death.

REDUCES STRESS
STIMULATES IMMUNE SYSTEM
IMPROVES MUSCLE STRENGTH
IMPROVES APPEARANCE
IMPROVES CONFIDENCE
UTILIZES FAT FOR FUEL
INCREASES OXYGEN FLOW
STABILIZES BLOOD SUGAR
INCREASES BLOOD FLOW
GROWS MUSCLES
PREVENTS CARDIOVASCULAR DISEASE
SUPPORTS BONE STRENGTH
INCREASES LUNG CAPACITY
STIMULATES NERVE GROWTH FACTOR

Becca

Becca was a vibrant smart-ass who talked more than I did, and I was the professor. A blurt-y gal with a big heart, Becca's sweet and confident nature won me over the first day of class. A few weeks into the semester, she become quieter and more sullen. Her excellent attendance began to slip. After her third absence, we talked. I asked her about her classes and assignments. These seemed fine and manageable. No teachers or assignments from hell. She got along with her roommate. She didn't hate the cafeteria food. No long-distance romance brought her down. We kept talking, and I asked if she played any sports in high school. She didn't. So, I let her know I was available to her and excused her.

A week later, students gave presentations on learning styles where they shared a personal area of strength and challenge. Becca's challenge was inhibition (no doubt), but her strength was the interesting part. Becca's passion was archery; she had been practicing the sport for years. She even brought in her bow and arrow and offered us a demonstration. At the end of class, we talked again. I asked her if she was practicing her archery, since arriving on campus. Becca responded that, no, she hadn't and, in fact, this presentation was the first time in she had handled her equipment in several weeks.

We discussed the relationship of her recent funk with her lack of archery, and she easily agreed. Archery had been her rock, her go-to, her place of confidence and stress release, for years. Suddenly, she was living without it, and furthermore, living in a place with new and much greater stressors than she had previously encountered in high school. She realized how

> important it was to reunite with her integral strategy. She did, and the rest of her semester soared into success, a veritable bulls-eye.

One of the reasons that college may be so detrimental is because of the sudden lack of movement. Students may miss this connection and instead focus on the poor food and mountainous stress. High school students who persist into college need extracurricular activities, demonstrating a "well-rounded personality" to their new institution. These extracurricular activities often include participation on sports teams, which require great amounts of daily exercise and physical vigor. Students enter college and this physical activity abruptly ceases. Stress builds up and diet breaks down, and pretty soon, the student feels tired, foggy, and irritable. Digestion is off, too. It's like they are living in a different body, and in a way, they are. Ever see a typical college dorm room? Pretty messy. That's your body, without movement.

I remember reading how it's better to exercise and eat junk food than to eat a perfect diet while lying on your butt. Not that I'm condoning either scenario, but it was an interesting observation to illustrate the importance of movement upon body health. This is a helpful reminder, as I spend my gazillionth hour sitting on my duff editing. One of the best things about writing a book about health is that it inspires the author to practice what they preach. At this particular moment, my brain is beginning to feel rather sluggish. So, if you'll excuse me, I will save this draft, turn off my screen, consume some whole foods, and head outside for a walk. You've read enough. I suggest you do the same!

SLEEP

"After all the research I've done on sleep problems over the past four decades, my most significant finding is that ignorance is the worst sleep disorder of them all. People lack the most basic information about how to manage their sleep, leading to a huge amount of unnecessary suffering."
—William C. Dement, MD, PhD, *The Promise of Sleep*

"Sleep, those little slices of death—how I loathe them."
—Edgar Allan Poe

"Sleep is my lover now, my forgetting, my opiate, my oblivion."
—Audrey Niffenegger, *The Time Traveler's Wife*

"I wonder why I don't go to bed and go to sleep. But then it would be tomorrow, so I decide that no matter how tired, no matter how incoherent I am, I can skip an hour more of sleep and live."
—Sylvia Plath, *The Unabridged Journals of Sylvia Plath*

"Early to bed, early to rise, makes a man healthy, wealthy, and wise."
—Benjamin Franklin

You are how you rest.

Other than stress, food, and movement, the most important lifestyle factor to one's academic success is sleep.

You've been a good college student, managing your stress, eating a balanced diet, and moving your body. Now you need to rest.

"I'll sleep when I'm dead," cries the college student, as he pushes himself to face yet another day of awakening too early and staying up too late. He is not alone. In a culture that rewards productivity and abhors lassitude, sleep seems to be a nuisance, an obligatory interruption in our crazybusy schedules. In college, sleep is more strained than in any other time in the young adult's life. With friends, partying, sex, video games, and studying, why on earth would anyone prioritize sleep?

Defending this psychonutrient is a major losing battle. Stress is a bully; everyone agrees in the logic of taming it. Food and movement are pretty easy sells, but there is something about sleep . . . something we love to hate. Telling a college student to sleep is like . . . well, like telling a college student to sleep. College students are notorious vampires, resisting sleep in favor of hedonistic pleasures and forsaking sleep for sadistic assignments. Sleep is surrendered only under protest in a complete collapse of the SBM. **To most of the civilized world, sleep is regarded as a waste of time, a wormhole for productivity.** There is simply too much to stay awake for.

LD students fare even worse. The typical ADHD profile faces a lifetime of erratic sleep patterns: wackily wound internal sleep clocks, bouncing between abnormally small or large amounts of sleep, and chronic insomnia. These sleep issues may worsen with co-occurring diagnoses like depression or bipolar disorder. Many college students I've spoken with report sleeping an average of four hours a night!

If a student is blessed with healthy sleep patterns, there is a good chance their slumber is challenged due to their roommate's sleep issues. If you are both lucky enough to be sleep-healthy, you have the rest of your world to contend with. In college, there is no separation between social and personal life. You are interacting with others 24/7. Unlike being home or living off campus, your social life is in the bed next to you, next door, across the hall, etc. There is no real down time, only a "quiet time" that is difficult to enforce.

Add to that fire drills, drama triangles, booze-laden brawls and just ... college. Nineteen-year-olds are a loud, obnoxious, egotistically oblivious lot. They generally don't mean any harm, but are sorely lacking self-awareness. How many babies have you met who "keep it down" if they're in the mood to cry? If these students do know, they often don't care or have not yet learned to inhibit their behavior. And "they" are everywhere: in your room, suite, resident hall, fraternity, or worse ... maybe "they" is you? Are you that annoying punk who gets regular visits from your RD? Bless your heart.

Sleep Your Way to an A

What you do in bed is as important as what you do in the classroom. We get as much done during these dreamy subconscious hours as we do during the day. Sleep is the shadow side of productivity. Picture the graveyard shift: while Baby brain is snug in his crib, an entire network of engineers and construction crews are bustling around the brain. We do our major regeneration at night: repairing injuries, replacing body parts, removing dead cells and toxins, and, for the college student, we make memories.

When it comes to sleep, both size and timing matter. Eight emerges as the magic health number. Every day, we need eight glasses of water and every night, eight hours of sleep. But it's not enough to have eight hour per day, nor is it okay to fit in naps after pulling all-nighters; *when* we sleep makes or breaks the system. From the discussion on elimination, recall the wisdom, **"Every hour before midnight is worth two after."**

The natural world flows with windows of opportunity. Dandelions awaken in spring. Hibernation comes when cool weather envelops. Humans follow similar rhythms—developmental times when growth is most readily available. The human body has windows for learning language and reading, daily cycles for digestion, and circadian rhythms for sleep. In an ideal world, a human goes to bed at 10:00 p.m. and rises at 6:00 a.m. How many college students do you know who honor this natural rhythm? In fifteen years of teaching, I think I've met three.

Sleep is divided into two main stages: deep and light. Deep sleep is vital for repairing and cleansing the body, while lighter sleep rejuvenates the soul and mind. Deeper cycles occurs first, between the hours of 10:00 p.m.–2:00 a.m. Deep sleep is like dining hall hours; if you want dinner, you have to eat when the doors are open. Deep sleep occurs first, then lighter sleep occurs where we enter the dreaming phase, called Rapid Eye Movement (REM). Memory-making occurs throughout the night.

We experience our lightest sleep just before waking. During the eight-hour cycle lasting from 10:00 p.m.–6:00 a.m., humans experience several sleep phases, generally known as stages 1, 2, 3, 4, and REM. These phases show different brainwaves and accordingly, are responsible for different sleep tasks.

Stage 1 is the relaxed wakeful state experienced as you begin your descent. It is a meditative state, often the time when ideas come to you. Next comes **stage 2**, a fugue-like state where consciousness shuts off. You may actually respond to someone during this stage, although you will likely not remember. Stage 2 puts the body to sleep, then awakens the soul. It is the time of intuitive receptivity. With the rational mind asleep, the subconscious is free to roam. During times of intense creativity, our minds rely heavily on stage 2 sleep. When we suffer from stress and anxiety, we rely heavily on stage 2 to filter excess stress chemicals. Due to its connection with spirit, stage 2 is also the time where we receive insight into problem solving. Insomnia is an abnormal extension of stage 2, as we obsess on life's issues.

Stage 3 is our carpenter, preoccupied with regeneration, rebuilding neurons, and constructing new pathways, including making new memories. Memory consolidation is higher in stage 3. Stage 3 is also the janitor, collecting waste and eliminating dead cells and toxins from the curbs. Minds are filtered, cleared of clutter to make room for tomorrow's information.

Soon comes **stage 4 or Delta**, the deepest sleep. During delta, we do the heavy lifting: major body repair and memory-storage. If

THE STAGES OF SLEEP

STAGE 1
(WAKING)

STAGE 2
(ALPHA)

STAGE 3
(THETA)

STAGE 4
(DELTA)

= REM
SLEEP

HOUR   1   2   3   4   5   6   7   8

you are suffering from a serious disease, delta is the stage that helps you heal. Delta sleep is also the time we create muscle memories, building skills and procedures.

REM sleep is your dreaming stage, which increases throughout the night. REM shuts down the frontal lobe, which could help explain why dreams are irrational. REM is lighter sleep, similar to stage 2. REM bypasses our conscious minds and communicates with spirit. We open the portal to the collective consciousness and allow it to enter through our subconscious mind. During REM, our physical body paralyzes. This is a good thing, if you've ever recalled a flying dream.

Delta sleep occurs in the first half of the night, between 10:00 p.m. and 2:00 a.m. Most college students go to bed around 2:00 a.m. See the problem? Students completely eliminate the most restorative time of the night and final stage of making memories. If you miss delta, you miss storing memories and will lose all that precious studying. Sleeping from 2:00 a.m. to 10:00 a.m. is not the same. It's not enough to sleep for eight hours per night; you have to begin them at a certain time. Even if you are a diligent student athlete who attends all classes and practices, if you stay up until 2:00 a.m., it's like skipping. It's as if you weren't even there.

Making Memories

"We find that the biochemical changes are simply not happening in the neurons of animals that are awake, and when the animal goes to sleep it's like you've thrown a switch, and all of a sudden, everything is turned on that's necessary for making synaptic changes that form the basis of memory formation. It's very striking." (*Marcos Frank, PhD University of Pennsylvania, www.ultracrepidate.com*)

We discussed how memories are made and how stress affects them, but what we haven't explored is *when* memories are made—when all that studying transforms into memory. That is during sleep. **During sleep, some executive decisions are made about how you are going to remember your life**. The brain retains the valuable and expels the "un-valuable."

What determines if information is valuable? Valuable is vital, helpful, and useful, while non-valuable is expendable and useless. Information is personal. What is valuable to me may be non-valuable to you. Sense and meaning are critical in memory consolidation, which is why training perception is vital in college.

Memory is tricky to the college student. If you hate a class, you will attach less meaning to it, thereby reducing the mind's motivation to encode information into memory. For instance, if you struggle with math and are taking college algebra, your emotional responses resist attention. This is simple logic; we tend to avoid or discard things we don't like. If you don't like spiders, you don't seek a career in entomology. If you are expected to learn data that you're not interested in and have trouble keeping in order, then the information lacks sense, and you are less likely to encode it. "Less meaning and sense" translates into less likely to become a memory. Sense and meaning, both heavily guarded by emotion, are key factors in encoding information and memory consolidation.

On the other hand, let's say you take a class you love, perhaps a ceramics class. You have a cool teacher who is creative and innovative. She lets you run with your imagination. The professor allows students access to the studio 24 hours a day; you are able to create any time the spirit moves you. It is an inspirational place. Even when you make mistakes, the professor celebrates how you took a chance and tried something new. She says that is just as important as making a perfect bowl.

This class offers a wealth of sense and meaning; therefore, the experiences may be strongly encoded. You may remember much more of that class than some required course needed for graduation. Even if you don't become a potter or touch a piece of clay ever again, you may remember more about that one class than all of your other classes, combined. Emotionally charged information is easy to remember and is easily encoded. For the less emotional information, we have to trick the mind into caring.

When sense and meaning are absent, as they often are in college, students need to rely on incessant repetition and mnemonics to make memories. Anyone who recalls The Pledge of Allegiance understands the power of incessant repetition. Flash cards, rehearsal, summary writing, and drawing notes are all examples of mnemonic devices. The brain is tricked into thinking that the information is interesting, makes sense, or is meaningful to you.

In fifth grade, I was a wicked pain in the ass, always talking throughout class and teasing poor Mr. Wilson, my social studies teacher. One day, he'd had enough of my disruptive tendencies and sent me out to the hallway, where I was to write the Preamble to the Constitution 100 times before returning to class. By the end of the week, I had memorized that damned paragraph, and to this day, still have it stored:

> We the People, in order to form a more perfect union
> Establish justice, insure domestic tranquility
> Provide for the common defense
> Promote the general welfare and
> Secure the blessings of liberty
> To ourselves and our posterity
> Do ordain and establish
> This constitution for the United States of America

To a fifty-year-old, this preamble is rather like a beautiful poem. What minds these men possessed! What foresight and wisdom! To the fifth grader, that stupid preamble was a mountainous waste of time and only made me more obnoxious in poor Mr. Wilson's class. (Mr. Wilson, thank you for the valuable lesson!) In moments without sense or meaning, incessant repetition is your studying savior.

* * *

Sometimes tricking the mind works. For this, we call on my personal favorite brain part, the hippocampus. How cute is that name? Who wouldn't love that brain part? In fifth grade, I bet I would have loved it. You'll really love it, when you hear what it does.

The hippocampus is the captain sailing the memory ship. It is the yeast that converts flour, water, and salt into bread. At night, while resting snuggly in your cozy college bed (scrunched up on your foam cutout mattress, mashed against the concrete wall, trying hard not to fall off the top bunk), this little guy works its magic. The hippocampus biochemically treats sensory information with enzymes and neurotransmitters and then shoots memories out to the cortical area, filling our filing cabinets with long-term memories.

We store information, not as whole experiences, but in sensory blocks: my mother's visual features are stored in one spot, the sound of her voice in another, and even the word "mom" in another place. My emotional response—how I feel about my mother—is stored in yet another place. Memories are like chains: when one link is pulled on or activated, it causes a chain reaction, pulling the entire chain back together, and I transfer "mother" into my active working memory.

The hippocampus is a weigh station, temporarily holding onto information, sometimes for years. Working as a cashier at a grocery store, we used PLU codes for ringing up produce. I remember thinking, *These hold no meaning for me.* Ironically, I ranted on about the meaninglessness of PLU codes and how I would never remember them, and now have used two as examples. They became novel, and anger stimulated my attentive state. Thanks to this memory trick, the PLU codes for cauliflower (530) and bananas (4009) are now successfully filed in my long-term memory. On my death bed, if you hold up a head of cauliflower and bunch of bananas, the PLU codes will be uttered with my final breath.

As long as I worked in the store, I needed to access this information, so the hippocampus served as a holding station, a kind of "long-term limbo." But, Mama didn't raise no dummies; as soon as I quit the job, the information stopped having meaning, and the hippocampus promptly discarded it. (All except for the two PLU codes that were associated with the strong emotions of my heated tirade.) This is why you forget the facts you cram each semester. After you take the final exam, the hippocampus eagerly dumps all that pesky brain-clogging data.

Much of college falls into this category, unfortunately. After you leave, all the facts you learn in your classes—all the papers you write, the tests you take, the facts you memorize, the jargon you practice—are swiftly deleted. By the time fall comes around, you'll have forgotten everything from the previous school year. You weren't using the information, and it held little sense or meaning. Being a smart creature, you deleted the files.

Maybe it's because we pay good money to attend, maybe it's because parents are still heavily involved in the process, but college information is expected to be retained and used. The truth is, every time we leave a job, we forget most of the information. Very little of our life actually gets through the hippocampus's tight security.

* * *

Let's say information *is* important to you and by golly, you fully intend to remember it forever. In healthy brain conditions, information travels from the frontal lobe to the hippocampus for temporary storage. When it is determined to be important enough for long-term memory, it is encoded in the hippocampus and travels from the hippocampus to the cortex, where it is stored for future use. When the information is needed, we open our files. The file travels back down through the hippocampus to the frontal lobe—the active working memory, where you place your attention. When we take an exam, we open our filing cabinets and retrieve the information to pay attention to it (take the test). When we use transfer—the cognitive ability to transfer previous skills into new learning experiences—we also rely on this memory highway system. Under normal conditions, highways are clear of traffic, well-paved, and ready for safe travel.

College is abnormal conditions. Cortisol hurricanes wreak havoc. You must manage your stress, or your hippocampus is unable to manage your memories. One of the most effective stress reducers? Sleep. Sleep eliminates cortisol's damage, thereby allowing greater memory-making and recall, which happens when you sleep.

College students who deprive themselves of sleep are throwing their education away. You are choosing to drive on a road with the bridge out. It doesn't matter how prepared you were for class or how well you paid attention and how much you participated; you have to complete the memory transaction. Without sleep, the day never happened. Sleep is as important as class attendance. For college success, students must consider sleep a life or death matter.

Jason

Jason was a bright, polite student who entered college a mere six credits away from graduating with a Bachelor's degree. He suffered from anxiety so severely that he regulated it with medication. Jason also suffered other problems: medication abuse and gaming addiction. He would take his medication and then stay up all night playing his online game, until morning. When his roommates were beginning to awaken for their long days, Jason collapsed into bed and slept until dinner time, when he'd rise, eat, and do it all again. This was a battle that Jason did not win, and he eventually withdrew from college three credits short of graduation.

THE PERILS OF SLEEP DEPRIVATION

HALLUCINATIONS

IRRITABILITY

MEMORY LAPSE OR LOSS

IMPAIRED MORAL JUDGEMENT

RISK OF HEART DISEASE

INCREASED HEART RATE

DECREASED REACTION TIME & ACCURACY

DECREASED BODY TEMPERATURE

COGNITIVE IMPAIRMENT

SYMPTOMS SIMILAR TO ADHD

IMPAIRED IMMUNE SYSTEM

RISK OF OBESITY

TREMORS AND ACHES

RISK OF DIABETES TYPE 2

GROWTH SUPRESSION

Sleep Debt: Pay Up

If you manage lifestyle sufficiently during the day, you earn enough "sleep debt" to warrant eight hours of slumber. Each day, we accumulate eight hours of debt and then sleep it off. If you miss a night of sleep, you go into *excessive* sleep debt, commonly known as sleep deprivation. The fewer hours of sleep you have, the more debt you owe.

Most people live a life of sleep deprivation, beginning in college. Students are overwhelmed with sleep debt. Sleep expert Dr. William Dement, author of *The Promise of Sleep,* explains how sleep debt does not fade away on its own. **The only cure for sleep debt is sleep.** The best strategy is prevention, honoring sleep each and every night.

All psychonutrients share the Sweet Spot ideal: not too much and not too little. Good health is just right. Good food, clear mind, ample movement, and stress management all prepare the body for healthy sleep. We need to earn our fatigue, working the SBM with physical and mental activity in Cycle Two, between 12:00 p.m. and 8:00 p.m. (the intake cycle).

Excessive sleep debt hastens aging, loses memories, causes disease, stresses us out, and makes us crazy. It impairs judgment, balance, and coordination, as if being constantly intoxicated. If you *are* constantly intoxicated, it's as if you've consumed twice the amount of alcohol. Excessive sleep debt begins with one night. Imagine the sleep debt you accumulate by graduation!

* * *

There is another strange but central symptom of sleep debt: misperception or cognitive stubbornness. **Sleep deprivation increases the subjects' belief that they were right, especially when they were wrong.** Apply that to a college student, and you can imagine the complications with academic, residential, and social issues. Disequilibrium requires cognitive flexibility and self-awareness of perception. Excessive sleep debt destroys the ultimate purpose of college.

Sleep-deprived students get into trouble and cannot comprehend the reality of the situation. They lose inhibition, which may be fine for socializing, but can be deadly for self-awareness ("I'm *fine* to drive!"). Sleep deprivation encourages **external locus of control**, a view of the world where you blame external forces for your problems. Sleep-deprived students are unable to accurately consolidate memories, which leads to misconstruing facts—facts both in and out of the academic arena. Dealing with a sleep-deprived person is like dealing with a mean drunk. Their senses are delayed, cognition is impaired, and perception is garbled. Sleep-deprived students still enter the classroom, engage in class discussions, do their homework, and take tests, but have little memory of these activities, being stuck in the netherworld of their fugue-state. The swiftest way to waste your college education is to lack sleep. You already face a mountain of financial debt upon graduation. Save yourself from a mountain of sleep debt.

The Dangers of Sleep Debt (less sleep you get, the greater the health risks)	
Hours of Sleep	**Health Outcomes**
8	Refreshed mood, alert, peak physical performance, memories made, immune system recharged, stress chemicals discharged
7	Moody, occasional trouble concentrating, reduced short-term memory, some drowsiness while driving, in class, and at work
6	Testy, irritable, poor decision-making, weight gain, reduced motor skills, inability to focus in class, memory consolidation disrupted (memories not made)
5	Depressed mood, 50% slower reaction time, stressed out, greater chance of heart and stomach ailments, physical performance akin to someone legally drunk
4	Extremely irritable, exhaustion, higher risk for ulcers, diabetes, heart attack, and obesity, dangerous to self and others on the job and while driving.

Sleep researcher James B. Maes, PhD and Mark Rosekind, former president of NASA's Fatigue Countermeasures Program, 2001

Don't go to bed too hungry or too full.

Keep bedroom dark and quiet.

Reduce your Caffeine intake.

Get regular exercise.

Make your bedroom your sanctuary.

Maintain a Consistent Daily Schedule.

Turn off the TV and the Computer

Listen to your internal Clock.

Limit your liquid intake before bedtime.

CONNECT

"If one is truly to succeed in leading a person to a specific place, one must first and foremost take care to find him where he is and begin there. This is the secret in the entire art of helping."

—Søren Kierkegaard

"Tell me who your friends are, and I'll tell you who you are."

—Confucius

"My mom says that any choice I make is OK because I love myself."
"Your mom is wrong."

—Louis CK, talking to (young boy) Never, on *Louie*

You are how you belong.

Other than stress, food, movement, and sleep, the most important lifestyle factor to one's academic success is connection.

Connection is a function of humanity. We require connection to some loving presence, whether it be human, animal, or spirit. On a deeper level, we need something that loves and cares about us and we need to connect with that presence on a regular basis. Connection to others allows the sharing of souls.

For academic purposes, spirit is connection. That's it. No need to be afraid of the word or what it means. No religious zealot is knocking on the door seeking your conversion, and no one's asking for money. We are being spiritual when we are connected—energy to energy, person-to-person, person-to-God, tree, pet, rock, paper, or scissor.

Connection steadies us. When we learn, we are in disequilibrium. Connection provides the support and structure to realign our balance. **Sharing our goals and dreams with others not only makes us feel good and motivated, but it actually helps the goal to be achieved.** Like the neurons in your brain, it takes two to make a connection.

Powerful forces

Connections stimulate mysterious forces called entrainment and coherence. Energy waves seek patterns, aligning with similar frequency. Researchers at the HeartMath Institute describe this energetic alignment:

> We see this phenomenon when flocks of birds or schools of fish synchronize their movements to more efficiently transport themselves. We also observe entrainment when the motion of several pendulum clocks in a room synchronize with the wave pattern produced by the largest one. And we know a baby's heartbeat patterns can eventually entrain to those of its mother when it is held closely.

Christiaan Huygens, an inventor in the seventeenth century, invented the pendulum clock. As he began building more clocks, he stored them in a room together. He began to notice an interesting phenomenon. At night when he'd retire, the clock pendulums would be swinging at different intervals. In the morning when he returned, all the pendulums swung in sync. Intrigued, he disrupted their "in-sync-ness," having the pendulums swing in alternating, erratic ways. In the morning, they'd all be back in synch. Huygens, inventor of the pendulum clock, also discovered a cool concept: entrainment. **Entrainment** is the way that energy connects and aligns with other energy.

What determines which energy wave entrains? With pendulums, it's easy. Throughout the work day, Huygens noticed how the largest pendulum with the strongest rhythm pulled the smaller pendulums into sync. It's survival of the fittest. Surrounding wavelengths gravitate toward the more powerful oscillating frequencies. This plays out on macro levels. Charismatic people exude irresistible energy, and people are drawn to them. The moon's cycles affect the tides.

Connection seems to be ruled by the conative domain; **we are driven to connect with a primal urge, often prioritizing it over basic physiological functions.** College students deny themselves sleep over connecting in social media. Students leave their phones on while sleeping and will awaken to respond. The motivation to connect can be greater than anything else. People often say that in the first flushes of love, they are unable to eat and sleep; all they can do is think of this person and want to be with them. Lust is the ultimate entrainment, and may be more addictive than anything.

Some entrainment is more basic. We understand this as "role modeling." Role modeling activates mirror neurons. Mirror neurons activate as if we are participating, but we are merely observers. Initially, that is. After we entrain, we may adopt the behavior. Role modeling entrainment includes yawning when someone else yawns or succumbing to peer pressure. Some people begin to favor one foot when walking with someone who is limping. We may also "observe" subconsciously. Remember in overnight camp, when some poor kid peed in his bed after some jerk placed poor kid's fingers in a cup of warm water? The warm water's suggestion to pee was powerful entrainment.

A pendulum is just a pendulum, but entrainment and temptation are practical playmates. **When polled about why they first started smoking cigarettes, a young smoker's common reply is that they identified with a smoking role model.** The person's values and attitudes mirrored their own, and smoking became a natural extension of the entrainment.

As Baby brain matures, his job includes overriding negative or harmful suggestions and recognizing positive behaviors and role models. Yawning or playing an instrument is okay, but smoking cigarettes or cheating on a test, not so much. As for peeing in bed, well, hey. That's camp for ya. Maybe better to be the one holding the cup.

Coherence is a bit more than alignment. It suggests a harmonious balanced state. When we are engaged in flow, soul is coherent with spirit. Learning occurs when coherence exists between learner and teacher. It's interesting that we also define coherence as being lucid or attentive, for we define a positive state of learning also as being attentive.

College requires maintaining coherence between social and academic commitments. Friends and lovers constantly vie for a student's attention, and they usually win out. Social life is a 24/7 onslaught, right outside our doors and in the next bed. In the classroom, students spend more time texting and messaging than note-taking. **Many students fail their first semester because they are succeeding so well socially.** What's a Baby to do? Pizza always trumps Psychology.

Coherence is tricky to achieve and even trickier to maintain. Since energy aligns to more powerful influences, we may veer off our paths under the force of more powerful oscillating frequencies. In academic terms, students entrain under the control of parents, teachers, partners, and friends. Learning is a fragile coherent system: too strong an energetic wave will manipulate how the student thinks and behaves. The student's conative domain is ignored for the stronger-willed supporter's agenda. In a spiritual sense, they entrain the student's soul, living the student's lives.

Author's note: The rest of the Connect chapter is primarily directed toward the supporters of college students, rather than the students themselves. Students may find this chapter validating (which may mean parents find it challenging). Either way, students should enjoy reading it, but please do share with your supporters!

The Sweet Spot of Support

Whether support comes from advisor, parent, friend, or mentor, one factor is key: balance. The key to balance? The Sweet Spot. Remember our friend, the Sweet Spot? Coined by researchers Yerkes and Dodson, the Sweet Spot indicates the sweet amount of stress that is just stimulating enough to initiate action, but not so stimulating that it overwhelms. All psychonutrients have their Sweet Spots: glucose balance, eight-hour sleep debt maintenance, ample movement to stimulate and relax, and creative flow. In terms of connection, the Sweet Spot refers to coherence. Supporters must offer enough entrainment for the student to grow, but not so much that they interrupt and retard the student's growth.

Abandon: Too Cold

Why is guidance important? College students don't know a lot, despite what they think. At eighteen, my son was so intellectually reasonable, I often forgot what an ignorant little turd he was. I mean, here I am, the mature, wizened forty-something mother, acquiescing to the rantings of this pot-infused nutball. Transfer more spending money? Fully sponsor another semester, after failing all classes, due to incompetent professors? Of course, anything for my Precious Flower. Eighteen-year-old US American males talk a wicked good talk. They are also raised to be autonomous: never seek help. They enter college, don't know what they are doing, and swiftly drown in a sea of freedom and unclear expectations.

Most mistakes are annoying, but some can be destructive or fatal. My inability to seek clarity in a simple assignment resulted in failing out of Bryn Mawr. If someone had been there to check in, see why I was not submitting work . . . if someone had shown me an example of a college essay, to clarify this abstract idea in my head . . . if someone had advised me to avoid early admissions to Duke University . . . who knows where I would be today? Doesn't it seem amazing that not asking a simple question could paralyze someone so completely and be so path-shifting? Happens all the time.

If students are given no support, they often won't do it: the Bryn Mawr Essay syndrome. "It" can seem like a simple task to others—emailing a teacher, talking to a roommate, or texting mother to request that she stop texting you in class. But "it" is in the eye of the perceiver; what is daunting for you may be simple for me. This is the danger in judging where others need support. Supporters must validate what is truly hard for their supportees.

Parents will sometimes threaten their children, saying "Get all Bs or we're through paying for college." This tough love may work, but it may also be laying a judgment over the student's stretch zone. There may be significant reasons why the student is not able to perform, and a threat may only threaten their affective and conative domains, rather than stimulate their cognition. When a teacher demands that a dyslexic student "read harder," it is lunacy. A student needs to have the ability to proceed and succeed.

Teachers may refer to this as the **breakdown point**—the developmental place where a student is at and must be met in order for support to be effective. For me, the breakdown point was assignment clarity. If I had known what an essay was, I could have submitted the assignment. Without that support, other issues piled up until, until the obstacles were too overwhelming for even the best support.

Social psychology describes the **Zone of Proximal Development** (ZPD), the Sweet Spot of learning. The ZPD is the zone where we move from what we already know to what we want or need to know. It moves us from the comfort zone into the stretch zone. ZPD is disequilibrium with guidance.

Humans learn how to be human from other humans. **If the whole point of college is to expose young adults to new ideas and ways of doing things, how on earth should they be expected to know how to do those things?** It's such a delicate balance to demonstrate something, then let the person do it. They will do it badly at first. They may do it badly for a while. Neurons take a while for their paths to become highways. Watch a toddler trying to crawl or eat with a fork. Supporters often supply the belief that students so desperately need to succeed.

Tucker

Tucker nailed the learning style presentation, when illustrating social support with his attendance record. He and his long-time girlfriend started the semester strong, and academically, it showed. Attendance was perfect, assignments submitted, and participation was engaging. His GPA was in the A range.

Around mid-semester, he and his girlfriend broke up, sending Tucker into a tailspin. Without his touchstone, he had no social compass to guide him as a positive influence. Tucker pointed to the graph where the line dropped swiftly in the middle: attendance plummeted, assignments ignored. Participation was obviously nil, as his presence was non-existent. Tucker also lost touch, cutting himself off from friends and family and stopping all email contact with his professors. His average class grade dropped to C range, and his communications class, where his girlfriend was also enrolled, dropped below a D. All interaction in that class ceased, completely.

A few weeks later, they reconciled and that graph got all better. Academic markers bounced back, and Tucker returned to the silly, exuberant wacko we all knew and loved. The significance was not lost on Tucker, thankfully. He applied this experience to academic performance, with a new profound respect for the power of social connection, but also with a guarded attention to its powerful entrainment.

Enable: Too Hot

College may be the most daunting event of young adults' lives, because the illusion of freedom is so complicated. Students crave it, luxuriate in the fantasy world of doing whatever it is they want to do. It's unbridled hedonism. On the other hand, they've never had this freedom before, so they don't know how to manage it. Add to that the strain of adapting to an entirely new culture. It's no wonder that parents want to support their young adults in this tender transition of the self.

When students enter college, parents, too, enter a new phase, the **Empty Nest**. Learning how to support a young adult is equally challenging for the parent. Parents, if you're reading this, remember when you dropped off your plucky cherub in kindergarten? Remember how you cried, realizing that the only thing worse than them being upset at your leaving was them being *okay*? Remember how it felt to have your child *not* need you, how you took their growth as personal rejection? Well, you're doing it again. Time to rechannel your creativity. Find another chrysalis to nurture.

Children need to become adults and the only way they can become adults is if you stop being adults for them. They'll make all the stupid mistakes you did, and just like you, they will live. Support is key, but not too much. Too much support becomes the dreaded "enabling," sweeping us out of the Sweet Spot.

Enabling sounds like such a positive word, yes? I am "enabling" you. Sounds like I am giving you the ability to learn something in your Zone of Proximal Development, but really, enabling is the opposite. The term **enabling** refers to the act of hindering a person with a helpful act. I am doing it *for* you, so you won't have to do it. Why would I do that? "It" may cause you emotional stress: fear, anxiety, worry, depression, and anger. As your supporter, I like you and don't want you to suffer; therefore, if I know how to do the thing, I will.

I'll call you in the morning to wake you up. I'll deposit spending money in your bank account. I'll send you care packages. I'll do your homework. I'll email teachers and insist they raise your grade. I'll call your roommate's parents and tell them that *their* delinquent is smoking pot in the room, thereby putting my Precious Flower at risk. I'll fill out your FAFSA and file your taxes and make your travel arrangements and manage your grades and create Excel spreadsheets of all your current homework and regularly call or text you to make sure you're going to class and doing your homework and submitting it and taking tests and seeking professor's office hours and joining extracurricular activities and managing a part-time job and seeing a counselor and attending the Writing Center and Science and Math Support and checking in with your Resident Dean and taking your meds appropriately and refraining from drugs and illegal substances and leaving your dorm room to make socially positive friends and finding deep and meaningful ways to connect with your academic journey. Basically, I'll program your life and make all your decisions and you will ambivalently stumble along in the process, pretending to be involved.

Parents, I'm not telling you to abandon your children, but I am recommending you stop being them. Parents were raised on the phrase, "Never do for your children what they can do for themselves." Somewhere, we replaced that motto for a hyper-involved relationship with parenting. Parents expect to be all things to their children: parent, role model, disciplinarian and mentor, and now, best friend. Parents hate to see their best friend suffer and will do anything in their power to avoid this.

That's too bad. What they are forgetting is that the "suffering" is growth. We fall while learning to walk. We touch hot stoves, discovering stoves are dangerous. We fall in and out of love and friendships, understanding how emotions are temporary and malleable. Children need to develop a relationship to inconvenience and pain, as these experiences are vital cogs in the machinery of humanity. Suffering breeds so many lessons: wisdom, empathy, humility, tolerance, patience, and passion. Why would you want to deprive your child of these gifts?

In Eastern philosophies, suffering yields blessings and honor—to encounter difficult moments, confront them, and navigate through. Disequilibrium involves suffering, and it's empowering to realize we *can and do* overcome obstacles. This makes us stronger and able to tackle new challenges. Young adults are still acquiring thousands of details, in learning the art of adulthood. When we enable our children, we stunt their lives.

Baby Boomers became parents during the psychology boom and civil rights movements. Humanistic values pervaded. Children became the center of the family universe, and Boomers began to live through their kids. Boomers are great problem-solvers, and they readily solve their children's problems. Problem-solving, as we will learn in our next chapter, is a creative outlet and feels good. When parents solve their children's problems, Baby brain remains a baby. **As long as parents take care of you, you won't take care of yourself.**

Another cultural phenomenon presents added distress: older parents. People are having babies at an increasingly older age. Previous generations had children in their 20s. Parents now put off having kids until their late 30s and 40s. Some even dip their procreative toe in their 50s. People are having babies at the same age their parents became grandparents. One student's father was 89! Whoa.

My sons mirror this modern view of procreation. They want to have fun as long as they can and don't want the chore of parenting to burden their shot at a good career. Valid points to consider, but there are valid points in support of having children when we are younger. Older parenting brings a different vat of stress, with age-related diseases and early death (early in their children's lives). College graduations are beginning to show parents in their 60s and 70s. Grandparents die sooner in the child's life, previously a source of love, inspiration, and guidance. Parents are dying when young people are in their 20s—a critical time in executive function development. Now that parents are becoming older and older, they'll be dying off before Baby brain fully develops. How will that play out?

If people insist on waiting to have children, they better allow their children to quickly mature. But the opposite is occurring, and the consequences worsen. Since the parents act as Baby's EF, society is left with 30-year-olds dealing with developmental issues that should have been addressed at 18. In fact, this is likely the reason that we keep pushing the EF maturation age forward. You don't grow up until you have to. When 18-year-olds had children, they had to grow up, fast. If you put off having children until your mid-30s and 40s, you put off having to grow up, yourself. Prolonging a family serves parents, not children. It's ironic; modern parents will do anything for their children, except have them when they are young.

Enabling causes dysfunctional entrainment and incoherence. **The mother who texts several times a night to "make sure you are on track with your homework" actually knocks you off-track each time she interrupts your studying.** Each text interrupts your active working memory, splashing worry, anger, and guilt into your SBM. This cognitive interference and body disruption also wastes glucose, the prized brain food. Next time your mother "helps you stay on track," copy this paragraph and send it to her. Go on; I'll take the heat on this one.

TMI: Too Much Involvement

It could be a lot of things. Maybe it's because parents are waiting to have babies. Because they've waited so long to have babies, maybe they experience fertility issues. Because of these fertility issues, maybe gestation takes several years and involves costly treatments. Maybe parents turn to adoption, which also requires major feats of endurance, patience, and finance. Because parents are so much older and the procreating journey has been so arduous, maybe they have only one child. Maybe because they have had so much trouble procreating, the child becomes a symbol of parental adversity and triumph. So much effort has gone into the acquisition of this child that they become a valued treasure, a Precious Flower.

I acquired my children the old-fashioned way: out-of-wedlock, under the influence of alcohol, and against all better judgment. I actually conceived my children while actively trying *not* to get pregnant, with herbal birth control. I had them in my 20s, so now I have the energy to write books and will hopefully be alive long enough to see some grandchildren.

If you plan to wait until your 40s to have your babies, all I can say is, *illlch*. Talk to anyone who tries to have kids in their 40s. If they even *can* conceive, the raising of kids at that age is . . . *illlch*. Students, there are physiological reasons you're always so horny! That window of opportunity for childbirth bursts open in your late teens and remains wide open in the twenties. Every decade that window shuts a bit more. Physiology is always at odds with culture, and shucks if culture always wins. For some odd reason, **society chooses to honor lifestyle values over physiological needs. I am reminded of this every time I need to desperately pee in a lecture hall and, instead, politely sit there.** So much for the "intelligent species."

Much has been written about over-parenting, a.k.a., "**helicopter parents**": well-meaning parents who hover mercilessly over their child's every move. Sometimes, parenting goes even further, when a child is diagnosed with a learning disorder or health issue. "Black Hawk Down" parents are not only fastidious in their intervention, but aggressive in their advocating. On one hand, you cannot blame them. They worked very hard to acquire their children, only to discover their child developed impediments. If they've suffered through years of dealing with fertility challenges, they and their children are now faced with decades of academic challenges and are forced into the role of advocating. Too much adversity causes detrimental behavior changes in even the most well-meaning person. Still, to allow Black Hawk Down behavior is to enable the parents. **Parents must practice wise stress responses to their children's stressors.** While remaining present and available to offer suggestions, parents need to allow their child to do the actual solving.

Parents, when tempted to help solve your children's problems, ask yourselves:

- Is my child in danger or are they inconvenienced?
- If they are in danger, and you have the skills to help, intervene.
- If they are in danger and you do not have the skills to help, seek support.
- If they are inconvenienced, let them be.

If your son or daughter waits until the last minute to do a paper, let them receive an F. When they are inconvenienced, allow them this emotionally stimulating experience, and let them learn. Let them be inconvenienced, so that the next time a paper is assigned, they are motivated to seek help. If they are safe, let them feel a little threatened, and Baby brain will pay close attention, activating the stretch zone. When they live through the experience, they will arrive more humble on the other side. One day, they will lecture their own kids about how they overcame this difficult obstacle. They'll tell their story with pride.

Here's a helpful flow chart for parents and other supporters to navigate through the difficult and confusing terrain of empowerment:

IS MY CHILD IN DANGER
OR
IS HE/SHE INCONVENIENCED?

Help vs. *Help!*

From *American Red Cross Standard First Aid Workbook,* 1988–1992

You must first decide if the situation is safe for you.
You cannot help the victim by becoming a victim yourself. Know your abilities. If you cannot get to the victim because of extreme hazards, call EMS. In addition to sending medical care, the EMS dispatcher can contact other services needed to handle the specific life-threatening hazard.

Are you prepared? Know yourself, know your limitations, etc.

Before you act, you should consider certain aspects of giving first aid before you are confronted with a crisis. By thinking through these points ahead of time, you'll be able to move smoothly and effectively when your actions really count.

Be Realistic

Most people are intrigued by the idea of rescuing someone from an emergency—after all, giving emergency care can be very rewarding. We'd all like to believe that the rescuer is a hero and the grateful victim will live happily ever after.

The reality can be very different. The rescuer may find he or she can do very little to help, or the victim may be uncooperative, or the situation may be extremely upsetting, or your best attempts at first aid may fail. But if you are motivated by a concern for others, you'll always have the satisfaction of knowing that you did your best to help.

Know Yourself

Before helping someone, you need to know and understand yourself—your strengths and your limitations, both physical and emotional. How much can you push, carry, or drag? If you have physical problems—a bad back, for example—your efforts could make an emergency situation worse instead of better. If you have an excitable personality, you may worry that you'll panic in an emergency. In fact, you may find that you're stronger under pressure than you realize. Many people are, especially if they are helping a family member or friend.

To be truly effective, you need a sound understanding of yourself, if you recognize that you don't cope well with certain situations, you'll know when to turn over the rescuing to someone else.

On the other hand, you may find that if you pause, take a few deep breaths, and focus on what brings you strength—for example, your concern for another person—you are able to use your knowledge and skills when they are most needed.

Remember, there is one very important step you can take in any emergency: calling for help.

The First Aid Guide to Academic Success

Empowerment: Just Right

Empowerment allows the person to take care of himself. Using the Zone of Proximal Development, we support the person as they do that thing they want or need to do. We don't walk for them, but we may steady them as they falter. Then we guide them back up and let them try again. Empowerment is often more painful for the supporter than the student. Parents have to put our own suffering aside to let our children suffer. Ha, that came out a little oddly, but I think you get it.

We have to ignore our inner critic who hates to see our kid suffer and worries that every time they misspell a word or miss a goal or don't get invited to a party they will give up and take drugs and become homeless and die a horrible, miserable death. We may sit by them while they grieve, but we don't pick up the phone and insist the teacher give Joey an A on a C paper or insist the coach plays Joey when Joey stinks or insist that Joey invite Billy to the party when Joey clearly hates Billy. We may offer advice, but they have to live the experience. In summary, parents have to stop fixing every single problem in their kid's life.

Children require what Harvard professor Tal Ben-Shahar calls **"The Privilege of Hardship."** Adversity is not only a part of life, but a necessary one. Challenge and struggle are how we develop our soul's purpose. Crisis and tragedy transform us into who we are to become. These are integral to our being, but to Western perspectives, they are not seen that way. To Western perspectives, challenge wastes time, interfering with productivity. Suffering is pain to be avoided at all costs. In the slow-living slow-living movie *Fresh*, a farmer relates food production to something his Pakistani college roommate once said to him: **"Americans fear only one thing. Inconvenience."** Disequilibrium is inconvenience and requires the Privilege of Hardship.

Parents have the tools and skills to reduce and prevent suffering. "We have the money, so why wouldn't we share it with our children?" Western views are afraid of adversity, convinced it will break the Precious Flower's spirit; but life works the other way. At first they feel broken, but if encouraged to persist, they transform. **Parents often mistake problem solving for love, and in doing so, cripple their children.** If parents constantly hold the bicycle wheel, sure, their kid never suffers a scraped knee—but he also never learns to ride the bike.

The Privilege of Hardship is needed now, more than ever. Since parents are waiting much longer to have children, by the time these children graduate college, parents will be in their 60s, senior citizens beginning their descent into illness, dementia, and death. If parents are going to become sick and die when their children are in their mid-20s, parents better make sure their children have the skills to live independently.

Parents, remember your life? Remember all your hardships? We tell our stories with pride. We lived through them. We endured, and we are the better for it. Allow your children the same pride and growth. You let them learn to walk; now, let them learn to walk away. Give them the privilege of hardship. They will thank you for it. (Eventually.)

Empowerment: A How-To

If you're the parent, repeat as necessary:

1. I am not my child.
2. One day, I will die.
3. When I die, my child will need to know how to do basic life stuff that I always do for him.
4. If I stop doing these things for my child, he/she will be forced to learn them.
5. While my child learns them, things may become messy.
6. Just because things become messy doesn't mean my child will end up homeless and addicted to heroin.
7. When my child learns this basic life stuff, he/she becomes an adult.
8. When my child has children, he/she will know basic life stuff and be able to teach his/her own kids.
9. Then, I can die.

If you're the child, repeat as necessary:

1. I am not my parents.
2. One day, they will die.
3. When they die, I will need to know how to do basic life stuff that they always do for me.
4. If they stop doing these things for me, I will learn them.
5. While I learn them, things may become messy.
6. Just because things become messy doesn't mean I will end up homeless and addicted to heroin.
7. When I learn this basic life stuff, I will become an adult.
8. When I have children, I will know basic life stuff and be able to teach my own kids.
9. Then, I can die.

Academic Connection: The Advisor

Susan Vogel, an educational consultant, identified the key common factor contributing to college student retention: connection. Successful students found someone to whom they could confide in and be themselves—someone providing entrainment and coherence. Some savvier colleges train academic advisors for this reason, more than just someone to sign off on their registration. Students are expected to meet weekly with their academic advisors, an unheard of luxury, compared with other colleges. The advisor wears many hats: advisor, coach, counselor, educator, advocator . . . and yes, friend. The advisor is often the student's confidante. Advisors model problem solving through questions, listening, and empathy. They offer tutelage in Socratic methods, asking open-ended questions and allowing students opportunities to explore their own experiences and come to their own solutions.

Advisors model metacognition, prompting the student's executive function. This is done with guided questions: *What happened? What was your role (what could you control)? What do you need to let go of (what's out of your control)? What could you do differently, next time?* Advisors also help reflect on successful moments. *What would you continue to do, next time?* Advisors encourage students to face their fears and overcome obstacles, whether it be confronting a difficult roommate or scheduling an office hour appointment. Together, they create a plan of action that the student completes.

One advisor and my personal mentor, Kathy D'Alessio, offers a *carpe diem* attitude. She understands that when a student makes a plan to carry out later, it often doesn't happen. **"I'll do it later,"** **means, "I'll do it, never."** Kathy seizes the moment, saying, "Do it now." With her there for moral support, the student takes action and confronts the problem. Taking action may be so empowering, stress immediately reduces, and confidence returns.

On a more basic level, these colleges understand how sometimes a student doesn't have their *one confidante*, that one special person in their lives to whom they can tell anything and be themselves. Advisors do not guarantee that intimate connection, but they offer the opportunity, and, often, it does happen. Some graduation ceremonies feature student speeches, where they have the opportunity to address the community and give thanks. The majority of students thank their advisors as the primary person in their academic journey—their touchstone, go-to person . . . their connection. Kathy is often the last 30 seconds in the two minutes that her students share with the world.

Support also plays another role, less valued but equally vital: validation. When students are growing, they need encouragement—not false praise plastered on every single attempt, but genuine acknowledgment and celebration when growth happens. The following dialogue with a former student illustrates this type of support:

A Conversation with Crowther and former student, Julie

Julie

So when I was at college I had this friend named Kayla. We were roommates during that first semester when we were living in the dorms. During that time she treated me really crappy. She recently Facebook messaged and asked me why I haven't talked to her since she and I had left. I told her how and why she treated me really crappy. Kayla is bipolar and she told me that it was the bipolar and not the real her treating me really crappy. I think that she is using her bipolar as an excuse for the way she treated me. I feel like that was actually her. But that could just be me. . . . What do you think?

Crowther

I think your gut is accurate. Bipolar is not a "get out of jail free" card. It's a label to help people take control and guide them through their otherwise out-of-control behavior.

Listen from the gut, speak through your heart, honestly and kindly. Your honesty with her will help her see her own areas of growth. It may hurt doing it, but it's better in the long run—for both of your development. These kinds of dialogues are good practice to becoming a confident woman.

Good luck, be calm and centered, and let me know how it goes.

Julie

Thanks so much Crowther. Also, when I told her that she was using her bipolar as an excuse she told me that I was being ignorant and that I didn't know what bipolar is when I actually do know what it is. I tried to be honest with her after that but she just wouldn't listen. In the end we basically ended our communication with each other.

Crowther

Yes. And that's how you separate the friends from the lessons! Sounds like you're well on your way to trusting yourself in these moments! Atta girl! (It only took me 20 years longer than you!) xo

To reiterate, this was a former student whom I have not seen in years, but we still keep in touch. Support extends well beyond the classroom. "Once a student, always a student." I imagine many instructors practice this philosophy.

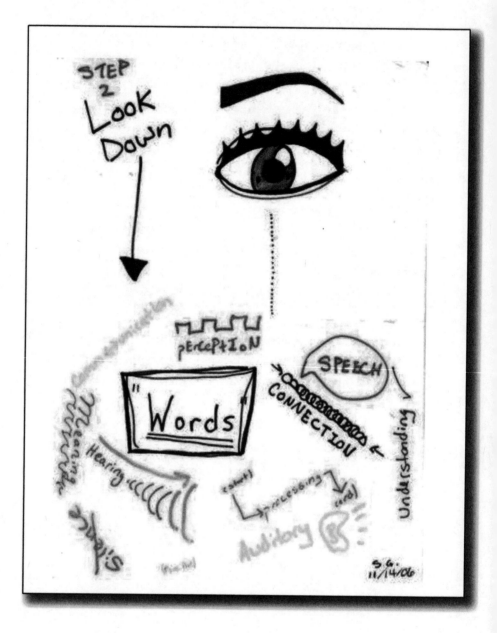

CREATE

"When you're in the studio painting, there are a lot of people in there with you. Your teachers, friends, painters from history, critics. . . . and one by one, if you're really painting, they walk out. And if you're really painting, you walk out."

—Audrey Flack, *Art & Soul*

"Go into the arts. I'm not kidding. The arts are not a way to make a living. They are a very human way of making life more bearable. Practicing an art, no matter how well or badly, is a way to make your soul grow, for heaven's sake.

Sing in the shower. Dance to the radio. Tell stories. Write a poem to a friend, even a lousy poem. Do it as well as you possibly can. You will get an enormous reward. You will have created something."

—Kurt Vonnegut

"You want to be a writer, don't know how or when? Find a quiet place, use a humble pen."

—Paul Simon

You are how you express.

Other than stress, food, movement, sleep, and connection, the most important lifestyle factor to one's academic success is creativity.

What on earth does creativity have to do with academic success? Okay, besides what crunchy granola hippie progressive teachers say— we need creativity to free our soul's release into the sacred universe— why does creativity warrant an entire chapter in terms of improving academic performance? Be creative; take a guess.

Let's review a few things. First, college is tough. It is volatile and arduous. College is filled with allostatic and catastrophic, chronic and acute stressors. It is boring and long-lasting. When we encounter something volatile, arduous, stressful, or boring—in other words, *tough*—we express. Volatile things make us angry. Arduous things make us frustrated. Stressful things make us anxious. Boring things make us bored. We release these difficult emotions through expression, and we feel better, returning to balance. Facebook is so popular because it is an easy way to express emotions.

Creativity is Intelligent Output

So far with our lifestyles, we are "inputting": information is received, perceived, processed, encoded, and stored, then recalled for later use. Creation is our "later use," the way we utilize our life experiences. Creation is the way that we "output" into our worlds. We "output" in how we view the world and what we do in the world. For our purposes, we will define "creation" in two ways:

1. Divergent perspectives
2. Output of experiences

Creativity may be defined as intelligence, which is the act of problem solving and adapting to one's environment.

Creativity redefines our views of intelligence. Howard Gardner burst the IQ bubble when he introduced the concept of Multiple Intelligences: humans may be "smart" in ways other than thinking and reasoning. Daniel Goleman popularized the theory of Emotional Intelligence, which is how to navigate through life emotionally, or applying the definition of intelligence, how emotions help us adapt to our environment and solve problems.

My elder son earned straight As in high school. I ranked ninth in my graduating class. At 12 years, I marveled at my 164 IQ, and my son's is probably higher; yet, we both flunked out of college. Clearly, our Intelligent Quotients did not guarantee success.

What *does* create happy and successful people? Creativity is key, tempered with wisdom. Wise, creative people get things done. They know how to succeed when things are tough. They use what they have to get what they want. They know how to recognize good opportunities, and they are courageous in taking chances. They understand when to face difficulties head on and when to seek support. They take time for celebration and pleasure.

As a chef and educator, I've encountered dozens of barely literate young adults who managed to graduate high school. How did they do it? Honing interpersonal skill, they charmed their way through. Hey, I'm not ripping on them; they freely admit to it. These struggling young adults were likeable, and they used their emotional intelligence to navigate the terrain of parents and educators. This is not a bad thing, but a *creative* thing. They used creativity to adapt to their environment (high school) and solve the problem (graduation).

Creativity is the ability to shift perspectives, to reframe a distress into a eustress. It is the ability to see the positive lesson in a crappy experience, to help develop an **internal locus of control**, which is to take ownership for how we may change the situation. Creativity makes lemonade out of those lemons, then figures out how to sell the beverage at a tasty profit.

Creativity allows us to solve the same problem in many different ways, what author Malcolm Gladwell describes as divergent thinkers. Students diagnosed with ADHD are often judged as being "random," but random suggests divergent thinking—understanding that problems have multiple solutions and questions have multiple answers. Schools often emphasize learning focused on identifying a single correct answer, but life's problems require more divergent approaches.

Divergent thinking does not apply to all experiences. Students who find divergent ways to succeed in one area are unable to see other things. I failed at Bryn Mawr because I could not see a way to solve the problem of identifying what an essay was. We all suffer blind spots, victims of convergent or one-way thinking. Students know one way to write a paper or read a book, one place to study, one way to "be" in a class, handle a teacher or difficult roommate, etc. When their one way fails, they become stuck. They may shut down, and this leads to the crippling behavior, learned helplessness, a warped version of the "My Way or the Highway" philosophy. They cannot succeed their way; therefore, they fail. The Cognitive Belief System suffers an autoimmune disease, turning on itself and attacking one's confidence, motivation, and abilities. Our perceptions become our own worst enemies.

Academia has a funny relationship with creativity. Once a pillar for intellectual pursuit, the institution begrudgingly concedes that humans do not live on logic alone. Man is a beast who naturally feels emotion and seeks connection. Therefore, these factors must be part of an intellectual pursuit. **Academics espouse critical thinking, which absolutely relies on the creative process: challenge ideas, see divergent perspectives, discover gaps, identify flaws, and improve situations. In this sense, creativity and critical thinking are the same.** Creativity is the expression of the whole person; therefore, creativity is key for developing the whole person, which is the objective in today's college experience.

Creativity is also vital in an academic setting for decision-making. We often rely on intuitive messages to guide us through life. Intuitive messages enter our energetic fields through the collective spirit to the soul. They are felt in our bodies and then interpreted in our minds. This may sound *foo foo,* but ask anyone if they have ever experienced an intuitive moment in their lives. They will smile, *yes,* with a sweet glint in their eyes. We love sharing our intuitive experiences and they connect us, universally.

Creativity is the language of intuition, because it is non-judgmental. Baby brain is gently hushed while information enters. We suspend rational thought while we accept intuitive messages; otherwise, we would discount them. When you speak with people about how listening to their intuition affected them, typically their experience resulted in a beneficial outcome. Because disequilibrium stresses cognition, the soul needs help seeing through the difficult moments. Consider intuition another supporter, helping you grow.

I explore intuition in depth, in an upcoming book. For now, let us entertain the idea that intuition is important in decision-making and problem solving, and the way we receive intuitive messages is through creativity.

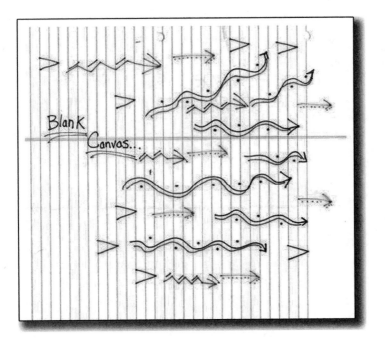

Visual Journaling: SBM + ART

Creativity is the output of experience, playing with innate talents. Creativity is two-fold: navigating your outer world and expressing your inner world. It's about surviving what life slings your way and about slinging what you want back into life!

Barbara Ganim, co-founder of the Expressive and Creative Arts programs with Susan Fox at Salve Regina University, uses the acronym ART to describe art: Access, Release, and Transform. When we allow ourselves to hear the language of art, we begin to hear our authentic voices. Art is our primal language.

In westernized societies, the order got reversed. Cognition received all the credit for knowing, when actually, Baby brain is merely our stenographer, recording what our souls and bodies have just experienced. Thinking is not experiencing; it is documenting and analyzing. Creativity, on the other hand, is experiencing. Creativity embraces the primal languages of emotion, body sensations, energetic fields, and intuitive messages. It uses all this information to create things. That's why creativity is often judged as being weird or unnecessary; it does not rely on rational thought, so it threatens our social boundaries of what is acceptable. But, that is also why creativity is so crucial to our survival. Without it, we spend our lives fondling information and following flocks, living more like computers and lambs than humans.

College is so intellectual and mind-based, it is healthful to balance these mind experiences with soul and body expression. The images in this chapter are examples of **Visual Journaling**, an expressive arts technique taught by Ms. Ganim, co-author of *Visual Journaling* with Susan Fox. Visual Journaling illustrates both output of experience and divergent thinking. It uses bilateral or whole-brain processing. Image is an effective way to activate our affective and conative domains. Visual Journaling is a simple and fun way to communicate with the soul and subconscious, tapping into our intuitive pathways.

The images represented throughout this chapter were created by one of my students, the dear Sara Goldsmith. She took to Visual Journaling with a natural vigor, delighting both our sensibilities. The following two images represent the personal energetic field. Sara noticed sensations and represented them. Visual Journaling does not require artistic talent, per se; rather, it is about accessing and releasing in order to free ourselves of energetic blocks and challenges. (Although, I happen to think her images are uber-cool.)

The great thing about Visual Journaling is how approachable it is. You can do it anywhere! I've *VJed* in airports, bank lines, and sons' baseball games (zzzz). It's a fun way to blow off steam anywhere, and if people see you do it, it makes a great conversation starter.

Visual Journaling Instructions

It's your turn. Take a risk and try Visual Journaling!

Grab something to draw with. Color is great, if you have a few markers, crayons, etc.

Settle into a comfy chair. Breathe deeply.

Ask yourself, "How am I?"

As you breathe deeply, feel the answer in your body.

It will arrive as a sensation or seem like a movement, a swirling or wave. Be still and open, and you'll notice it.

Begin to transfer the body movement onto the paper, representing the shape. As you do, keep asking yourself, "How am I?" Let the answer guide your drawing.

The movement on the paper may start to take a shape, as you begin to see things in your mind's eye.

An image or shape may appear. Just keep drawing movement or images, whatever comes out.

When you feel done, be done.

Sit back and reflect on the image. What's the message? Be open, and you may surprise yourself with what you discover.

VISUAL JOURNAL ACTIVITY: HOW ARE YOU?

Creativity or Procrastination?

Ask any wildly successful person how they arrived; you will find a creative piece to their puzzle. Conversely, ask someone who is unhappy or unsuccessful how they arrived there. They often respond with some kind of variation on, "My soul has been suppressed." People devoid of creative outlets lead lives of quiet desperation, as Thoreau lamented.

I don't know why I write. The money is drivel, the time commitment is enormous, and the publishing world is dying. I began my professional career as a writer at the age of 50, when every neuron and body part suffers sagging and decay. It's ridiculous. There remains no rational reason to continue writing. But, I write. It's what I do. If someone gave me one million dollars today and I never had to work another day, the next day I would wake up and write. **What is it that you feel driven or compelled to do?** What do you do that makes you feel like you? After you do it, do you feel more alive and calm, more complete and centered?

Happiness researcher Mihaly Csikszentmihalyi coined the concept of "**flow**"—when we're in that connected zone and disappear into creation. Cooking also plays a role in my flow. I am me, when practicing health: foraging wild mushrooms, making herbal teas, giving a massage, and writing about health topics. Writing, Cooking, Health . . . these are my flow. What about *you*? How do you flow? Discover those things.

Be careful about the word "love" when identifying creative outlets. Popular self-help books embrace the advice to *"Do what you love and the money will follow."* I'd like to gently challenge this concept. One's creative outlets are less about love and more about volition. **Creativity resides in the conative domain, while love is ruled by the affective domain.** What I *love* to do is sit on my ass, watching chick flicks and binge-watching *Parks and Recreation*. What I *desire* to do is write.

To be clear, creativity is *not* procrastination. I'm talking about the things we are *called to do.* Writing is something I am called to do, even though I often don't want to do it. **It's the output that compels me: the only thing worse than writing is not writing.** It's odd, but most people understand what I'm talking about. Once I begin writing, I fall into that "me-ness."

Differentiate between your creativity and your procrastination. Creativity is expression and procrastination is avoidance. Playing video games instead of doing homework is not being creative; it is avoiding work you should be doing. I love health, but reading about health is not creativity. Creativity isn't input, it's *output*. Creativity is your vocation, how you express your conative domain. There is a critical difference, sometimes between life and death.

You might counter, "When I'm playing video games, I'm solving problems and adapting to my environment." I'll give you that. You are thinking divergently in order to win the video game, but you are not creating. If you play video games to avoid a problem, it is a negative coping strategy for stress. If you play video games to avoid schoolwork, it is procrastination. If you repeatedly play video games to avoid your work or deal with the stressor and are unable to stop, then it is an addiction. Creation is a contribution, while addiction is a distraction. Creating gives; addiction takes. Be honest with yourself.

Creation has been compared to conceiving a child. We don't know the exact moment of conception. You cannot control most aspects of the gestation. It will arrive on its own time. Sometimes it keeps you up all night. Sometimes it demands your time, taking priority over everything else, including eating and sleeping. When editing this book, I often forgot to brush my teeth until dinner time, but by end of the day, when I completed twenty pages of writing, I created. And, I slept well.

We must complete our creative endeavors, but not haphazardly. We must complete them, completely. This is an extraordinarily difficult thing to do, and it is why creativity is so integral to our wellbeing.

Jim

In a recent conversation, Jim Fallone, a mentor in the publishing field, offered one key piece of advice for creative projects: complete them.

The best thing you can to is complete it. "It" can suck, be utter crap, but just complete it. Once you get it done, you can go back and fix and tweak it. The number of unfinished novels compared to the amount of published work is astronomical. Complete it and then it will get found. If it needs to get found, it will get found. That's really the main thing. Everything else starts to fall into place. The thing you create, once it's complete, starts to take a life of its own—it has a personality, it's almost like having child. Every revision, every tweak starts to make sense in its own organic way.

Creativity is the most intimate pursuit in the Privilege of Hardship.

Self-expression is using whatever is in *you*—your unique compilation of thoughts, feelings, experiences, beliefs, and interpretations. You will therefore be able to problem solve and adapt to your environment in ways only you on this planet at this time in history are able to do. This is not only creativity, but also destiny.

Art Makes You Smart

Create Balance

The body reacts to stress in polarized ways, regulated by the **parasympathetic** and **sympathetic** systems. I could never distinguish between the two, until I came across a mnemonic from Dr. Morter. He says that we *Power down with parasympathetic* and *Speed up* *with sympathetic.* That clinched it for my hippocampus. People tend to have default systems for stress response. Some speed up, while others power down.

Ever notice how some people seem more relaxed during stressful times? In fact, they seem almost absurdly under-reactive? You thwack their heads like a microphone, saying "Hello, hello? Is this thing *on?*" They are experiencing high levels of parasympathetic intervention. The parasympathetic system powers us down, lowering blood pressure, increasing blood flow to the inner organs, and decreasing attention. The parasympathetic system aids in digestion. We need the parasympathetic system to activate after eating, but if you are under intense stress and your *sympathetic* system activates, it will draw blood away from the digestive system to the limbs, to prepare for battle. High stress levels often manifest in digestive disorders, diarrhea, and constipation.

You've met people who gravitate toward the sympathetic response. Their default mode is stuck in *fight or flight.* (Most of these people live in New Jersey. Kidding. Of course.) These are "fly off the handle" types who overreact to any situation. In sympathetic response, aggressive stress hormones flood the system, and you feel a rush of emotions and sensations. You are ready to pounce: heart races and blood vessels dilate with a rush of blood, sugar, and oxygen, turbo-charged; lungs open widely, gathering great gulps of air. The sympathetic system causes a government shutdown. All non-essential areas are temporarily constricted: digestion, hair, skin, and nails.

Too much of a good thing in either direction works against us. We want to remain in our Sweet Spot, somewhat activated and ready to handle stress, but after the stress is over, we need to be able to relax and carry on regular bodily functions. Creativity stimulates the parasympathetic system, relaxing SBM, and also invigorates the sympathetic system, offering attentive focus.

To understand the effect of creativity on cognition, we need a basic understanding of how minds run. Researchers from the HeartMath Institute and other progressive mind-body organizations have conducted some pretty amazing work in supporting creativity, exploring our four brain states: Beta, Alpha, Theta, and Delta. You may remember Delta stage from sleep. One stage we do not experience during waking states is REM, thankfully; otherwise, we would all be certified schizophrenics.

Beta: The Panic Zone

Beta is our most alert state. It's fifth gear, high-octane, crazybusy. Beta waves control alertness, concentration, and cognition. It narrows focus. When driving in traffic during an ice storm, your mind is in Beta. It is highly-aroused thinking, helping us during cramming sessions and test-taking. We need Beta waves for simple, mundane tasks, like doing laundry and in academics, when things seem easy or irrelevant. *"What does this have to do with my major?"* is the common lament to what students perceive as busy work. Mr. Miyagi's *Wax on, Wax off* chores are easy cognitively, but difficult affectively and conatively. The assignments themselves make sense, but doing them makes no sense. *What's the point?* Beta brain is there to save the day, allowing us to hyper-focus and power through that resistance. Even the act of dealing with a cantankerous parent uses Beta waves to supply the extra boost of glucose needed to deal with Mom's tantrums. We tend to put boring or hard tasks off until the last minute, then rely on Beta to get the job done. Beta may be great for getting the job done, but not so great with problem solving or creative thought. When riding in a car at high speeds, you can't see the landscape. **In Beta mode, you miss the situational landscape, because you are going too fast.**

Due to the rush of exciting hormones, Beta can become addicting; observe drama queens or chronically anxious folk. Many people prefer keeping busy to avoid resolving issues. People often become neurotically stuck in Beta—story fondling, obsessing, and doing anything but dealing with a problem. That's unfortunate, because Beta junkies are missing out. As soon as the problem is dealt with, our minds may relax and ease into delicious Alpha.

225

Alpha: The Stretch Zone

Aah, divine Alpha: calm, centered balance. Alpha states ignite relaxation, creativity, and awareness. The way to reach Alpha is through the breath. When we breathe, we activate the relaxation response, and begin to slow our Beta waves. Alpha regulates the vagus nerve, our main nerve highway of the nervous systems, which has a profound effect in keeping the body's energy traffic flowing. Heartbeat and pulse slow down, muscles relax, and stress fades. Then, our minds begin to clear.

In Alpha, our minds expand their focus, literally; visual capacity diffuses, increasing peripheral vision and allowing us to see a wider view of a situation. **Alpha states are where problem solving occurs, because we are moving slowly enough to see the problem, and we are relaxed enough to hear the solution.** While Beta executes the solution, Alpha discovers it. An episode in the television series *Scrubs* illustrates these two states. The low-key JD is the better doctor, but somehow neurotic Elliot is better able to handle highly stressful medical situations. JD hounds Elliot until she finally reveals her secret. It's quite simple, actually. Elliot takes a deep breath. Things slow down around her, and she can see again. Elliot, through deep breaths, reconfigures her brain activity from Beta to Alpha. She retains her cool, and can now see the situation presenting.

Alpha state is necessary for working our stretch zone: learn new tasks, challenge ourselves, and lean into problems. Alpha is also key for more complex tasks, where a steady hand and centered disposition are needed. It's great for solving puzzles and improves divergent thinking. Lower arousal is also good for things that are easy and automated, when they are enjoyable—art, PE, reading, classroom discussion—anything that comes naturally.

Alpha state is flow state, when we are in the zone. Alpha waves are slower, calmer, centered, akin to walking on the road—able to see more clearly. When you turn the sound down, you can hear more clearly; therefore, Alpha is the state for analyzing a situation and understanding

your intuition. People may think of Beta as the college mode, but really, Alpha states create more successful students, overall. College students need to be able to shift into Beta mode, while residing in Alpha.

Theta: The Comfort Zone

We interpret intuition in Alpha, but we receive it in Theta. Theta state is where we receive the solutions to problems that we understand through Alpha and then execute in Beta. Theta is vital to creativity, as it listens to the spirit world, bypassing your rational brain, who judges you for wasting time being creative. **If Beta is the speeding car and Alpha is the slow walk, Theta is sitting quietly by the river, taking in the whole world.** Shamans consider Theta to be where magical awakening occurs. Theta is the fugue state, when we are lucid yet not fully aware. Theta waves are not quite asleep, but you don't want to be operating heavy machinery.

Theta waves fully activate the parasympathetic system. It is a very comforting and therapeutic state. When we sink into our procrastinations, we dip into Theta. Because it feels so relaxing and restorative, some people become quite dependent upon it, never reaching into their stretch zones, denying their potential. A little Theta can go a long way, and we have to respect its restorative powers.

Delta: The Resting Zone

Delta is the time to regenerate, the healing state. Delta is our resting zone, free of challenge, growth, and transformation. No intuitive insight, no creativity . . . but Delta is vital to both. Since creativity can be an outlet for emotional distress, keeping well-rested will free

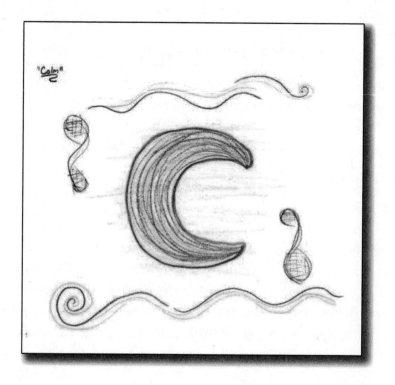

up creativity to be what it is truly meant to be: an outlet for your own personal experiences, versus your internal psychotherapist and primary caregiver.

A creative person sleeps better and a well-rested person creates better. It's true that creativity will often consume us, like raising a newborn, and that may mean temporarily depriving us of sleep (or brushing our teeth). But like any caregiver, it's vital to stay healthy, or else the caregiver needs care! Honor creative bursts as short-term periods that must be balanced with long-term Delta renewal.

Marginalized Students & Troubled Teens

My first year of teaching was at a middle-high school in a rural Vermont town. With a background in health sciences and culinary arts, I wore several hats: teacher of health, family consumer science, and electives like cooking and sewing (I didn't know how to sew, but that's another story). Teaching electives allowed me to observe something that I encountered time and time again: **students with academic issues often thrive in creative classes**.

Isaac

Isaac comes to mind. What a pain in the ass. In health class, Isaac fidgeted, poked his neighbors, blurted out stupid jokes, and ignored homework. When he signed up for cooking, I considered quitting. Ignorance is bliss, but money is money, so I showed up the next day with an open mind and clenched jaw.

The story turns out as you might imagine: Isaac was my knight in stainless steel armor. He took to cooking like a nerd takes to physics. Isaac possessed exceptional spatial skills, able to multi-task cooking's many steps and working deftly around other students. He intuitively placed utensils in a left-to-right flow, to avoid crossing his

> hands. Isaac came to life in the kitchen, navigating his terrain. I will always remember this and thank him for challenging my convergent thinking about all those "troubled" students we encounter.
>
> In college, I often encounter this discrepancy. During study abroad programs, the students who struggled with verbal-auditory-based assignments would flourish in experiential assignments, such as service learning activities. In Habitat for Humanity and Rescue Centers, students found themselves nourishing their tactile senses, interacting with buildings, monkeys, and snakes. They applied interpersonal intelligence to the social challenges of communicating effectively with host families who did not share a common verbal language (lots of pointing, hand gestures, and laughing involved). Despite no language, they became role models to young children.

Art makes you smart, when we define intelligence as problem solving and adapting to one's environment. Art changes brain plasticity, which improves general neural function and increases cognitive function. Temple Grandin says, "As language gets wrecked, art comes out." Art creates a healthy cycle, allowing students a way to express information, which then helps them regain the ability to think and reason, cognitively. Art is a spiritual reboot of our systems. For many years, practicing art has been correlated with enhancing intelligence.

Art reaches the fringe, students who are otherwise dismissed. Often, the arts are the primary reason that fringe students persist in school. An engaged student is a better student. When more students are reached, disciplinary issues are reduced. Arts provide a community and sense of belonging, a sense of purpose and self.

Because students learn differently or divergently, we need divergent teaching. It's not just for the students' benefits. Teaching something is the best way to retain information. We'll explore this in the Giving chapter. When a teacher is encouraged to teach the same material in different ways, she learns the information much more fully.

Art Makes You Smart!

- Students who took arts classes had higher math, verbal, and composite SAT scores than students who did not take arts classes.
- SAT scores increased linearly with the addition of more years of arts classes, that is, the more years of arts classes, the higher the SAT scores.
- The strongest relationship with SAT scores was found with students who took four or more years of arts classes.
- Acting classes had the strongest correlation with verbal SAT scores. Acting classes and music history, theory, or appreciation had the strongest relationship with math SAT scores.
- All classifications of arts classes were found to have significant relationships with both verbal and math SAT scores.

(Vaughn & Winner, 2000)

Music and the God Spot

God resides in our brain. How does God reside in our brain, you may ask? (My two atheist sons will definitely ask.) When research subjects are asked to "summon God"—pray, chant, send loving kindness, or describe a time when they helped someone—a small area located in the upper right temporal (side) lobe lights up. It's been coined, "**The God Spot.**" The God Spot is also the place where we process music and emotions.

It's no coincidence that teens explode with a passion for music at a time when they are exploding emotionally and spiritually. Emotions *are* explosive in the teen world, new and untethered. Listening to music is a positive coping strategy and creating music, singing or playing, is a creative outlet. Music is the teenager's way to God, a portal for solace. Music lifts us outside of ourselves; we are a song away from being connected.

The teen years are also the time when a mind explodes with divergence. Cognitively, the mind begins to grasp metaphorical and abstract thinking—something could be like something else or that something could have many meanings. Concrete thinking refers to a literal object, universally described. Concrete thinking sees things as black and white, while abstract thinking considers 50 shades of grey.

One way I illustrate the difference between concrete and abstract is to have students close their eyes and picture an apple. Next, I ask them to picture a banana, and after that, maybe a pencil. Then, I ask them to picture balance. I give them a few minutes with this one. After some time, I'll ask a few students to describe what they imagined when they pictured balance. The images may be similar in quality, but they are different. Every student imagined their own situation, based on their unique perception and Cognitive Belief System. Granted, there may be 50 shades of apple (especially in Vermont), but an apple is basically an apple, banana's banana and pencil, pencil. When we imagine balance, love, or respect, we engage in the abstract. There are as many interpretations and situations as there are opinions.

Life gets confusing when we begin thinking abstractly. Suddenly, life is not right and wrong. Suddenly, you have a soul, body, and mind of your own, distinct from your parents and family. You realize you are, ultimately, on your own. These shifts are chaotic and catastrophic. Teenagers need help, and receiving help may be a life or death matter.

Because music affects SBM, it affects our health. Music calms us. When Mama and Baby are calm, Papa also calms down, relaxing basic bodily functions. Notice how immediately music affects you. When you listen to loud rock, you pump up. When you listen to sweet classical music, you soften. Music directly alters physiological functions in both the sympathetic and parasympathetic systems: changing heart rate, breathing, blood pressure, and even pain tolerance. It alters our perception, thereby manipulating stress. Music affects blood and

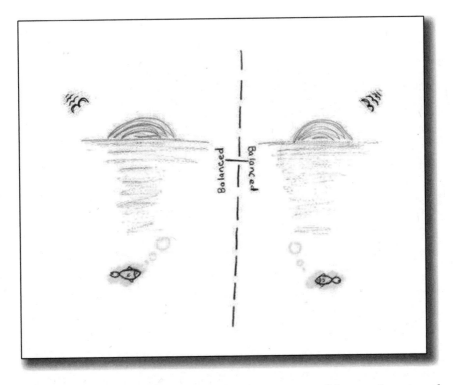

neurological currents, lowering blood pressure and improving neural strength, tickling the brain. Remember the cerebellum, who drove you home when you were drunk? (Of course you don't; how could you?) Music stimulates the cerebellum and improves coordination, including coordinated academic skills of reading, writing, and speaking.

Music's energy waves influence our energetic fields. It's been shown to relieve stress, process trauma, and reduce pain. It's used in massage to increase efficacy. Music is played in doctors' offices to allay fear and tension. Musical research has moved into more clinical areas, exploring its effects on treatment of neurological diseases and sensory impairments. Stroke patients unable to speak and people who stutter may be able to sing. Speech therapists use music's neurological pathways to retrain the speech centers of the brain. Music is a language detour, while the highways are repairing.

In a society that increasingly disassociates from religion, our souls crave an outlet for connection. For young adults, that outlet is often creativity—music and art. What do parents do? Admonish kids to "turn down that noise" and to "dress like a real person." Music, dress, art, even piercing and tattoos are creative expressions allowing the young adult to mature. (Just keep the tattoos off the face. No one needs to be *that* mature.)

* * *

We are at the threshold of understanding creativity and its role in promoting academic success. In reductionist organizations, we compartmentalize information and relegate creativity to the art class. In a 120-credit college program, students are typically required to earn only three credits of "creativity." *Go be creative, there. Then, return to your core classes and get to work.*

Creativity extends way beyond that sentiment and needs to be part of every course objective, practiced as naturally as critical thinking. For instance, summary and response papers are both logical and creative. Summaries are important; understanding the essence of something is helpful in communicating a message. However, the response is personal, where you enter the assignment. In order to respond to something, you have to see it from your point of view, which is a creative or divergent perspective from the convergent or author's point of view.

Creativity allows us to live with the crisis of college, beyond its campus. College students face external situations out of their control: parents moving and divorcing, grandparents and family pets dying, and best friends transitioning into their own lives. Money is a chronic stressor. Students juggle their already full schedules with part-time jobs and work study. **Creativity allows you to express distress and in doing so, releases the crisis.** Once the stress is outside, you may experience it objectively. We control it, instead of it controlling us.

Why do college students like to drink alcohol and smoke pot so much? These substances calm the frontal lobe and relax the intellect.

As one student says, "It makes the painful and uncomfortable things . . . tolerable." Being in college is a struggle for most students. I don't know if I've ever met anyone who embraces every class, assignment, and exam with unbridled joy. Everybody hates college at least just a little, and for that, there is creativity. If students are denied creative expression, they find release elsewhere.

CONTROL

"An over-indulgence of anything, even something as pure as water, can intoxicate."

—Criss Jami, *Venus in Arms*

"Every form of addiction is bad, no matter whether the narcotic be alcohol or morphine or idealism."

—Carl Jung, *Memories, Dreams, Reflections*

"Invisible threads are the strongest ties."

—Friedrich Nietzsche

"If someone jumps into shark-infested waters... you can't jump in after them."

—Prison guard Sam Healy, *Orange Is the New Black*

You are what you do.

Other than stress, food, movement, sleep, connection, and creativity, the most important lifestyle factor to one's academic success is control.

Our focus of control is addictions. Addictions go beyond affecting SBM; they obliterate the self. Addictions are coping strategies gone wild. Where a strategy may have initially reduced stress and enhanced health, the addiction now enhances stress and reduces health.

What are addictions? **Addictions** are behaviors people do repeatedly that result in problems in one or more major areas of their lives. How do you know you are addicted? It boils down to three things: response, repetition, and result. Stress management involves managing responses to stimuli. Addiction's response to stress is to anesthetize. The stimulus remains and we continue to ignore it, responding instead with the numbing behavior. This addictive response becomes automated, like other procedures. The cerebellum takes over and coordinates this behavior without your attention or control. Baby brain is completely removed from managing the addictive experience. People who have overcome addictions often have few memories of the addictive time. The addictive period is one giant black out.

Addictions tend to be considered substance-specific, but addiction can involve *anything* you (or those who observe you) perceive as a negative influence. From *Invitation to Holistic Health* (Charlotte Eliopoulos, 2009):

> The repetitious behaviors that constitute an addiction include misuse, overuse, and abuse of alcohol, food, work, sex, shopping, smoking, money, internet, power, relationships, exercise, drugs (prescription, nonprescription, and "street" drugs), and collections of "stuff."

Feel free to add your own personal substances, items, and behaviors. I would certainly include screens: television, computers, phones, tablets, video games, and the number one addiction in contemporary culture, social media.

Sources vary, stating 10–20 percent of all people suffer from addiction. I would contest that everybody is addicted to *something*. Since addiction is defined by the inability to control a behavior resulting in a negative effect on our SBM, we all have at least one area in our lives fitting that criteria. You don't need to change anything at this moment, but at least be honest with yourself. Take a moment. Sit back. Take a deep breath, slowly release, then ask yourself: *What do I do repeatedly, that I am unable to stop, and that feeds my procrastination?* Listen with your gut; it never lies.

***

What defines "a negative influence?" In terms of psychonutrients, **a positive coping strategy encourages creativity, while a negative influence encourages procrastination.** If the behavior interrupts your goals, erodes your potential, and you are unable to stop (or recognize this), chances are you're addicted.

Addictions are personalized: what may be addicting to one person may be totally innocuous to another. Your roommate may stay up all night playing video games and sleeping all day. You may think, "*Why doesn't he just turn off the computer at 1:00 a.m., go to bed, and then play again tomorrow?*" The "why" is the addiction, a madness that discriminates. Addiction may be anything, so may be difficult to recognize and more difficult to confront through the lens of judgment. "*Why don't they just stop?*" the observer wonders, shaking her head. In judgment, we abandon, and the addict loses support.

Addiction is sometimes abstract and obscure. Defining addiction as a negative repeated response to a stimulus could be a lot of things. We may be addicted to certain defense mechanisms. Do you crack a joke or change the subject to avoid a difficult situation? Humor

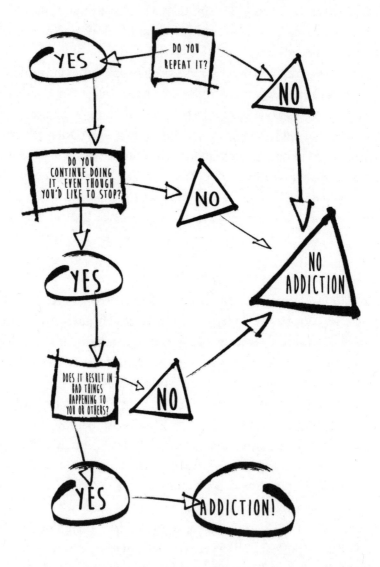

IS THIS BEHAVIOR AN ADDICTION?

and deflection addiction. Are you the door mat in your relationships, always saying yes and putting others before yourself? Approval addiction. Do you avoid doing things you dislike? Procrastination is the hallmark academic addiction.

Sometimes life decisions prompt addictive behavior. Take college, for instance. You want to be in college, but you are struggling. The work is difficult and your roommate is even more difficult. A positive coping strategy would help you to succeed, while the negative coping strategy would make these difficult issues become unmanageable. On the other hand, maybe you do *not* want to be in college. Your SBM fights against it, but your parents are devoted to the belief that college equates with happiness and proper child-raising, so, here you are. Being off our paths and in others' control can be so painful to our souls, it prompts addictions. **When students are failing at college, they are often succeeding in addiction.**

People are willing to die for their addictions. Hundreds of thousands of drivers die while texting—more deaths than alcohol-related vehicular accidents and heart attacks, combined.

Texting While Driving Causes:

1. 1,600,000 accidents per year (National Safety Council)
2. 330,000 injuries per year (Harvard Center for Risk Analysis Study)
3. 11 teen deaths *every day* (Ins. Institute for Hwy Safety Fatality Facts)
4. Nearly 25% of *all* car accidents (www.textinganddrivingsafety.com/ texting-and-driving-stats)

Do these facts stop people? Are you kidding? I text while driving and recently nearly smashed into a tree. When they pull my dead body out of the car with the Jaws of Life, they'll find a phone in my hand. My last message on earth will be a text addressed to my son declaring, "Your butt smells." Social recognition—the act of being witnessed—is one of the most primal of all human desires. When

Papa brain is addicted, nothing stops him. The desire to be seen is stronger than life itself. No offense to Mark Zuckerberg, but that dude caused over half a billion addictions and counting. **Facebook's motto should be, "Always addicting and always will be."**

Baby, Drugs, and Rock and Roll

Contemporary health books discuss specific "psychoactive" substances in detail. For our purposes—exploring how lifestyle factors affect academic performance—we are going to review drugs in one great big pile. Certainly they affect the SBM in different ways, but the point is that they *affect*. Drugs are **psychoactive**; they play an "active" role on our "psycho" or mental function. Many drugs are synthetically manufactured, but our bodies are the largest producing pharmaceutical plants. We produce all the chemicals necessary to conduct basic life functions.

The word "drug" originates from the verb *drogge,* meaning, "to dry." The first synthetic drugs were derived from animal sources and foodstuffs, especially herbs and spices. All food contains nutrients, which affect and alter the body chemistry. Food is medicine, so the healthiest way to medicate is to eat healthy foods: garlic, onion, turmeric, parsley, cranberry, etc.

Eating foods that FARE WELL—fresh, ripe, whole, and local—maintains balance during normal times. When we are knocked off balance, we need stronger doses to intervene and heal. One way is to eat the most nutrient-dense foods, but sometimes we turn to more potent measures. Food, herbs, and spices are harvested and dried, then made into different preparations: juices, teas, tinctures, poultices, and capsules.

This strategy worked pretty well for a few thousand years, but not quickly enough for westernized lifestyles. Modern science accelerated healing, providing a slew of medicines that isolate and concentrate the active ingredients from foods. Valium comes from the herb Valerian; Aspirin is derived from White Willow bark, and magical Penicillin was first discovered from the humble cantaloupe mold. *Feel better, faster.* The problem with medicine is the problem with anything concentrated; it's supersized, more for the body to deal with all at once.

Imagine going to a rock concert every day. You think that would be fun. Every single day you have to get all punked out and spend $20 driving 90 minutes to the arena and spend 30 minutes finding a parking space and pay $25 to park and walk a mile to get to the entrance and hand them your $89 ticket and blow $47 on snacks and merchandise. Then, the concert begins, and you begin standing among thousands of people in an excruciatingly loud venue, screaming at the top of your lungs and jumping around in a frenzy, then finding your way back to your car and making your way home and passing out at 3:00 a.m.

Sounds like a blast for a night, maybe two. Imagine doing this every night for a year. Or two years. Or ten. Imagine what would be sacrificed in your life, to make time and energy to keep up this lifestyle. This can be how drugs react in the body. Whether prescribed

---

Sam

Back in 1990, my husband was given Paul McCartney tickets. Did I want to go? Hells, yeah! There was one problem: our six-week old son, Sam. What to do with the baby? We decided to bring him. I'd carry him in a sling and nurse him privately right in our seats, in the dark. Baby's first concert!

Sir Paul McCartney, you may recall, is a financially successful bass player (your parents will definitely recall). This concert was majorly produced, with townhouse-sized speakers lining the stage. The concert began with the eerily blaring James Bond soundtrack tune, *Live and Let Die.* McCartney's bass notes smashed through the air like Godzilla. Lasers swirled maniacally around the stadium. Thousands of fans shrieked and cheered at the tops of their lungs. It was quite intoxicating.

Sam seemed so calm in that sling, and I thought to myself, "Aww, our little Rock 'n Roller is a Beatle's fan!" When I leaned to give him a kiss, I felt a gentle rumbling. I leaned in closer, and now heard the rumbling. I looked up to see if it was part of the song. It wasn't. I leaned in closer and the loud rumbling grew louder, sounding something like this:

WAAAAAAAAH!!!! WAAAAAAAAH!!!!!
WAAAAAAAAH!!!! WAAAAAAAAH!!!!!
WAAAAAAAAH!!!! WAAAAAAAAH!!!!!
WAAAAAAAAH!!!! WAAAAAAAAH!!!!!

I leapt up, squishing my way through the row, down the aisle, up the stairs, down the corridor, and into the women's bathroom. There was a long line, but I pushed through the girls and wedged my way to a corner of the room, squatting on the beer-soaked floor. While Sam screamed, I pulled out my boob and frantically tried to nurse him. It took a while for him to settle down, but after several minutes of frustration, he finally began nursing. I sat there for some time, cooing him with, "Booby Sammy, booby Sammy. It's okay. You're okay." The milling party gals looked on, half smiling, half shaking their heads. I was too freaked out to care. After a half hour or so, we got up to leave. Outside the bathroom was dad, standing there with both our coats. "Guess it's time to go, huh?"

or illicit, drugs interfere with the body's natural functioning. "Side effects" is also a misnomer; an effect is an effect. Pharmaceutical marketing may determine which effect will be singled out for prescriptive use.

Drugs love to party with all areas of the brain: rage with Papa, laugh and cry with Mama, but Baby brain is especially susceptible. Baby is the most malleable, but also the most fragile and vulnerable.

It's a baby, after all. Developing neurons are easy to kill, and drugs do just that, causing neurodegenesis. Neurodegenesis is the opposite of genesis, neurologically. Imagine taking a baby to a concert. Who would be crying by the end of the night, you or the baby?

Babies are not meant to attend rock concerts. Duh. But, hey, new mom. Live and learn. Babies freak out at rock and roll concerts, just like Baby brain does every time you give it drugs.

The pre-frontal cortex—Baby brain—while the last brain area to mature, is essential for college. College demands that we constantly manage our body functions (stay awake in class) and emotions (drama maintenance). College requires an extra level, a "higher order" of regulation—the Executive Functioning (EF), which was basically supplied by your folks and teachers for the first eighteen years of your life: wake you up, get you out of bed, make you a healthy breakfast, give you vitamins or medication, remind you of your chores, organize your school work, organize your daily schedule, point out that your fly is unzipped, drive you to school, and insist you can do anything if you work hard enough and apply yourself. Our EF is also responsible for all those "civil" functions: holding the door open for the ladies, using a tissue when sneezing, refraining from farting in class or telling the teacher they are a boring jerk. When you punch a wall in anger, your EF is held captive by emotions, in one of those amygdala hijacks. EF's job is to talk the killer down safely off the roof.

Both prescription and non-prescription drugs may be taken to help regulate neurotransmission. Drugs override our EF and interrupt its natural development. Similar to the synthetic sugars and trans-fats, drugs can become power hungry and micromanaging. We've seen enough movies to see excessive power go wrong, and drugs may begin to do more damage than good. Drugs force the body into releasing valuable neuro-regulating chemicals like dopamine. They use up precious resources, and then they do something horrid. Drugs begin to alter neurotransmitter receptor sites—chemical release portals—to better suit the foreign drug. Drugs become the new roommate from hell who starts taking up all the space in the fridge, eating your food, "borrowing" money from your wallet, and wearing your clothes. Our own bodies cannot manage their own chemical distribution. It's very much like how we become "addicted" to antibiotics; our bodies lose the ability to kill off bacteria and viruses independently. Antibiotics do work, but if used to kill every bacteria, they enable our immune systems in the process. Our immune systems also need the Privilege of Hardship, in order to strengthen. Over-reliance on drugs eventually results in our bodies being unable to function independently; our bodies become helpless.

Studies demonstrate how **nicotine** helps regulate neurotransmitters and may benefit EF symptoms commonly found with ADHD and other behavioral disorders. Transdermal nicotine is currently being used in ADHD therapy. It's common for students to begin smoking cigarettes in college or wait to quit until college is over. The fact that nicotine may help to regulate these brain chemicals and improve EF is tempting for a college student. ***Smoking equals better grades!*** **This reasoning supports the addictive behavior, however, at the cost of cancer, emphysema, stroke, and death. There are healthier ways to pay attention.**

Drugs, antibiotics, and over-protective parents all do the same thing: enable. It's something else doing something for you that you should be doing yourself. The 1993 movie *Boxing Helena* exposed the horror of control: an obsessed, scorned doctor surgically dismembers a woman, in order to keep her in his life. This analogy may feel like a stretch, but enabling reduces the victim in a similar way. The person is left unable to take care of herself without outside help. She is unable to control her behavior. Her behavior controls her, which is frightening. **When you think, "enable," think "unable**." Medication can be valuable and has its place in the academic world, but only as a last resort. Lifestyle factors must be regulated before one is medicated.

Risk and Self-Medication

Addicts often partake in risky behavior. Students diagnosed with ADHD have long been associated as risk-takers. The key may lie in self-medication. Students diagnosed with ADHD struggle with proper neurotransmitter function, and risk may be the key to regulation. Risk-taking is exciting, which is a casual way of saying "neurochemically stimulating." Excitement brought on by daring ventures elevates mood-altering neurotransmitters like epinephrine and adrenaline.

Ever notice how kids with ADHD move around a lot? Fidgeting is actually one of the criteria used for establishing their diagnosis. One explanation suggests that when ADHD kids wiggle in their seats, the wiggling activates chemical releases of synovial fluid, which releases serotonin, a pleasurable and calming chemical. ADHD students also spin, which may seem peculiar to observers. Spinning stimulates cochlear fluid release in the ear, which aids in physical and mental balance.

When the child wiggles and spins, how does the authoritarian respond? "Stop moving around and sit still!" The child has just been forced to stop self-medicating and judged to be bad, in the process. In effect, well-meaning but frustrated parents and teachers sentence the ADHD child to a life of neurological torment, because wiggling seems weird. Students with ADHD don't have the luxury to regulate brain chemicals like their normal counterparts. Personally, I'd take a spin over Ritalin any day.

Students with ADHD struggle with chemical imbalances in general, and in particular, with glucose. They cannot metabolize it as efficiently, especially in the brain. They require more glucose to keep the same amount of brain activity at an even plateau. Risk causes a rush of aldosterone and cortisol, which signal glucose release. Again, the student is self-medicating without awareness or intention of malice. Unfortunately, this creative strategy of stimulating glucose release comes with terrible side effects: hangovers, unwanted pregnancy, car wrecks, and sometimes, even death. At the very least, homework is put off.

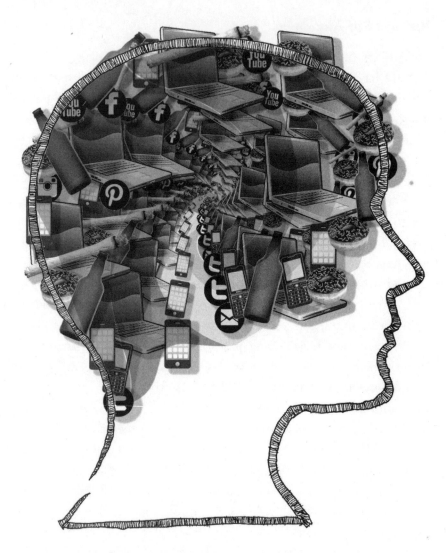

Parents might say, "Well, my son or daughter does not suffer from ADHD." I would retort, "Oh, yeah? **If a primary biological determination of ADHD is the 'inability to regulate and modulate neurotransmitter function in the frontal lobes,' then, while in college, every young adult suffers temporarily from ADHD.**" And, if college students *are* diagnosed with ADHD? Well, their "self-medicating" just doubled.

Addiction: The Opposite of Pleasure

Why do addicts continue to do something they hate doing? The quandary plagues our human condition. The more dependent they grow upon the addiction, the less enjoyment they receive. The key lies, once again, in the Sweet Spot.

Addiction involves two main neurotransmitters: dopamine and serotonin. For decades, scientists have been researching the roles that these two brain chemicals play in addiction. During brain scans, dopamine activation was found to be the common denominator in addictive behaviors such as drug and alcohol abuse. Dopamine releases when these substances were taken, but there was more to it. *When subjects would simply describe their experiences of taking these substances, dopamine would release.* Just thinking about the behavior would cause a chemical reaction.

It's one of the reasons addiction rehabilitation strategies strongly encourage avoiding the addicts' "old haunts." Alcoholics are advised to avoid their favorite bar or club, even if they refrain from drinking. Relocation can be a positive strategy for the recovering addicts. When addicts return to their addictive locations, the environments trigger State Dependent Learning flare-ups. Transfer floods the brain with dopamine, like Pavlov's dog, who inadvertently began drooling when a bell rang before suppertime. Like Dr. Selye, this discovery happened by accident (as do many scientific discoveries). Pavlov observed his dog drooling before suppertime. Every time he fed the dog, a bell rang at the same time. Pretty soon, just the sound of the bell would initiate the drooling. The bell conditioned the dog's brain to respond with "suppertime mode," which, in turn, activated "drool mode."

Dopamine is such an interesting neurochemical, because it swings both ways. Dopamine is secreted in times of *fight-or-flight,* released during both eustress and distress. We've long-associated dopamine with the first flushes of love. Using this new view of dopamine, love could be considered a stressor, an extreme change in SBM. With change comes dopamine release, and we begin to associate the chemical with the reaction. Unfortunately, love is not all birds and bees; it's also bats in belfries. When eustress shifts to distress, dopamine's function shifts, as well.

Dopamine is considered to be the pleasure chemical, but it's a bit more complicated. Brain scans also showed that subjects could experience pleasure without dopamine release. In one dopamine study, University of Michigan psychology professor Kent Berridge, PhD researched what happens in the brain when rats ate their favorite foods.

Rats typically make a facial expression in response to preferred tastes, a rodent "grin." Researchers figured that rats with normal dopamine release would smile when they ate yummy food and rats who'd had their dopamine systems blocked would not be capable of enjoying it. Instead they found that, while rats without dopamine wouldn't seek food, they still smiled like normal rats if rodent-preferred delicacies were hand-fed to them. In fact, the dopamine-depleted rats were so lacking in any type of desire that if the researchers hadn't placed food in their mouths, they would have starved. But the rats' delight in dining didn't seem to be diminished. "Originally, we didn't believe our results," Berridge says. "There was so much reason to believe that dopamine was pleasure."

Dopamine itself does not produce pleasant feelings; it causes *desire* for pleasure and focuses attention on getting it. Berridge aptly describes this as "wanting." Dopamine, therefore, is intimately engaged with the conative domain. When we desire, dopamine ignites. Dopamine is the chemical of desire and motivation, the heat-seeking missile. There are at least two types of pleasure: pleasure of the hunt and pleasure of the kill. Hunting is wanting and killing is enjoyment, and this creates confusion. The dopamine hunt is pleasure in the pursuit, not the result. The actual "pleasure" or "enjoyment" chemicals are the opioids, specifically, serotonin.

The presence of separate systems for "wanting" and "enjoyment" cause problems; dopamine (want) levels increase, and serotonin (enjoy) levels decrease. Desire for the drug grows as the drug's effects become less enjoyable. The addict finds himself passionately wanting an experience that he no longer likes, and that he may, in fact, genuinely dread.

Addicts speak intimately about this phenomenon. When you first try the addictive behavior—take a drink, inhale a cigarette, place a bet—there's not much to it. It might even make you sick. You may wonder what all the fuss is about. If you persist through these initial reactions, the chemical or behavior begins to stimulate dopamine release. You may experience a pleasurable moment that accelerates dopamine production: horse wins big at the track; medical-grade bud melts your anxiety; listening to a friend's problems makes you feel important; sexual orgasm is awesome.

When these experiences feel good, we "tag" them with dopamine, associating them with pleasure. The next time we do this addictive behavior, we release dopamine. Each time we do it, we release a tiny bit more dopamine, as tolerance increases. Then, like Pavlov's dog, we begin to fool our SBMs. Our cognitive belief systems change. We believe that if we do that behavior, then we'll feel good. Soon, just thinking about the addictive thing releases dopamine, and wanting soars. Then, it gets really screwy. Every time we release dopamine, we begin to associate it with that addictive thing, which stimulates the craving. Addiction, like academics, relies intimately on State Dependent Learning.

The problem with this scenario is that we are increasing dopamine production, not serotonin production. In addictive states, when dopamine increases, it crowds out other neurotransmitters, and serotonin decreases. The same behavior does not yield the same feeling anymore. We are not gumball machines; inserting dopamine does not yield a "serotonin gumball" every time. Addictions are more like slot machines; sometimes the behavior yields a positive result, but most times, you just waste your quarters.

Try telling this to an addicted brain. One main problem with addiction is that it changes the structure of the brain. It is exactly like trying to reason with a drunk. The addicted brain now "chemically believes" that the addictive behavior breeds pleasure. Dopamine rules his world, even when serotonin knows otherwise. This is why an addict is often concurrently rationally lucid about his situation and unable to stop. Mama and Papa are addicted, and Baby has no say in the matter. It's a Dr. Jekyll–Mr. Hyde kind of situation.

Not only does the brain break off into an altered personality, but the chemical regulators inverse. Addiction starts with no desire, just pure pleasure: you take your first hit off a joint, and soon you feel good. There is no wanting or desire, just the behavior and the result; but it felt good, so we try it again. And again. We begin "chasing the dream" or "chasing the dragon"—terms associated with wanting to recapture those first few awesome experiences. Pretty soon, Mr. Hyde says, "Hey, Jekyll. Remember that cool feeling with that joint? Wasn't that the bomb?" Our dopamine remembers the pleasant feeling and is stimulated. We take another hit, and we receive another pleasant boost of serotonin.

For a while, it's evenly balanced: we receive as much pleasure as we desire. We reach the Sweet Spot of addiction, a gold mine of balanced desire and pleasure. Good times. But, **eventually the downward slope begins. We begin to desire the feeling more than the pleasure we receive from the feeling.** The slope begins its nasty descent. The stronger the craving, the worse the feeling. We are left to wonder, in addictive stagger: Why are we craving something so much when it causes us to feel like crap?

Relationships may also take on properties of addiction. In healthy partnerships, the mechanisms of wanting and liking serve to cement healthy interdependence and romantic empowerment. In unhealthy relationships, desire escalates while happiness plummets into dysfunctional enabling and abandonment.

It's all the same, with whatever the addiction. Eventually, our desire to do it is stronger than the enjoyment we derive from doing it. Dopamine completely takes over and serotonin supplies are depleted, causing an odd cocktail: abundance of desire and lack of pleasure, leading to depression. As Berridge puts it, "Addicts don't say that the drugs get better and better," adding that if this was their experience, "they'd be rational not to quit because the drugs would be becoming increasingly wonderful." Stated another way, if the feeling worsens, a rational person would stop. Our affective domain naturally revolts against negative feelings, but addiction hijacks these emotional messages.

Baby brain may understand the situation, and Mama may feel awful about the addiction, but these chemical reactions bypass rational processes. Nothing is more powerful than Papa's primal urges. As much as we like to think we need the civilized brain for survival, we don't. Jack Nicholson creepily illustrated this after his lobotomy, in *One Flew Over the Cookoo's Nest*. Addicts will sound so reasonable, analyzing their behavior while they are doing it! If I had a nickel for every time I heard a cigarette smoker say, "I know, I know I should quit," I could buy a copy of this book. Baby knows, but Papa is clueless.

Too bad. **Addiction is one time where having one's civilized brain would come in mighty handy.** We could effectively reflect, *Oh hey, ol' sport. Recently, I have noticed how you are increasing your activity of this particularly negative behavior, even as the behavior becomes increasingly unsatisfying and in fact, detrimental. You may want to reconsider that particular choice.* Our primal brains would promptly reply, *Golly! That makes sense! Thanks, ol' chap! Behavior aborted! Tally ho!*

Some evolutionary psychologists theorize that depression evolved as a way to pull people away from making bad choices to help break the addictive cycle. If addicts force themselves to engage in previously healthy activities, they reclaim pleasure. Unfortunately, it's nearly impossible to convince yourself to take action and make a radical change when depressed. It's akin to the biological *"Death vs. Diabetes"* conundrum. The body must choose survival first, so if depression reduces the deadly addiction, the body takes it. Depression won't make us healthy, but it may keep us alive. Sometimes, too, the "depression strategy" backfires: Addiction fuels depression, which in turn, feeds the addiction.

Depression, itself, may be addicting. Depression is actually an excitatory response. Our environments become victims of excitotoxicity, that fancy term for TMI. The overwatered soul has to mull through this inundation of information (the addictive behavior and avoidant issues piling up). It takes energy to misperceive all the time, and depression is a parasympathetic response to divert fuel away from all that stimulation. Tranquilizers are typically given for depression, rather than stimulants.

Psychoactive substances increase depression. A sedentary life increases depression. A poor diet malnourishes the SBM, increasing depression. Lack of sleep certainly increases depression, but also, psychosis. The last thing an addictive person needs to be is psychotic. Addicts are already out of touch with rational thought; they don't need lighter fluid on that bonfire. Psychonutrients are key in changing addiction, due to their symbiotic relationship and powerful balancing of psychoactive substances. Adding positive lifestyle changes will begin easing addictive behaviors, regardless of what the addict wants.

Here again, we revisit William Glasser's theory: We first act, *then* think and feel better. Altering our state begins with change. Depressed addicts face another absurd Catch-22. **The way to break depression and recover is to change behavior, and depressed people wait to feel better before they change their behavior.**

This happens with many positive changes, such as exercise. No one wants to work out, but everyone is happier after they do. *In essence, we like it, but we don't want it.* "We have to be motivated to exercise in more cognitive ways. We want the outcome of having exercised, rather than the process," Berridge says. Choosing to do something on the basis of outcome is completely rational, but often not as motivating as more basic dopamine-based incentives. This is the vicious cycle for lifestyle change, and the crux of this book. **Students must act on blind faith, accepting that radically changing their lifestyle will make them feel better and help them to believe in themselves.** They have to thoroughly believe in something while everything in their souls, bodies, and minds is convincing them otherwise. Convincing a typical student to embrace lifestyle change is like trying to convince a depressed addict to stop smoking pot.

While searching for addiction quotes, I realized that I had been searching for over an hour, instead of selecting a few satisfactory ones and then returning to writing. That's the thing about procrastination and addiction. It's not the behavior, but the perception. Do you repeat it? Can you stop? Does it affect you adversely? These are the questions of control that must be answered, honestly.

The Way Out

The college experience is one of cognitive, affective, and conative dissonance—what you thought, felt, and believed would happen is different than what actually is happening. Sometimes this is good: more fun, more excitement, and more interest. Sometimes, this is bad: more isolation, more confusion, harder work, and less support. Ideas are challenged. Beliefs you grew up with are belittled by condescending professors. Years of friendships may vanish in an instant.

Cognitive dissonance and disequilibrium rewire our entire circuitry, and that rewiring is both exhilarating and terrifying—two emotions that crave addictive responses. Without proper support and guidance, college is an addictive trap. The escape is through control, and ironically, that's what starts the addiction. **We control the scary, disorienting experience with something that makes us feel better, and pretty soon, what "makes us feel better" is a scary disorienting experience.**

By this part of the chapter, I've probably made you feel pretty awful about your addictions, so let's externalize this locus of control. Time for a scapegoat! I'll blame my favorite: society. Our country's motto could be, "Anything worth doing is worth overdoing." As an Irish friend once said, "I love drinking so much, I would never abuse it." A moderate Irishman? Seriously? This one man has more sense than an entire nation. The United States has never been the poster child for moderation.

Wake up! I know, I just said moderation, which is scientifically proven to be the world's most boring word in college, the US, and most developing nations. Moderation is even more boring than "sleep," if you can fathom. My son plays a drinking game with his fraternity buddies. Every time I text, "pace yourself," they take a shot of Jack Daniels. If they and you only knew the magical powers that await with moderation . . . well, they'd probably become addicted to it.

To control addiction's controlling presence, we need a few things. Certainly, we need to embrace the lifestyle factors presented, but addiction is a full-on attack on balance. We need physiological Martial Law. We need addiction's kryptonite . . . moderation.

Moderation is a wonderful strategy for some, yet fatal denial for others. Proponents of moderation tout its "have your cake and eat it too" compromise, but if you are already addicted or feel unable to behave moderately, the point may be moot. For many people, moderation is not an option. Moderation is like being "moderately pregnant." Alcoholics Anonymous uses the metaphor of a pickle. Once a cucumber is pickled, it never re-cucumbers. Some therapies disagree, offering attenuation models, where reducing the addictive behavior is allowed versus a complete eradication, the "Cold Turkey" method. **One of the reasons I support moderation is that some behaviors, such as laptop use or approval seeking, may have to be tolerated, since they are commonly used in everyday life.**

Whether moderation or eradication, recovery involves reducing the behavior. Reduction calls on a few more strategies, beginning with resiliency. Resiliency is key in all successful endeavors, especially with breaking addiction. Resiliency is persistence until we achieve our goal, requiring united dedication of SBM. Resiliency solicits all our brains and domains.

Resiliency is such an effective recovery method, because its experiences are as delicious and satisfying as the addiction. Resiliency stimulates both dopamine and serotonin. Repeated resistance diminishes the addictive wanting and increases EF control. The brain is like a muscle: use it or lose it. Engaged areas grow, while neglected areas shrink.

The first few attempts at stopping often feel like holding your breath, when every cell in your body is screaming for oxygen. Keep trying. Keep trying, thousands of times. Act, then feel and think, and finally, you will believe you can do it. **You will believe you can break the addiction *after* the addiction is broken.** Funny how it works. Spirit is watching and waiting to lend a hand. As you change your experiences, you change your self, and the universe changes around you. AA mandates belief in a higher power. Higher power wants to help, and your energy needs it.

I vaguely remember some energetic law in some high school science class, probably chemistry. Understanding the hierarchy of attention, it should be obvious why I remember so little; my mind perpetually focused on all the cute guys in class. Regardless, one concept wormed its way into my psyche, which dealt with the amount of energy required for transforming a substance from solid to gas. It seems that the energy needed to maintain one state is more than the energy needed to transform from one state to another. Transformation takes less energy than maintenance. This makes sense, in terms of the Information Processing System. Transformation is new and exciting and captures the attention of Baby brain. Maintenance, however, is automated, controlled by the cerebellum. We don't need to pay attention to automatic procedures, so we lose interest, and this makes maintenance more difficult. The Dalai Lama was asked, "What is the meaning of life?" The revered one's response? *Routines.* Drama is way sexier than routines; therefore, we give it our attention.

As an advisor and life coach, I use the Appreciation Theory in dealing with addictive behavior. **Appreciation Theory** reminds us that negative behavior has positive aspects, at least initially. The addictive behavior must be validated before we label both behavior and addict as "bad." If supporters move right into judgment, the addict sends up warning shots of protection and defends the behavior, reinforcing loyalty to their addiction. Instead, we begin by recognizing that addictions were, at first, productive coping strategies to some of life's challenging stimuli: a car accident, a fight with a boyfriend, and a college experience that is not what one expected.

We previously explored connection and the power of social support. Connection is key in overcoming addiction. The supporter supplies energy to the addict's depleted soul. The supporter supplies the energy for the addict to travel through the painful process of transformation. Addicts sometimes change on their own, but it's rare. I would challenge the "alone" philosophy, hypothesizing that these addicts possessed either a strong conative domain, spiritual connection, or both. They had the support that allowed them to believe in themselves and carry them through to wellness.

Support is a very tight rope, needing extreme attention to balance. Support must empower, never enable. Supporters may be so eager to help the addict recover that they interfere with the work of transformation. Interestingly, recovery sometimes happens after the "support" stops. The partner leaves and the addict is forced to deal with the reality of the situation. The supporter's energy, while well-meaning, may breed resentment and obligation. Once freed of this oppressive entrainment, the addict may channel their energy on healing, rather than guilt. Addicts may become caught up in defending their behavior to a supporter. When this dynamic is removed, the addict gets on with the work ahead.

My father, a martial arts instructor, used to marvel at how, when students would skip several classes, he administratively withdrew them, and *then* they began to show up. After months of berating my son for refusing health care, I gave up. The next month, he applied for health care. This shift happens with or without addiction. Once our soul's energy is unblocked, movement surges. Long-time couples split, then a former partner meets and marries a new person. We quit a job that has been dragging us down for years, and a surprising opportunity unexpectedly presents itself.

Human connection is key in overcoming addiction, but spiritual connection is also vital. God and nature are common forms of spirit, but any connection with one's creativity may overcome an addiction. **Some believe this is the root cause of addiction— disconnection from our callings.** We step off our paths, forsake our creativity, and BAM! The separation is too painful to endure. Until we reconnect with our path, we drown our depression and anxiety with distracting addictive behaviors. Once we face the truth and re-engage with our paths, an energetic sigh is released. We are back in ourselves and able to let go of the addiction.

Careful, though . . . even the conative domain faces addiction, since dopamine rules this arena. Our sacred path in life, our goals and creative pursuits are fueled by desire. We may become addicted to "following our bliss." In truth, "walking our paths" involves a lot of walking. Realizing one's goals is a tiresome, unromantic pursuit, fulfilled by day-in, day-out dedication; but, the delicious secret comes at the end of the day, when we feel *good*. Dedicated behavior stimulates subtler serotonin, but dopamine is stronger and sexier, always pulling us away from our paths. Think of dopamine as instant gratification and serotonin as delayed gratification.

Dopamine may rule the soul, but serotonin is fueled by spirit. "Being present" has gained popularity in the eyes of stress management. Yet another Sweet Spot, being present also refers to balancing wanting and enjoying, reducing the need for dopamine production and increasing our serotonin levels. Our focus remains in the present moment, away from dopamine's lure of past and future wanting. In order to truly break free from addiction, you have to do what you enjoy doing and stop doing what you want to do.

* * *

The bulimia and drug addiction I suffered in college persisted for several years, until a curious thing happened. I ate sea creatures. I heard about lichen, a type of mossy plant that supposedly got you high. I was weaning myself off of cocaine and cigarettes and willing to try anything. Ironically, I held a passion for both psychoactive substances *and* health foods. Go figure. This lichen stuff was supposedly uber-rich in a multitude of nutrients just waiting to stimulate brain activity. It was legal. I couldn't wait to try it.

I couldn't find lichen in any natural foods store and wasn't about to go picking it off logs; but I did find something at the store that caught my attention: spirulina. Spirulina is an algae. This blue-green algae is reputed to contain a bounty of nutrients that boost energy and improve mood. If you drank a spoonful in water, it'd give you a healthy high. My addictive mind took over. I bought some, went home and tried it. I *did* get high—a nice buzz and burst of energy. My mind felt clear, alert, and relaxed, all at the same time. I took more. I took more each day and continued to feel better. In a few weeks, I noticed that I had been forgetting to make myself throw up. Cocaine's craving lessened from dull roar to annoying murmur. I was even smoking fewer cigarettes. Spirulina was my portal into a healthy lifestyle.

I didn't intend to become a health food nut, but after seeing how a repeated behavior could yield positive results, it didn't make sense to continue behaving negatively. There are many healthy ways to feel the "natural high" that replenishes brain chemicals rather than depletes them. Since that time, I've tried just about every substance sold in health food stores. Maybe I'm addicted to health? Yeah, maybe, but it's an addiction I can live with. These days, I stick to herbs that grow around my yard—red clover, dandelion, and other herbs that are nutritionally packed. Spirulina is great, but it is expensive, and writers are not pro-football players, after all.

The more psychonutrients are mismanaged, the stronger addictions manifest. You don't have to consume sea creatures to cure addiction. Following the lifestyle strategies outlined in this book is a super start. **A life that actively and continuously manages its lifestyle factors may be free of addiction.**

Creativity is a must; addicts need an expressive outlet and navigational map back to their paths. The more attentive we are with ourselves, the less dependent we become on distracting addictions. Our life paths—callings, vocations, however you wish to label them—share something in common. They involve doing things we are drawn to do and have a natural ability in doing. They may not be easy, but life is harder when we avoid them. We create our gifts to share with the world. There is such a natural high in this doing and sharing, more powerful than any drug, behavior, or sea creature.

This brings us to our final lifestyle factor.

GIVE

"If anyone on the verge of action should judge himself according to the outcome, he would never begin. Even though the result may gladden the whole world, that cannot help the hero; for he knows the result only when the whole thing is over, and that is not how he became a hero, but by virtue of the fact that he began."

—Søren Kierkegaard, *Fear and Trembling*

"Our deepest fear is not that we are inadequate. Our deepest fear is that we are powerful beyond measure. It is our light, not our darkness that most frightens us. We ask ourselves, Who am I to be brilliant, gorgeous, talented, and fabulous? Actually, who are you not to be? You are a child of God. Your playing small does not serve the world. There is nothing enlightened about shrinking so that other people will not feel insecure around you. We are all meant to shine, as children do. We were born to make manifest the glory of God that is within us. It is not just in some of us; it is in everyone and as we let our own light shine, we unconsciously give others permission to do the same. As we are liberated from our own fear, our presence automatically liberates others."

—Marianne Williamson, *A Return to Love: Reflections on the Principles of "A Course in Miracles"*

Joy
"I slept and dreamt that life was joy.
I awoke and saw that life was service.
I acted and behold, service was joy."

—Rabindranath Tagore

"It is more blessed to give than to receive."

—Jesus Christ

You are how you give.

Other than stress, food, movement, sleep, connection, creativity, and control, the most important lifestyle factor to one's academic success is giving.

The final phase of psychonutrient health completes the circle. With everything in place, we are in a place of fulfillment. We have an outpouring of health, love, information, skills, abilities, creativity, and motivation, and so, we give.

Humans are programmed to give. It's in our nature. Giving is half of the human experience, equal to receiving. As delightful as receiving feels, giving actually feels a bit better. All the other lifestyle factors are oriented around the self and how you handle the world. Giving is different; the focus is outside of yourself. Suddenly, the focus shifts to how the whole world handles you.

There is no finer joy than when we give, probably because when we give, at least two souls feel better, so the joy multiplies. We crave it as much as recognition, which many psychologists and business analysts believe to be the number one factor to personal and professional satisfaction. In fact, giving can become as addicting as sugar or cigarettes. The warm glow we receive from a selfless act is stunning, and so must be balanced.

An article in *Spirituality and Health* magazine described the link between volunteering and health. It claimed that **volunteering increased energy levels and stamina, decreased depression and anxiety, and improved the immune system and well-being.** Participants volunteered four hours per month. Several markers were monitored pre- and post-volunteering: immune markers of T- and B-Cell counts, macrophage counts, and cortisol levels. General feelings of mood and depression levels were analyzed, as well as number of absences from work or school.

One key to the study required subjects to volunteer with strangers or people outside of their "circle." Fixing your parents' computer was not considered volunteering. That type of activity is considered a duty rather than a gift. Volunteering involved some outside organization or person. One group of volunteers was encouraged to offer service in ways that expressed their creativity: voracious readers might read to young kids at the library; cooks might serve soup at a drop-in center; musicians might teach music to seniors at the community center. Another group was encouraged to volunteer in areas where they wanted to gain experience. Someone wanting to learn yoga might volunteer assisting a yoga instructor at a nursing home. Other volunteers simply offered service to an outside organization.

As you may imagine, the results were impressive. After three months, volunteer markers were measured. Immune systems strengthened, cortisol dropped, and well-being soared. While all three groups demonstrated health improvements, positive markers significantly increased in correlation to utilizing one's creativity. The most dramatic improvements occurred when volunteers gave with their passions. Plus, an unintended finding emerged. Most participants from all groups continued volunteering after the study completed.

When one volunteers, the sense of well-being lingers long after the activity stops. It is similar to the glow after intercourse, resonating within our energetic fields. This makes sense, as volunteering and intercourse share a common bond: two people join and make love. When one volunteers with their unique creative expression, then the real magic begins. This is what the article described. One's energetic fields are so stimulated and elevated, it biochemically changes us, in soul, body, and mind. Our life purposes begin to align. We feel better and stronger. We are more resistant to disease. We appreciate others and are receptive to love. In short, we awaken and come alive.

The premise illustrates what I call the **interface,** a cosmic Sweet Spot of sorts. In soulful endeavors, there is an energetic halfway point where the giver and receiver "meet." The giver gives as much as the receiver receives. The receiver appreciates the gift as much as the giver appreciates the offering. This is the interface—a delicious moment of energetic equality and sharing, a co-mingling. At that moment, the giver becomes spirit, giving to the receiver's soul. When you give, you are the entire universe! (At least for that moment.)

* * *

Kids are receivers. It's their job; that's how they survive. From the moment a zygote explodes into existence, it receives. It takes space, nutrients, and time. Kids are born taking and they continue taking. They are designed to soak up sensory information and experiences and skills and procedures and language and behaviors. They take and take and take, and supporters are their Giving Trees.

At some point, the energy shifts. Even young children begin taking in enough to be able to give back. He may receive enough love to hug his mommy or be full enough to share a carrot. She may help a friend on a swing or teach someone how to play a new game. Just as we are programmed to receive and learn, we are also programmed to give . . . and teach.

Those Who Can, Teach

The best way to learn something is to teach it. Teaching is highly creative, requiring divergent thinking and problem solving to adapt the student to the environment of a new skill or idea. Teaching requires being outside of yourself. It requires that you have to convey this "something" to someone, figure out how to communicate the information in a way they will understand. In a sense, you have to become the learner. Teaching engages our **Theory of Mind—** having to consider someone else's perspective. It requires empathy, feeling, and understanding others' experiences. These "outer self" experiences require us to think outside our soul.

That is hard. Broken down simply, teaching A to B is having A become B, temporarily. Respecting the interface, B also has to become A; that is, B has to be receptive to A's gift. Part of the gift is in motivation. Somehow, the teacher has to offer both the lesson and the motivation. This is why teachers cry in their first year of teaching. The job is a bitch.

Teachers must meet students halfway, but no more. No enabling, no abandonment . . . teaching must empower. Students have to meet teachers halfway, as well. We've all experienced jaded teachers and needy students, in and out of school. This imbalance disrupts the interface.

Why is giving integral in academic achievement? Let's consult the learning pyramid. The learning pyramid illustrates information retention rate with different modalities. Basically, the learning pyramid says, "Let's take some information, do different things with it, and see how well each thing tricks your hippocampus into making a long-term memory."

Let's use the example of painting. You attend a lecture. You read an article on it. You listen to a tape or watch a film. You observe a painting demonstration. You participate in a discussion group. You practice painting. Finally, you must teach painting. The learning pyramid theory postulates that the more interactive we become with the information, the more likely we are to retain it. All three brains engage with all three domains in our SBM. The more active you are with information, the more involved Baby gets in paying attention. Imagine trying to teach a baby how to walk by lecturing him on the merits and techniques of walking. Good luck. When you teach, your sense and meaning of the information skyrocket; the hippocampus pays close attention and memory easily consolidates. When teaching something, you don't even have to try to make a memory. The memory makes itself.

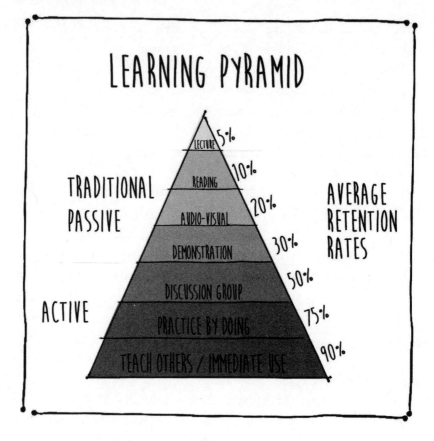

Giving must be taught

A few years ago, I was switching offices at the end of the semester, which entailed moving my stuff. I packed up several totes filled with books, office supplies, and other memorabilia. In order to transfer the totes into my new office, I needed to move them out to my car, a few hundred yards away. These totes were large and heavy. I dragged one about 25 feet, then would go back and retrieve the next one, repeating the process. I would drag totes down the hall, through the building's front door, and then towards the parking lot. As I lugged my totes in this cumbersome manner, I passed several male students hanging out on the lawn. They were laughing and bantering, enjoying the warm May air. I noticed them. They did not seem to notice me.

As I laboriously dragged my totes, they continued their easy-breezy languishing on the lawn. I couldn't believe they didn't offer to help, yet felt paralyzed in asking them. The drama began to swell inside me. In typical female fashion (sorry ladies, but you know this is true), I fumed silently, sending psychic guilt beams into their minds, demanding their souls awaken and offer to help.

They didn't.

The totes became immediately heavier. Each tote now weighed several trillion tons. I was close to exploding each time I passed by them. I suppose the anger supplied me with the energy needed to get the job done, but the anger also compounded my stubbornness. Instead of asking them to please help, I insisted on remaining fully pissed off, personally affronted that, *not only had they not offered to help, but they hadn't even yet acknowledged me, traipsing back and forth right in front of them!* I blamed them, their stupid parents, their stupid parents' parents, their home towns, their home states, and the entire culture that raised those selfish good-for-nothing bastards.

Later, I realized who was the stupidest one of all. **Giving is a natural tendency, but first needs to be taught.** Giving needs opportunities to practice, like all learning experiences. We have to teach kids how to give as explicitly as we teach them how to tie a shoe, read a book, and wash their hands. Young children learn to give in a mechanical way. *Billy, share your toys with Johnny.* Eventually, their giving progresses. I, a professor at that college, missed a teaching moment, because I was too busy judging untaught students.

Should they have known better? Perhaps by eighteen years of age, yes. Maybe they *did* know better, and they truly didn't notice me. Who knows? If they didn't notice me, then it was my job to be noticed. If they didn't know better, then I received a moment to teach them about giving. Did I miss an interface moment? I would have found out, by their reaction. My money says that they would have leapt right up and helped the nice lady out. The only selfish bastard was pouting inside my head.

* * *

College is organically a self-centered pursuit. Ask students why they are in college and their answers invariably are self-serving: *get my degree, secure a good job, make loads of money, and be happy.* Some goals may be more immediate: *avoid parents, make friends, and party.* The common bond appears to be the individualistic mindset, the *"What's in it for me?"* If I ever heard a student respond with, "I attend college to learn how to give back to my nuclear tribe and greater community in ways that are unique to my current incarnation on this planet," I would spit up a lung. In defense of the young mind, you sure wouldn't have heard me uttering *that* sentiment at Bryn Mawr.

That's okay. Young adults are *supposed* to be selfish little turds. College is their window of opportunity for turd-dom. It is the supporter's job to transform these little bastards into Integral Giving Cogs within their greater community. Being selfless must be modeled, learned, and practiced, and *then* appreciated.

In college, there are a slew of giving opportunities: group activities, leadership conferences, peer mentoring, community service, and fraternities. Students join academic groups, such as Phi Beta Kappa. There are extracurricular media groups: newspapers and radio stations. There are special interest clubs: chess, gardening, and anime. There are spirituality groups, political groups, and social activist organizations.

Joining groups is a good beginning for learning how to give. Giving starts with serving the self, which evolves into serving others. Belonging to a group means that you are now accountable for someone or something beyond yourself. **We are more likely to hold ourselves accountable for someone else than for ourselves.** There is an inherent connectedness to our human nature. Raised in a hyper-individualistic competitive culture, we may be less aware of this natural tendency. Add to that a decline in religious affiliation and we reduce opportunities to practice being accountable with a community.

Discovering your role in life definitely requires the Sweet Spot. Following your unique personal path involves belonging to a group, while breaking free from their conventions. As we refine who we are, we refine how we give. **Giving distinguishes us from our tribe, and in the same moment, allows us to give back and support the tribe.** We give more of our true selves, and this completes our human sense of self and purpose.

Giving doesn't have to be organized or group-oriented. Giving starts with smiling at a sad person. Giving is handing someone a pencil. Giving is listening to your roommate when they are in pain. The point of giving is to do something for someone. The giving interface is that you use your creativity and meet the receiver halfway. Giving is the key to personal transformation, flipping the Zone of Proximal Development.

Give in ways that place you in your stretch zone. If you are afraid of heights and want to overcome this, you may offer to help a friend with a ropes course training. Only give of yourself what you can afford to give, or else you become the enabler and they learn helplessness. You are not giving if you forsake an important homework assignment in order to give your time to a friend in need. Be careful; you may be masking altruism for procrastination. Then, you plead with the professor, *I need more time. My friend was in need.* The reality is, you don't need more time; you need better boundaries. Enabling is not giving; it is self-serving and fear-based. Next time, have your friend call someone else for help, and finish your assignment. If they are a true friend, they will understand.

Give when you are in a solid place, when your needs are met, and you have time and energy to give. Meet the receiver halfway, only. Keep it a gift, for both sides.

Interface.

Luc

The *Lifestyles for Learning* course is highly interactive and experiential. Students found themselves cooking, meditating, practicing yoga, and climbing walls. For our stress unit, I illustrated the stress response by having students climb the rock wall. Nothing says stress like hanging 30 feet in the air while your classmates watch safely on the floor.

Every student had their turn, and we had some class time left. One of the students, Luc, happened to notice that I hadn't taken a turn. He called me out. I smiled politely and said, "No thank you, I'm good." He persisted, and a few other students looked over. I persisted, too, but these students were undeterred by gentle social cues. Finally, I blurted, "I am afraid of heights. I tried this wall a few years ago and got about ten feet up, and that was plenty, so, let's just drop it."

Luc, bless his heart, wouldn't just drop it. "But, Crowther," he retorted, "you keep telling us the best way to make a fear go away is to face it. Right? Shouldn't you do that, too? Come on, I'll help you."

The little bastard had a valid point. (I hate it when they pay attention in class.) Before I knew it, a few students were holding up the harness and straps, pushing and pulling my limbs through various loops and belts. I felt like a puppet with some very weird masters yanking on body parts in a considerably non-academic fashion.

I began my ascent, placing one foot in front of the other. The first ten feet were fine, and I felt the sensations of moving from comfort to stretch zone. With the students' encouragement, I continued until about fifteen feet, and then stopped. The terror of height crept in quickly, rushing through my veins with an electric buzzing. It's amazing how we go from fine to fear, instantaneously. Staring straight at the wall in front of me, my feet gave out. Dangling there like a massive ornament, I shouted, "Okay, I'm all set. Ready to come down, now!"

"Keep going, Crowther!" Luc the bastard called out.

"No, I'm good. This is great. I'm fine. Down, please!"

But, Luc would not be swayed. He raced up the wall like a monkey and within a minute, was hanging beside me. "Crowther, you can do this. I know you can. I'll be with you every step of the way. Trust me."

By now the façade of professorial decorum had been fully replaced with raw human emotion. I began to stubbornly babble like a toddler, shaking my head vigorously. "Nuh uh. I can't do it. I can't do it!"

Luc didn't seem to hear it and instead began placing my feet back onto the jutting rocks. Luc and I faced the wall, or rather, I stared straight at the wall, and Luc, by my side, stared straight at me. His gaze never wavered for even an instant, and his calm voice was constant. The gentle sound seemed to carry me up that wall, one rock at a time. We never spoke of the top, only the next step. I had no mind of my own.

Step by step by step, we made it about 30 feet up—a mere two feet away from the bell. By now I was openly sobbing, rather like my son Sam was during the Paul McCartney concert. I kept pleading with Luc that I could not make it. He told me I was fine, this was great. I made it 30 feet, for chrissake! Better than I could have imagined! I was exhausted and shaking and unable to breathe and ready to come down. But, Luc wasn't ready.

Staring right at me, he said, "Crowther. You are two feet away from the top. You will place your left foot there (pointing at a very close rock). Then, you will push yourself up, and put your right foot there (pointing at another very close rock). Then, you will reach out and ring the bell. And you will have done it! I'm going to do it with you. You're all set. Let's go."

Luc would not give up, and since he had taken control of my mind, neither could I. We placed my left foot there and the right foot there. I may have peed a little. In a great surge of energy that somehow was still in my body, I boosted myself up. I made it to the top. And, I rang the bell. I didn't dare move my gaze, but could tell through peripheral vision that Luc was smiling. The students were howling and cheering. He called out down below, "Okay, she's ready to come down."

Sometimes we don't want the gift and don't feel ready to receive it, but the giver is so confident in our ability to receive that we find ourselves able to grow. That is the ultimate sacrifice of both the giver and receiver. It is the ultimate goal of learning. It is the ultimate goal of life.

The Meaning of Life . . . (or at least, College)

The Meaning of Life is the giving interface. The giving interface remains balanced and sustained through healthy lifestyle. The healthier you are, the more actively and intimately you live. The swell thing about receiving is that it allows others to give, which keeps the giver's karma revving smoothly. This is why people feel good after giving. They are giving back to themselves, a spiritual investment on which they will later collect. That's the great irony: giving is the greatest high, unlike any other. It produces the most Alpha waves—that resplendent calm, attentive energy. Giving takes spirit's gift, nurtures it through our unique soul, and shares it with the world, back to spirit.

In giving, magic meets you halfway. Giving is the true expression of humanity. All you existentialists out there, please be open-minded. If you haven't given from your true innate sense of purpose, you haven't lived. Suddenly, the expression transforms into, "Everything matters, and so what if it does?"

We're all part of the same tribe, the human tribe. All humans thrive on the same basic psychonutrient factors: eat, move, sleep, connect, create, control, and give. We all need to manage responses to life's stimuli. We all need the courage to receive and give help. **Giving offers a sense of well-being, which reduces stress, which increases digestion, which gives more energy, which allows us to move, which allows us to rest, which allows us to awaken refreshed and ready to create what we share with others. It's a lovely closed-loop lifestyle cycle, self-sustaining.**

Giving is the true path to success, to happiness, to fulfillment. We must be giving in our unique way, in order to be truly happy humans. College offers the opportunity for students to mature into givers, allowing them to become teachers . . . to become human. In the end, it doesn't make us better learners, but better people.

And that, very well, may be worth the price of admission.

Until one is committed, there is hesitancy, the chance to draw back, always ineffectiveness. Concerning all acts of initiative and creation, there is one elementary truth the ignorance of which kills countless ideas and splendid plans: that the moment one definitely commits oneself, then providence moves too. All sorts of things occur to help one that would never otherwise have occurred. A whole stream of events issues from the decision, raising in one's favor all manner of unforeseen incidents, meetings and material assistance which no man could have dreamed would have come his way. Whatever you can do or dream you can, begin it.

Boldness has genius, power and magic in it. Begin it now.
—Johann Wolfgang Von Goethe

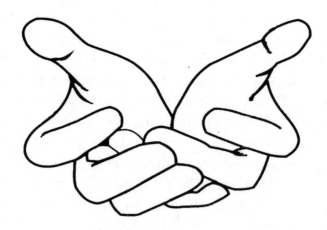

NORMAL

That, my friends, is college. If you're normal.

That is, if you are intentionally born into this world and into a family unit with healthy genes on both sides. Your parents long to have you, and your birth is planned. Your mother takes care of herself before, during, and after gestation. Your father also behaves himself before, during, and after your birth. Your mother carries you full-term, and your birth is unremarkable. Your APGAR score is 9 or 10. You are nursed for a minimum of one year. Your parents methodically introduce you to non-allergenic foods.

You possess a fine constitution and a sound soul, body, and mind. You experience the expected childhood illnesses and remain robust. Your height is in the 50-75th percentile and weight ranges around the 50th percentile. You are active and coordinated. You take no medication, are free from allergies, and require no surgery.

You develop along normal lines, meeting each and every developmental marker in growth and development, crawling by nine months and walking soon thereafter. Your sensorimotor state—moving and touching all that life has to offer—lasts about two years, followed by vibrant language skill development. Your siblings follow normal developmental paths as well. You encounter a healthy manageable dose of sibling rivalry—loving, competitive, and supportive.

Your parents remain in their monogamous, loving marriage, growing in communication, admiration, and respect. You have at least one pet and you help care for it. You have acquired a circle of friends and family who are around and involved in your upbringing. You don't watch too much television or play too many video games. Your computer and phone use is limited, controlled, and scrutinized. You remain active and curious, and are often encouraged to play outdoors.

You enter kindergarten and begin serious social-emotional development. You transition well, learning to count, speak, sit still, and interact with others. You learn rules and how to abide by them. You learn how to self-manage your behavior.

As you enter elementary school, your cognitive windows of opportunity continue to open and are filled with knowledge. In first grade, you begin reading, writing, and spelling. You are in the gold star group! You write and illustrate your own book: *My Book About Me.* You and your classmates host a book signing event. You read your book out loud to everyone in the auditorium. Reading out loud comes naturally, so although you are a bit nervous, you nail it! Everyone applauds at the end of the presentation. You go out for ice cream with your family and friends to celebrate.

In fourth grade, you develop research skills. In fifth grade, you continue acquiring a wide range of background knowledge, such as the US state capitols and Native American culture. You learn the Preamble to the Constitution of the United States. You enter the science fair and win first prize for your invention.

Your family takes regular vacations. Your parents focus on collecting experiences versus material goods. Your parents' careers are suited to their temperaments and personalities. They are happy with their work and believe they are manifesting their callings in life. Money is never an issue and is not discussed. You have all that you need and want.

You are not raised in a family of divorce, you are not adopted, and you are not an Army brat. You are not abused, and you are not a foster child. You are not bullied, nor do you bully. Your circle of friends is diverse and tolerant. You are accepting of all races, creeds, and denominations. You are not left-handed, gay, or gender-confused, and you do not wear glasses. These days, you are likely not male.

Although life flows easily, you receive the Privilege of Hardship— your parents do not micro-manage or behave as a helicopter, hovering over your every move. They allow freedom to grow, to make your own mistakes, and to recover and learn from them, thereby developing your resiliency and adaptability. Your self-esteem is honed and determined.

You are given opportunities to explore interests and passions. In high school you begin to travel and work. You take on leadership roles like Big Brother/Sister and Peer Counseling. You join clubs and play sports where you actively participate. You pursue creative endeavors, experimenting with music, art, and practical skills like cooking. You are encouraged to continue experimenting with new activities, and supported in developing pursuits you are drawn to. You are given the time and personal space to be creative.

As you continue to mature, you are drawn to academics. You love the scholarly pursuit of knowledge, challenge your own perspectives and mental models, and find gaps and flaws in your and other's knowledge. You gingerly harvest your critical thinking and analysis. Teachers enjoy your presence; the word "asset" is often used in describing your role in class. You are a role model in school.

You develop a strong rapport with your teachers and at least one in particular, with whom you consider a mentor. This mentor gently guides you, ignites your intuition, and encourages you listen to your own voice, while providing structure and input. You take risks and you learn from them. You are comfortable making mistakes, because that is how you learn most effectively. You are comfortable asking for help, because help is always available. You feel humble and grateful, while transforming into a fine young adult.

You are interested in college. You initiate the college search process independently. You research, visit, and select potential schools in your junior year and apply to college in your senior year. You maneuver this complex process without coercion from family or external prompting from counselors, friends, teachers, doctors, or coaches. You request their perspectives as a way to gauge your own decision-making. They offer guidance, while instilling your own particular values. They understand that this is your path, and they are there, empowering you to walk it.

You are accepted into the college of your choice. You visited this institution, and it felt like the right fit. The environment suits you—

geographically, culturally, economically, and politically. You have a clear idea of the path you plan to pursue, while remaining open-minded to new opportunities, interests, and influences. In short, you are trusting the process and letting go of the exact outcome that you will manifest, while steadfastly moving toward it.

In your first year at college, neither your grandparents nor your family pet dies. Your parents remain together in loving union and vibrant health, and they remain in your home town. Your siblings also share good health. Your best buddy is not deployed overseas, no friends die in fatal car accidents, and no major calamities occur, such as a college shooting, terrorist attack, or natural disaster.

Oh. Just one more thing.

You don't have a learning disability.

LIFESTYLES FOR LEARNING DIFFERENTLY

"I still live by the wisdom of Susan Crowther, and my grades are good at my new school. I am currently set to graduate in one year with a Bachelor's in Management and a Minor in Business Administration. Defend your education, Crowther."
  —Brian Fitzgerald, *graduate from Northern Kentucky University*

"Defend your education."
    —Susan Crowther

LD: WHAT IT IS (AND WHAT IT'S NOT)

One of the most misunderstood paradoxes of the learning-disabled (LD) student is that they are smart. In fact, legally, they are *required* to be smart. Learning-disabled students are typically as smart as or smarter than "normal" kids, because they have to be smart enough for something to be noticeably wrong. They must perform with an academic gap or deficit of 15 percent between their potential and their performance in order to be considered for diagnosis.

In plain English, that means you have to be an A-B student who receives C-D grades. Your potential has to be high enough so that, when you are not performing as you should, there is cause for concern. An average student who performs averagely is fine; but, if you have above-average intelligence performing academically at an average (or below) level, that is a call to action.

What is a Learning Disability?

The individual has a mental or physical impairment that substantially limits one or more major life activities. This determination is made by a team of knowledgeable individuals, including the parents, who are familiar with the student and his/her disability.
There is no list of "approved" disabling conditions. A person with a "disability" is simply one who (1) "has a physical or mental impairment, which substantially limits one or more major life activities," (2) has a record of such an impairment, or (3) is regarded as having such an impairment.

—*(LD Online: www.ldonline.org)*

What's happening? Something is an obstacle, preventing you from reaching your true potential. This "something" may be the result of many things: genetics, gestation, environment, concussions and other injuries. After we eliminate parents, wombs, power lines, and soccer fields, diagnosis gets tricky.

LD is an exclusionary concept, defined by what it is *not*. LD is not the result of sensory impairment, such as blindness or deafness. LD is not a cognitive impairment; students possess the ability to process information. LD excludes mental retardation; students must score over 80 on the IQ tests (in some states, a minimum of 70). LD is not a by-product of nurture. It is not caused by social or emotional factors. You don't develop an LD as a result of divorced parents or if your parent is in the military and you have to move several times. You don't get an LD because of a broken home, abusive father, or sexual assault. LD is not the result of bullying or being cut from the Little League team. LD is not a cultural disease. It does not happen after playing too many video games, watching too much television, or listening to heavy metal. It is not the result of bad parenting, lack of religious foundation, or neglect. Legally speaking, it is not caused by demonic spirits.

To recap, LD is *not* the result of a lot of things:

- Low IQ (you cannot be retarded)
- Sensory impairment (blind, deaf, or dumb conditions do not cause it)
- Social and emotional states (bullying, molestation, or some co-occurring diagnosis, such as depression or anxiety)
- Culture (moving, army brat, divorce, trauma, alcoholic parents, date-rape, sexual confusion, homosexuality, demonic spirits, bad karma, past life regression, etc.)

DO YOU DESERVE YOUR LD?

Let's say you are a bright, capable student who is performing abnormally. Something is an obstacle, preventing you from reaching your true potential. This "obstacle-to-potential" differential is the driving force behind LD accommodations, which are created to align and resign this learning roadblock.

Let's say you are diagnosed with a learning disability and you want to go to college. You should get accommodations, right? Maybe. First, you have to be "substantially limited" in at least one "major life activity."

"Major life activities" are defined as:
Caring for yourself, performing manual tasks, walking, seeing, hearing, speaking, breathing, learning, working, thinking, concentrating, and interacting with other people.

"Substantially limited" is defined as:
Significantly restricted as to the condition, manner, or duration for which an individual can perform a particular major life activity as compared to the condition, manner, or duration for which the average person in the general population can perform that same major life activity.
(*www.ldonline.org/ldbasics/whatisld*)

Wow. That definition of "significantly limited" makes me want to poke my eyes out. How on earth can one create a universal assessment tool for "significantly limited?" Remember apples, pencils, and balance? We're now dealing with a pretty abstract concept. Take fifty people with a similar experience, and you'll have fifty different degrees of struggle. LD is as subjective as pain; some people complain about every sniffle while others shake off a dismembered limb as a "flesh wound." In fifty different states with fifty different psychologists, you may receive fifty different diagnoses. **LD is tricky to diagnose, trickier to offer accommodations, and trickiest to receive these accommodations, in college.**

While a typical person will typically face learning challenges in their lifetime, what distinguishes a personality from a disorder is the *quality and quantity* of these significantly limiting experiences. The average person faces occasional challenges, but they find strategies to overcome the obstacles. These obstacles become amusing stories in a person's life. The person with an LD is not chuckling. They do not experience occasional issues; they live a chronic struggle. Every minute of every day contains these obstacles. Their learning disability *is* their life story.

"Great!" I hear you cry. "I'm totally significantly limited in at least one major life activity!" *Now* I can get my accommodations in college, right?

Not quite. Next, you must be otherwise qualified.

In order to receive accommodations for a particular job, you have to be qualified for the job. **"Otherwise qualified" means you have to be able to do the thing you are hired to do. In legal terms, you have to be able to perform** *the essential functions* **of that job.** A blind person would not be qualified to be hired as a bus driver. A physically disabled person may not be qualified to handle carrying 50 pound bags of flour up a flight of stairs. Students with LDs may not be essentially qualified for the job of college.

Essential functions relating to the job of college:

- reading
- writing
- mathematical calculations
- attending class (work) regularly each day
- coming in at a specific time
- estimating time and managing job requirements
- communicating effectively with others
- getting along with your boss, team leader, supervisor, or team
- maintaining the minimum grade point average
- maintaining the minimum required course load
- completing the degree requirements

A college student's job is attending college; therefore, you have to be qualified be in college: be accepted, perform the work, and succeed, with or without any accommodations. There's the rub, so let's repeat it: **Students with LDs must demonstrate the ability to be successful in college without accommodations, in order to be qualified to receive accommodations.**

As a US citizen, it is your legal right to a free and appropriate education, from kindergarten through 12th grade. You don't have to be "otherwise qualified" to attend high school; in fact, you are legally obligated to attend. Until they graduate high school, LD students are primarily covered by the IDEA, the Individual Disability Education Act. The IDEA offers accommodations, which support LD students in reaching their *own individual potential*. In K–12, the gap applies. LD laws support accommodations that allow the A-B student to perform with A-B grades.

Once a student graduates high school, they are covered by different laws. College students may receive accommodations *only* if they are qualified to be in college—if they can perform those essential college functions. And they only receive accommodations that allow them to perform as well as the average person—not any average *schmo* off the street, but the *average college person*. If a student is "otherwise qualified," he may receive accommodations to allow him to achieve average grades. We may live in a grade-inflated society, but "average" is still a C.

You have to be able to perform the job—pass college classes, earning a grade of C or better in all classes. You are only offered accommodations in college in order to perform as well as the average person in the population—in other words, receive a C. You only receive accommodations to bring your grade to a C, but must be able to earn a C without any accommodations. By this reasoning, colleges need never offer legal accommodations. It's an academic catch-22, and some colleges use this logic to their advantage.

What the law means, realistically, is that LD students may no longer receive accommodations in college. Gaps are gone; the average rules college law. If LD students are earning grades of C or better in high school, their college may be able to decline their accommodation requests. It's a messy procedure that involves methodical disclosure and advocacy. To further complicate matters, by law, the discloser is the one who has to advocate—the student with the LD. Suddenly, Baby has to be the parent.

The bad news for students diagnosed with an LD is that, the more successful you are, the less legal (and cultural) support you receive. If you are a student with an LD and you've made it to college, by most mainstream opinions, you don't have an LD. Why? *Well, you wouldn't have made it to college if you had an LD.* This is not just ignorant or outmoded thinking. Courts still refer to this type of logic. Try to advance your academic career and pursue a Master's or Doctoral degree, and you'll find even less tolerance for any institution or court to uphold accommodations.

The good news is that, even if you are refused accommodations in college, you still have strategies. What's the difference between accommodations and strategies? Freedom and control. Accommodations require legal approval and constant monitoring. Each individual institution determines accommodations, so every time you enter a new college, or even a new classroom at the same college, your accommodations may change depending on the "essential functions" required in that particular "workplace." By contrast, you control strategies. A student's best bet at success is to take matters into their own hands.

Strategies are all the things you do by yourself to help you succeed in school. Strategies aren't exclusively for the learning-challenged; every successful student uses them. An alarm clock is a strategy. The library is a strategy. Asking a question is a strategy. (*What is an essay?*) Strategies are the ultimate empowerment.

You can create most legal accommodations through strategies!

- Preferred seating? Arrive early.
- Tutorial? Use Academic Centers and Office Hours.

- Early Registration? Research classes and be ready to register the moment registration opens.
- Extended time? Manage your time.
- Time management support? Ask your RD, counselor, coach, or successful friend.
- Assisted support? Join study groups, friends.
- Additional resources? Access the web, PPT, and online study guides.
- Reduced course load? Allow extra studying time and/or take longer to complete college.

Accommodations are a bit of a myth: elusive, unpredictable, and unreliable. Success must be in your hands; like your health, you must defend your education. **Academic strategies are half of your success story. Developing and maintaining a balanced, healthy lifestyle completes the picture.**

ADHD OR A BOY?

What's the difference between ADHD and a personality? Does Joey suffer from a disability or is Joey just being a boy? Everybody experiences the symptoms of ADHD. Everybody loses their keys, becomes distracted, and blurts out inappropriate comments. We've all experienced social anxiety and struggled with decision-making. Why do some people receive this label? To answer this, let's first review the symptoms.

DSM-5 Criteria for ADHD—Attention-Deficit/ Hyperactivity Disorder:

People with ADHD show a persistent pattern of inattention and/ or hyperactivity-impulsivity that interferes with functioning or development:

The 9 inattentive symptoms are:

- Often fails to give close attention to details or makes careless mistakes in schoolwork, work, or during other activities (e.g. overlooks or misses details, work is inaccurate).
- Often has difficulty sustaining attention in tasks or play activities (e.g., has difficulty remaining focused during lectures, conversations, or lengthy reading).
- Often does not seem to listen when spoken to directly (e.g., mind seems elsewhere, even in the absence of any obvious distraction).
- Often does not follow through on instructions and fails to finish school work, chores, or duties in the work place (e.g., starts tasks but quickly loses focus and is easily sidetracked).
- Often has difficulty organizing tasks and activities (e.g., difficulty managing sequential tasks; difficulty keeping materials and belongings in order; messy, disorganized work; has poor time management; fails to meet deadlines).
- Often avoids or is reluctant to engage in tasks that require sustained mental effort (e.g. schoolwork or homework; for older adolescents and adults, preparing reports, completing forms, reviewing lengthy papers).
- Often loses things necessary for tasks or activities (e.g., school materials, pencils, books, tools, wallets, keys, paperwork, eyeglasses, and mobile telephones).
- Is often easily distracted by extraneous stimuli (e.g., for older adolescents and adults may include unrelated thoughts).
- Is often forgetful in daily activities (e.g., doing chores, running errands; for older adolescents and adults, returning calls, paying bills, keeping appointments).

The 9 hyperactive-impulsive symptoms are:

- Often fidgets with or taps hands or squirms in seat.
- Often leaves seat in situations when remaining seated is expected (e.g., leaves his or her place in the classroom, in the office or other workplace, or in other situations that require remaining in place).
- Often runs about or climbs in situations where it is inappropriate (e.g., in adolescents or adults, may be limited to feeling restless).
- Often unable to play or engage in leisure activities quietly.
- Is often "on the go" acting as if "driven by a motor" (e.g., is unable to be or is uncomfortable being still for extended time, as in restaurants, meetings; may be experienced by others as being restless or difficult to keep up with).
- Often talks excessively.
- Often blurts out answers before questions have been completed (e.g., completes people's sentences; cannot wait for turn in conversation).
- Often has difficulty awaiting turn (e.g., while waiting in line).
- Often interrupts or intrudes on others (e.g., butts into conversations, games, or activities; may start using other people's things without asking or receiving permission; for adolescents and adults, may intrude into or take over what others are doing).

(*www.add.org*)

In addition, the following conditions must be met:
- Several inattentive or hyperactive-impulsive symptoms were present before age 12 years.
- Several symptoms are present in two or more settings (e.g., at home, school, or work; with friends or relatives; in other activities).

- There is clear evidence that the symptoms interfere with, or reduce the quality of, social, school, or work functioning.
- The symptoms do not happen only during the course of schizophrenia or another psychotic disorder. The symptoms are not better explained by another mental disorder (e.g. mood disorder, anxiety disorder, dissociative disorder, or a personality disorder).

(*www.adhd-institute.com*)

ADHD: A Disorder of Perception

ADHD is not formally considered a learning disability, but students diagnosed with this disorder receive educational accommodations. They experience the same issues that the LD students do, with the addition of social alienation.

Kids diagnosed with ADHD are . . . annoying. They get on everyone's nerves. "We didn't have ADHD in the 80s," I tell my students. "You were just a pain in the ass." ADHD brings up cultural angst, challenging social-emotional interactions as much as cognitive and intellectual pursuits. Plainly put, kids with ADHD are just as obnoxious in and out of the classroom. You take away the dyslexic child's book, and you have a sweet, kind, thoughtful person. You take the ADHD child out to the park, and he's thwacking nearby kids and throwing dirt on peoples' shoes. Still, the LD criteria for accommodation applies.

Despite their symptoms, ADHD students have to be able to perform the essential functions, in order to receive accommodations. ADHD still has a stigma of being a "fake diagnosis." It may have something to do with perception.

Estrogen-Dominant Perception

There is another interesting phenomenon that may influence ADHD diagnosis. I refer to this as "Estrogen-Dominant Perception."

Today's children are immersed in an estrogen-dominant environment. From the moment children are born until their high school graduation, the primary gender who raises, observes, judges, and labels them is female.

More children are born into single-parent homes and homes of divorce. They are raised by their mothers, unless Mom has to return to work. Then, children are raised by friends and family—sisters, aunts, and grandmothers—all women. When older, children are placed into daycare centers and pre-school, primarily run by women. Children enter K-12 schools, where the vast majority of educators, counselors, paraprofessionals, and administrators are women. After-school daycare is run by women. Women also are fully ensconced in the workplace, so chances are the child's employer and/or co-workers will be female. Throughout their young life, these children are monitored by pediatricians, psychologists, and social workers, which are primarily female fields.

What does all this mean? In a word: women. Women are raising our children, and, in general, women are estrogen-dominant. ADHD, in general, is testosterone-dominant.

Women are perceiving and labeling children through their female lens. To a normal female, the normal male appears disabled. *All* males have ADHD; they are nuts! Review those ADHD symptoms. That's how women describe male behavior in everyday conversation. I wouldn't be surprised if a woman invented ADHD. At the very least, she nagged her husband into including it in the DSM.

* * *

Joking aside, you can see the disastrous implications of an estrogen-dominant perceiver being the deciding factor when diagnosing a student with testosterone-dominant behavioral disorder like ADHD. Put two females in a room with one young boy, and they'll agree; there is something wrong with that kid. The testing criteria lacks comprehensiveness; a male perspective should be required to be included for confirming diagnosis. **Advocacy swings both ways; if two men were about to diagnosis me with a behavioral disorder, there better damn well be a woman present to advocate for the female perspective.**

You may argue that men do work in these child-perceiving positions, but the majority of males who adopt these caretaker roles tend to be amply estrogenically-sensitive types, and if you believe the theory outlined in *Brain Sex,* their brain behavior is estrogen-dominant. I still want a guy's guy in the room, before you slap a label on my bratty son.

We know ADHD is not exclusively a male disease; females do receive that diagnosis. Interestingly, many females develop their ADHD symptoms during puberty and adolescence. In the past, diagnostic criteria required symptoms to manifest by the age of seven. **What may be the cause of an increase in female diagnosis of ADHD? The answer may lie with hormonal imbalances.** Recalling the hormonal theory for brain behavior in the video series *Brain Sex*, extreme and ongoing stress causes chronic hormonal imbalance, which may cause gender imbalance in genital assignment, sexual preferences, and for our purposes, hormone-dominant behavior. Females develop with more testosterone, and men, more estrogen. Hormonal imbalance and excessive hormone production has also been linked to animal consumption—too much meat and dairy in the diet—causing early onset puberty and other endocrine disruption. This change of dietary hormones may be an underlying cause of the sudden increase in LGBT populations.

Extrapolating the hormonal flooding theory of *Brain Sex* may help explain how young girls began to challenge young boys as heirs to the ADHD crown. Excessive and chronic stress directly affects hormonal balance. During gestational floodings, excessive stress hormones may affect the third trimester hormonal flooding, which, in turn, affects gender behavior. Simply put, when hormones are out of flux, boys may act like girls and girls like boys.

No matter how you, or your son or daughter, came to receive a learning or attentional disorder, one truth remains clear: the path of success is paved with academic and lifestyle strategies.

LD: LEARNING DISABLED OR LIFESTYLE DISABLED?

The legal criteria for LD and ADHD diagnosis rejects lifestyle or psychonutrients factors. The definition is exclusionary, asserting that LD *may not* be caused by poor diet or malnutrition, dehydration, sleep deprivation, stress, anxiety, low self-esteem, sedentary lifestyle, lack of creativity, addiction, or isolation. Lifestyle factors may exacerbate or alleviate, but not create or cure.

I disagree. If stress can turn a boy into a girl, it can turn a normal brain into an LD brain. This section brings a call to action in challenging the current LD paradigm. I'd like to invite a moment of disequilibrium and propose the following:

1. LD symptoms/diagnoses are directly affected by lifestyle factors.
2. LD symptoms/diagnosis may be caused by lifestyle factors
3. LD symptoms/diagnosis may be cured by lifestyle factors.

Epigenetics: A Permanent Solution to a Temporary Problem

In the article *You Can Change Your Genes: The Power of Epigenetics* (Fortson, Wellbeing Journal, 2013), author Leigh Fortson discusses the work of Dr. Dean Ornish, MD, who advocates for the direct eminence and influence of psychonutrient factors. "Doctor Ornish has taken conventional cardiovascular patients, provided them with important lifestyle insights (better diet, stress-reduction techniques, and so on), and without drugs, the cardiovascular disease was resolved."

Genetics experts say there is no rhyme or reason to why genetic mutation occurs. It's completely random, but there are known causes, such as traumatic stressors. Genes are incredibly adaptable. Fortson cites Dr. Bruce Lipton, PhD, "Your mind can alter the activity of your genes and create over thirty thousand variations of products from each gene" (Fortson, 2013). If, in epigenetics, genes "turn on" or express as a result of trauma or a significant stressor, perhaps genetic "mutation" is influenced in the same way, and psychonutrient distress causes the mutation. Otherwise, why would it mutate? Stress causes the change in the environment. Any change is stress, so genetic mutation is therefore caused by stress (change).

Some can cope with the stress, and some cannot. The "cannot" may translate to illness or mutation. Sometimes "cope" means adapting to a change—altering your state to eliminate or remove the stressor—*fight or flight*. In this way, "mutate" could be nature's way of adapting to that particular stressor, but with epigenetics, change can be fatal. **The coping strategy of genetic expression becomes a permanent solution to a temporary problem. Your genes permanently change, due to a temporarily stressful situation.**

Learning disabilities may be caused through epigenetic expression. The epigenetic expression may be caused by lifestyle factors; therefore, learning disabilities may be caused by lifestyle factors. A common causative agent responsible for genetic expression is stress-induced trauma. Since stress is in the eye of the perceiver, the intensity is personal. What may cause genetic expression in your genes may not in another person sharing a similar genetic abnormality. For many students, college is a major stress-induced trauma. For others, the trauma begins much earlier than college years.

It is time to recognize psychonutrient factors as acceptable causative criteria for LD diagnosis. Lifestyle factors may be directly responsible for LD symptoms, and therefore must be formally indoctrinated into the testing process and recommended accommodations. At the very least, we may fully acknowledge the direct role that lifestyle factors play in co-occurring diagnoses, such as Attention Deficit Hyperactive Disorder (ADHD), Traumatic Brain Injury, (TBI), Obsessive Compulsive Disorder (OCD), depression, anxiety, conduct disorders, personality disorders, substance addiction, and media dependencies. Psychonutrient factors may also be the missing link accounting for all the "unknown" causes or "non-specified" LDs. "Non-specified" is a common term used to describe an LD diagnosis with no clear label.

Since co-occurring diagnoses directly affect the severity of LD, and lifestyle directly affects co-occurring illnesses, then lifestyle directly affects the severity of LD.

Many students diagnosed with an LD suffer from a co-occurring diagnosis. Most people in the United States, in general, are diagnosed with *some* illness. Either the "co-occurring" diagnosis is the primary diagnosis, or it accompanies other health disorders such as allergies, asthma, diabetes, cancer, auto-immune disorders, etc. Being sick is stressful and traumatic; therefore, a persistent stress response is a logical consequence for the SBM.

If a student is suspected of having a learning disability, a new healthier protocol would recommend improving these lifestyle factors before LD testing. If they already have a diagnosis, recommend retesting after an appropriate period of time, say six months to a year. Furthermore, lifestyle factors must be included in LD recommendations for accommodations and be monitored by educational institutions, the student's family, and medical providers. If a student is not adhering to positive lifestyle changes, they may face the risk of losing their legal accommodations. Accountability would shift the focus onto the student, where it should be if a student is to take their primary education serioiusly, and where it must be if they are entertaining college.

Lifestyle-Disabled Is Learning-Disabled

Changes in lifestyle create changes in life. Some changes are profound and transformative. Lifestyle changes have the power to transform a "disorder that significantly limits major life activities" into a burden managed by strategies. If you have diabetes, you may diminish symptoms with psychonutrients, but you are still diagnosed with diabetes. You may just have diabetes with no symptoms, but are you cured? How do you know? Just change the psychonutrients; if you eat white sugar, avoid moving your body, and embrace social drama, watch your glucose count sail through the roof.

So, too, with LD. Lifestyle factors may greatly reduce the symptoms of a learning disability, but if you are diagnosed with an LD, you have one. You may be able to fully function in college with strategies and accommodations, but, you must still monitor your psychonutrients fastidiously to maintain academic success.

Lifestyle factors create dramatic effects equal to many medications, but are superior, as there are no negative side effects. First, and always, *they do good*. Movement reduces anxiety, stress, and depression, without causing impotency, weight gain, mood alteration (flat mood), and other detrimental side effects associated with medications given for these illnesses. It stimulates and calms the mind just as neuro-stimulators Ritalin and Adderall do, but without the over-stimulating effects of neurodegenesis, irritability, and appetite destruction. Movement's benefits are found in all lifestyle factors. Psychonutrients wake us up and chill us out. We maintain the smooth Alpha state and are able to shift into Beta and Theta smoothly, like a well-oiled Porsche.

When students are struggling on an assignment, the first question I ask is, "Will you please explain the assignment?" I want to know if they understand it and can articulate it to someone else. This helps to see where their breakdown points are, the "essay syndrome," if you will. Never assume students understand the assignment; often, the opposite is true. Once they do understand, the stress subsides, they return to Alpha state and are able to see more clearly. Then we make a plan to have them complete the assignment.

If students understand the assignment or are performing poorly in general—low attendance and grades—I go directly to lifestyles. I run through all the factors here and give the student a chance to check in. There is much to report on. I have never had a student report that their lifestyle factors are fine and dandy while they are doing poorly. It just doesn't happen. Reflecting on their lifestyle factors allows them the opportunity make the connections. It validates that these issues are real and significantly blocking their success. The recognition immediately initiates their parasympathetic system. Then, we share a couple deep belly breaths and make a plan.

For struggling students who insist they are fine, there is a guaranteed LD cure. **Students can completely eliminate their diagnosis of dyslexia, ADHD, or any learning-related diagnosis. The cure? Let the testing expire.** Students are required by law to update their diagnosis every three years in order to receive academic accommodations. Without legal documentation, there is no legal diagnosis. Without a diagnosis, there is no LD.

Of course, the symptoms don't disappear, just your access to legal academic support. This illustrates the fragile ecosystem of the LD landscape. LD management is not as simple as receiving a diagnosis, then receiving medication. For that matter, neither is diabetes or any health condition. Even possibly fatal diseases like cancer embrace holistic management.

The college student diagnosed with a learning disorder possesses an imbalance in wellness; but more accurately, *any* college student, regardless of learning ability, is in a permanent state of imbalance. Furthermore, every person is in a constant state of flux. Balance is an abstract ideal, tossed around casually. **Everyone is in a continual state of imbalance, with occasional moments of balance. A healthy successful life is the continual pursuit and constant adjustment.** Even so, the student labeled with the LD or ADHD continually faces particular attacks on their well-being. In terms of developmental wellness, there are many facets to consider: deficits and delays in motor, physical, behavioral, and social-emotional development, in every stage of the student's maturity. These challenges don't end with a college diploma; they accompany the person throughout their lives.

Certainly, lifestyle factors directly impact the successful maintenance of an LD and may help eliminate the need for legal accommodations. Returning to my original posit, I do believe that lifestyle may play a diagnostic role in first manifesting the LD. Psychonutrients change genes, cause death, and cure cancer.

It is audacious and legally blinding to negate lifestyle factors as a causative determinant. If LD laws pay homage to environmental, gestational, and genetic factors, modern science has advanced enough to now include lifestyle factors as viable causation in the diagnosis of a learning disability.

* * *

I had originally intended to explore lifestyle solely in the context of LD college students, because of my professional training. It seemed logical that I should explore wellness in terms of these students. Furthermore, LD students are typically discussed in research as a marginalized population with greater risk for social and emotional issues and potentially harmful lifestyle behaviors. I reasoned that if marginalized students were at greater risk for psychonutrient imbalance, and if lifestyle factors could greatly improve their academic performance, then "normal" functioning students would also benefit, perhaps with greater success.

I created the *Lifestyles for Learning* for college students with learning issues, because this is what I know. If lifestyle factors improve LD academic performance—a student who has withstood academic assault and a barrage of wellness onslaughts throughout their lives, a student who is significantly limited in the ability to learn and maintain the major activities of their lives—imagine how improving lifestyle factors would improve academic performance for the "normal" student. While improving psychonutrient health allows LD students to survive, these same factors allow "normal" students to thrive. Lifestyle factors have the potential to improve anyone's academic performance. Furthermore, if lifestyle factors can affect academic performance, they can affect performance, in general: the workplace, relationships . . . life. **If improving lifestyle factors works for college—the most volatile time in a person's life—it can work for you, anytime, anywhere, in anything.** Improving one's lifestyle factors will always result in improving one's life. *Lifestyles for Learning* is for college students and the people who love them, and it is for everyone. It is a guide for anyone seeking to increase their performance, in soul, body, and mind.

* * *

As my former student loved to quote his favorite professor, "Defend your education. Defend your health."

You are how you be.

Be well.

Epilogue

Remember Simon, the sweet student who loved drumming? Plan B? He and I reconnected years later. He shared his relationship with music, the creative process, and college:

Simon

I remember that conversation and not wanting to be there (college). I got really sick with mono that winter and on top of that went into a really bad mental place (severe depression/anxiety). Was the worst year and a half of my life. Once I came out of that I worked odd jobs for a few years. I practiced daily during that time. When I had enough saved up, I moved to LA. I went to Musicians Institute where I grew exponentially as a player. 24 hour facilities where I could play as late and as loud as I wanted without a second thought. During and after MI I have been in bands. I am now taking classes at Cape Cod Community College. I'm focusing on Psych. I'm cooking at the Colonial House Inn in Yarmouth Port nightly. The band I'm in out here is a killer blues band primarily but we like to branch out into other genres also.

Music has served me well. It is the vehicle in which I can communicate most openly and freely with my fellow musicians on stage as well as the audience. I will say though that playing in bars can present challenges. However, when it comes to what you are writing about, there isn't a more

---

powerful positive influence in my life than performing, being able to share my emotions with total strangers and bring them enjoyment.

I asked Simon, "You ever play with the idea of being a music therapist? Combine Psych and drumming?"

Funny you should ask. I'm really into psychology. More specifically group dynamic psych. With my experience in bands over the years there have been overachieving bands with modest talent and failed bands with exceptional talent. I'm focusing on learning about group process and how to maximize potential. Maybe a band manager post drum career??

I hope you are doing well Susan. I still follow your advice and bring a water bottle with me everywhere and stay hydrated! Haha. Let me know when you are finished with the book. I look forward to reading it! Take care.

Glad he is still drinking water. Fifteen years of teaching, and that's all these punks remember. Oh well, it's as good a legacy as any.

You take care too, Simon. I'm going to hold you to reading this book.

Simon playing his drums.

~Acknowledgments & Credits~

CREATIVE DESIGN AND ILLUSTRATION

Julie DuCharme Cover Design, Illustration, Creative Consultant

Julie prefers Apples to popsicles.
Julie and Susie have been friends for several lifetimes.
Visit Julie: *www.juliefallone.com*

THE MODELS

Natalie Knowles
Yoga & Wellness Educator: www.natalieknowleswellness.com

Lucas Thibodeau
Senior, East Tennessee State University, son of Susan

ACKNOWLEDGEMENTS

Grateful for husband Mark, who balances between manager, editor, and best friend. Breadsticks and besos, Schteino.

Thank you Abigail Gehring Lawrence, for your belief, sincerity, and enthusiasm.

Thank you Skyhorse, for your support in passionate pursuits.

Jim Fallone, again. I raise my glass to your humble expertise and willingness to share.

Thank you dear students, for sharing your stories. Thank you Kenneth, Shaelie, Colin, Brian, Caroline, and John, for also sharing your names.

Blessed to have known the late Robert Sargent Fay, integrity guru. Life's a party, dear one, and we'll continue to celebrate it together.

Appreciation to friends and family for their encouragement, humor, and patience.

Gratitude extends to our dogs, Libby and Bodo, for couch-snuggles during stressful editing moments and vehement persuasion of daily walks.

Thank you for listening.

May our children learn from their mistakes and gain from our wisdom.

May you empower the world with your own sweet souls.

Resources

"10 Tips for Better Sleep Infographic." A Health Blog. Accessed March 14, 2014. http://www.ahealthblog.com/10-tips-for-better-sleep-infographic.html.

"ADDA - Attention Deficit Disorder Association | ADDA, The Only Organization Dedicated Exclusively to Helping Adults with ADHD." ADDA Attention Deficit Disorder Association. Accessed June 19, 2014. http://www.add.org/.

American Red Cross Standard First Aid: Workbook. U.S.A.: American Red Cross, 1988.

Baker, Nena. *The Body Toxic: How the Hazardous Chemistry of Everyday Things Threatens Our Health and Well-being.* New York: North Point Press, 2008.

Baker, Sidney M., and Karen Baar. *The Circadian Prescription.* New York: G.P. Putnam Sons, 2000.

Barkley, Russell A. "Attention Deficit Disorders." Handbook of Developmental Psychopathology, 1990, 65–75. doi:10.1007/978-1-4615-7142-1_6.

Ben-Shahar, Tal. *Happier*. London, Eng.: McGraw-Hill, 2008.

Childre, Doc Lew, Howard Martin, and Donna Beech. *The HeartMath Solution*. San Francisco, CA: HarperSanFrancisco, 1999.

Crowther, Susan. *The No Recipe Cookbook: A Beginners Guide to the Art of Cooking*. New York: Skyhorse, 2013.

Csikszentmihalyi, Mihaly. *Flow: The Psychology of Optimal Experience*. New York: Harper & Row, 1990.

Dement, William C., and Christopher C. Vaughan. *The Promise of Sleep: A Pioneer in Sleep Medicine Explores the Vital Connection between Health, Happiness, and a Good Night's Sleep*. New York: Delacorte Press, 1999.

Dewey, John, and David Sidorsky. John Dewey: *The Essential Writings*. New York: Harper & Row, 1977.

Eliopoulos, Charlotte. *Invitation to Holistic Health: A Guide to Living a Balanced Life*. Sudbury, MA: Jones and Bartlett, 2004.

Food, Inc. Directed by Robert Kenner. Movie One, 2008. DVD.
Fresh. Directed by Ana Sofia Joanes. 2009. DVD.

Ganim, Barbara. *Art and Healing: Using Expressive Art to Heal Your Body, Mind, and Spirit*. New York: Three Rivers Press, 1999.

Ganim, Barbara, and Susan Fox. *Visual Journaling: Going Deeper than Words*. Wheaton, IL: Quest Books, Theosophical Pub. House, 1999.

Gladwell, Malcolm. *Outliers: The Story of Success*. New York: Little, Brown and Company, 2008.

Glasser, William. *Choice Theory: A New Psychology of Personal Freedom.* New York: HarperCollinsPublishers, 1998.

Harris, Jonathan, Anne Moir, and David Jessel. 2003. *Brain sex.* Princeton, NJ: Films for the Humanities & Sciences.

Henderson, A. Scott. "Boys in Crisis?" The Educational Forum 71, no. 2 (2007): 186-87. doi:10.1080/00131720708984931.

Hjortshoj, Keith. *Understanding Writing Blocks.* New York: Oxford University Press, 2001.

How Difficult Can This Be? The FAT City Workshop. Directed by Richard LaVoie. PDX/PBS Studio, 2004. DVD.

Jensen, Eric. *Teaching with the Brain in Mind.* Alexandria, VA: Association for Supervision and Curriculum Development, 1998.

Katz, Sandor Ellix. *Wild Fermentation: The Flavor, Nutrition, and Craft of Live-culture Foods.* White River Junction, VT: Chelsea Green Pub., 2003.

Kennedy, Robert Francis. *Thimerosal: Let the Science Speak: The Evidence Supporting the Immediate Removal of Mercury, a Known Neurotoxin, from Vaccines.* New York: Skyhorse Publishing, Inc., 2014.

Khalsa, Dharma Singh., and Cameron Stauth. *Brain Longevity: The Breakthrough Medical Program That Improves Your Mind and Memory.* New York: Warner Books, 1997.

Kotler, Steven. "The Perils of Higher Education." PsycEXTRA Dataset, 2005. doi:10.1037/e592272007-032.

Luks, Allan. "The Healthiest Way to Help: Face to Face." Spirituality and Health, May/June 2003, 30-37.

Marcus, Susan Archibald. *The Hungry Brain: The Nutrition/cognition Connection.* Thousand Oaks, CA: Corwin Press, 2007.

"Mind Over Medicine." October 01, 2013. Accessed November 6, 2013. https://www.wellbeingjournal.com/vol-22-no-6-november-december-2013/.

Morter, M. T. *Dynamic Health: Using Your Own Beliefs, Thoughts, and Memory to Create a Healthy Body.* Rogers, AR: Best Research, 1997.

Morter, M. T. *The Soul Purpose: Unlocking the Secret to Health, Happiness, and Success.* Rogers, AR: Dynamic Life, LLC, 2001.

Pennebaker, James W. *Opening Up: The Healing Power of Expressing Emotions.* New York: Guildford Press, 1997.

Philpott, William H., and Dwight K. Kalita. *Brain Allergies: The Psychonutrient and Magnetic Connections.* Los Angeles: Keats Pub., 2000.

Pope, Loren. *Colleges That Change Lives: 40 Schools That Will Change the Way You Think about Colleges.* New York, NY: Penguin Books, 2006.

"Psycho-Cybernetics - Zero Resistance Living." Psycho-Cybernetics - Zero Resistance Living. Accessed May 20, 2011. http://www.psycho-cybernetics.com/about.html.

Ratey, John J., and Eric Hagerman. *Spark: The Revolutionary New Science of Exercise and the Brain.* New York: Little, Brown, 2008.

"Relaxation Response." Accessed March/April 2014. http://www. bensonhenryinstitute.org/.

Restak, Richard M. *The New Brain: How the Modern Age Is Rewiring Your Mind*. Emmaus, PA: Rodale, 2003.

Sapolsky, Robert M. *Why Zebras Don't Get Ulcers: A Guide to Stress, Stress Related Diseases, and Coping*. New York: W.H. Freeman, 1994.

Schauss, Alexander G., Barbara Friedlander Meyer, and Arnold Meyer. *Eating for A's: A Delicious 12-week Nutrition Plan to Improve Your Child's Academic and Athletic Performance*. New York: Pocket Books, 1991.

Sousa, David A. *How the Brain Learns*. Thousand Oaks, CA: Corwin Press, 2006.

"Stages of Sleep." Neuroscience for Kids. Accessed May 20, 2015. http://faculty.washington.edu/chudler/sleep.html.

Taira, Karina. "Hurts so Good." Elle magazine, September 2002.

"Texting and Driving Statistics." Texting and Driving Statistics. Accessed December 3, 2014. http://www.textinganddrivingsaf

What the Bleep Do We Know!? Directed by William Arntz. Performed by Marlee Matlin. 2004. DVD.

Zimmerman, Marcia. *The ADD Nutrition Solution: A Drug-free Thirty-day Plan*. New York: Holt, 1999.

Index

Notes